SIXTEEN ACRES

Philip Nobel # SIXTEEN ACRES

ARCHITECTURE

AND THE OUTRAGEOUS STRUGGLE

FOR THE FUTURE OF GROUND ZERO

METROPOLITAN BOOKS

Henry Holt and Company

New York

ɱ

Metropolitan Books
Henry Holt and Company, LLC
Publishers since 1866
115 West 18th Street
New York, New York 10011

Metropolitan Books™ is a registered
trademark of Henry Holt and Company, LLC.

Library of Congress Cataloging-in-Publication Data
Nobel, Philip.
    Sixteen acres : architecture and the outrageous struggle for the future of Ground Zero /
Philip Nobel.—1st ed.
        p.   cm.
    Includes bibliographical references and index.
    ISBN-13: 978-0-8050-7494-9
    ISBN-10: 0-8050-7494-5
    1. World Trade Center Site (New York, N.Y.)   2. Architecture—New York (State)—
New York City—21st century—Designs and plans.   3. City planning—New York
(State)—New York City.   4. Architecture and society—New York (State)—New York
City.   5. New York (N.Y.)—Buildings, structures, etc.   6. Manhattan (New York, N.Y.)—
Buildings, structures, etc.   I. Title.
NA6233.N5W67488 2005
725'.23'097471—dc22   2004055239

Henry Holt books are available for special promotions and
premiums. For details contact: Director, Special Markets.

First Edition 2005

Designed by Fritz Metsch
Map by David Cain

Printed in the United States of America
1   3   5   7   9   10   8   6   4   2

To Caroline

CONTENTS

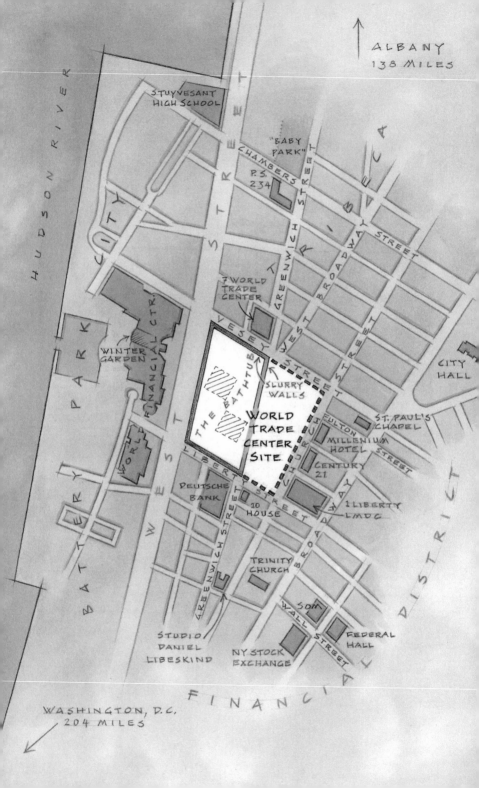

SIXTEEN ACRES

A few hundred feet from the Pyramid, I bent down, scooped up a handful of sand and then, a little farther away, let it silently spill. Under my breath I said: *I am modifying the Sahara.*

—JORGE LUIS BORGES, *Atlas*, 1984

PROLOGUE

THERE ARE 205,951 acres in New York City. On the morning of September 12, 2001, sixteen of those acres were in ruins. They had been wrecked and they were burning; they were the scene of an unprecedented crime. But they had not exactly been "erased,"[1] as so many papers reported, not "wiped off the map,"[2] as one writer, far away, would claim. Under the debris dominating what had already been named Ground Zero by the afternoon of the day before, the land and the right to rebuild on it remained, the deeds and leases still signed and countersigned. The towers were gone, shedding their tonnage in smoke and then, when they fell their quarter mile, in what we all agreed to call "dust." The surrounding buildings were cratered and condemned, and with them what was left of the World Trade Center, a city of sixty thousand, among which an unknown number were "missing." Beyond the bucket chains, the hopeful probing, the wildfire rumors of miraculous survival, their troubled redemption was gathering. It would come in the boiler plate of deals, in the exchange of memoranda, in handshakes and whispers and white papers, and, all too soon, in the siren songs of architectural fancy.

The city quietly ordered eleven thousand body bags two days after the attack, a day when the number of confirmed dead stood at eighty-two. Those five-figure fears became a four-digit reality as the count ticked down through the fall and early winter, leveling off at around three thousand in January, not long after the last fires were put out. Two years after the attack half the victims' families would have nothing to bury, nothing more tangible than Ground Zero itself. But despite that new burden, the site retained its principal, irresistible attribute: its value, as sixteen acres of well-placed land, rich in transit, in the nation's third-largest central business district and its first home to big-time money handling. The site was stilled, off the grid, newly haunted, but it was not out of the city's great game. Far from it—Ground Zero was the only game in town.

New York barely paused between that cataclysmic present and a speculative future. The city had its introspective revolution, but that sudden outbreak of grace was short-lived. The candles and itinerant yogis were swept out of the peaceable kingdom of Union Square within two weeks; the shrines were collected by curators, rushing downtown, getting there one step ahead of Sanitation. In Washington, too, the attack did not bring some stirring renovation of the city's soul. But only pride, not money, was on the line there, and the capital was spared the antagonism that consumed the World Trade Center site as its future was debated. The smashed wedge of the Pentagon was rebuilt within twelve months; if the fourth plane had found the Capitol, its assumed target, we would already have seen the great white dome rededicated in exquisite replica, flags whipping and Congress rising to applaud as the jets made their pass at the end of the president's speech. Such is the reverent hereafter uncomplicated icons can expect in a city that looks to them for meaning. The Twin Towers, however, were commercial buildings—real estate first and symbols last, and not even a taste of apocalypse could reverse that order. Regardless of the cause of the vacancy, we knew in our hearts and would learn again, New York only knows how to do one thing with a hole in the ground.

The city had greeted the blue morning of September 11 in its typical state: layer upon layer of potential and kinetic energy made manifest in plans and action. Polls had just opened for the Democratic primary in a contested race for mayor. Real estate developer Larry Silverstein, who six weeks earlier had leased the right to profit from the World Trade Center for ninety-nine long years, was dressing to go to the dermatologist to care for his yachting-ravaged skin. The white tents were in place for Fashion Week in Bryant Park. The Raelians, who believe that humans were synthesized by little green men, were preparing for a meeting that night in Greenwich Village. A dance company was setting up folding chairs for a lunchtime performance on the broad plaza under the Twin Towers. Wrapped up in itself, a great machine for the pursuit of happiness, New York City was particularly unprepared for what would come that day. The legal travails of Lizzie Grubman—that strangest of Manhattan creatures, a star publicist—continued to divert the city. As New York lay supine, dazed from the boom and bust of the years before, she was gobbling column inches with the story of her sixteen-count hit-and-run in the Hamptons.

Unlike other bouts of prosperity in the city, the 1990s had left no grand marks on the physical plant. In the 1980s, Reaganomic tax incentives had helped to sow a crop of glibly retrospective skyscrapers, among them the toy towers of the World Financial Center, a palisade rising between the World Trade Center and the Hudson River, on fill created from the excavation of the Twin Towers' deep "bathtub" foundation. In the era of irrational exuberance, though, the city had rationally retrenched, filling in the gaps and finishing up old business. The Flatiron district and stretches of Lower Broadway had been revamped to house the new economy. Industrial West Chelsea had come back to life, spurred by the resettlement of the Soho art world. Residential towers built in the city's own "lasagna" vernacular—in which the raw edges of concrete floor slabs are left exposed on the facade to speed construction and save a buck—completed the Upper East Side and displaced long-established flea markets in the wholesale flower

district. Times Square was reinvented as a family-friendly shopping center in the shadow of new towers that had been in process
for twenty years. Down around Wall Street, a decade of effort to
reimagine the area as a "24/7" destination was beginning to show
its doomed results.

None of these developments brought with it any progress in the
Mother Art; in the pristine aesthetics of architecture critics, each
could only be seen to have set it back. But Manhattan can take a
great deal of abuse. The island's primary grid (drawn in 1811 in a
spree of land-grab futurism) is so strong that individual buildings,
even the largest, are insignificant by comparison: the knickknacks
always subordinate themselves to the shelf. This is something that
Minoru Yamasaki, the architect of the World Trade Center, understood, a phenomenon that would serve those buildings well. "Manhattan itself is an ever-changing landscape," he wrote in 1979, six
years after his towers were complete. "A few of the buildings are
very handsome, most are mediocre; in certain lights, the silhouette
of the skyline is very beautiful, and even poorly designed buildings
become merged into the texture of this fascinating conglomeration
of structures surrounded by water."[3]

Within that fascinating, mediocre conglomeration, set off by it,
are the rare buildings—the Guggenheim, the Empire State—that
by design or default have come to epitomize a time. Significantly,
not one structure rose to reflect the surface-thin pleasures of the
nineties, except maybe the AOL Time Warner complex on Columbus Circle, shorn of its embarrassing dot-com prefix before opening in late 2003, somehow a more perfect symbol for having so
spectacularly missed its moment. Many other potential markers
remained unbuilt, affecting the city only as renderings in the real
estate pages, unable to navigate the pitfalls of politics and finance
to get as far as a ground-breaking.

In New York, increasingly, iconography became the business of
things other than architecture. Throughout the late 1990s, the city
was wallpapered with stretch-face signs of comical proportions—

five stories, ten stories, wrapping whole buildings in ad man's vinyl (sometimes cutting out holes for the windows if people still occupied the superseded structure). Often tributes to Panasonic or Nike, such signs bridged the gap between architecture's reticence and the open, ambient communication expected of the city. Contemporary buildings no longer say much to most people. It was easier before architects denied themselves the use of ornament; no one ever missed the point of that sculpture of Mr. Woolworth counting his nickels in the lobby of his Manhattan tower or misjudged the mood implied by the gothic confection of its facades. When it was completed, everyone called the building "The Cathedral of Commerce."

Despite this reticence, architecture remains the most prominent and most culturally engaged of all the arts. It is also the most contingent—an art that is neither high nor low, an art that gets to *art* only after locking lips with reality: satisfying a client, securing funds and permits and insurance, getting built. In New York City, no big building can go forward before a developer and his architects and lawyers have bartered with union leaders, placated the appropriate politicians, pacified the antsy neighbors, navigated the fickle press, and tamed whichever groups of civic watchdogs have taken on the defeat of the project as a righteous cause. These glamour-free facts-on-the-ground work to slow the already painstaking accumulation of materials on a construction site, beam on beam, pour on concrete pour, one crane hoist after another, until the wires can be slowly pulled, the pipes fitted end on end, the wallboard screwed, the carpets tacked—and mind the breaks and overtime, if you please. At last the ribbons can be cut and the keys turned over, and the patient citizens, kept at a distance behind plywood fences, can approach to take the measure of what private enterprise has wrought, just on the far side of that implacable frontier, the property line. That invisible line defines a building's footprint on the ground, and as it pulls up into the air, the structure molds itself to the zoning limitations devised by city planners to restrain bulk and make sure some dim light can reach the street; how high it goes is a function of what the market will bear. On all sides, office towers hug those lines and shelter safely behind them, making the exigencies of business visible. Manhattan is composed of little else. And so do architects create the experience of the city, filling up those invisible boxes.

The folkways of New York real estate carried over intact to the redevelopment of the World Trade Center site. With the world watching and fires erupting from the shifting pile, the debate over the future of Ground Zero was joined—by its owner, the powerful Port Authority of New York and New Jersey; by its primary leaseholder, Larry Silverstein; by politicians near and far; and by civic groups and a public expecting something more than business as usual. That last pursuit was given hope by the presence of a new faction: representatives of the September 11 dead. These players assembled, a bureaucracy was minted to oversee them, and in the din of clashing mandates the redevelopment follies began. A diverting pageant, driven by political bluffs and architectural bluster, this was not a preamble to some orderly, talent-driven planning cycle to come; these first years of brinksmanship were not an historical interlude to be filed away the morning an anointed architect woke up with some conclusive eureka. In any building project—and this was, in the end, mostly any building project—a design, a built thing, is the product of countless glancing conflicts. More than any architect's fever dream, the sum of those conflicts—the collision of interests and the echoes of their Band-Aid resolutions—is that final design. Yet from day one of the rebuilding process, those who trust in the power of architecture were waiting for genius ex machina, even as a new World Trade Center was being spun out of chance and constructed happenings. The shape of the future was determined by the shape of those happenings: the battle, the circus, the process.

In a city that was already home to numberless unmatched venues for the scrutiny of human conduct, Ground Zero became the main attraction. And, for a time, architects stood at the center of that stage. In response to the tragedy, in an attempt to defy it, they were asked to do something they no longer knew how to do: make buildings speak, give them meaning, create symbols for a culture with no common code. That effort fell short, as it had to, but even as they failed, architects were providing a singular look at the factors that shape their art. All the while the city was revealing its own prejudices and recording its likeness in the disposition of those sixteen acres. The redevelopment process and its architectural products were the most honest reflections of New York's reaction to September 11: what it wished to immortalize and what it wished to forget, how it was moved to change and how it refused to budge.

In time the site will be filled again, and when we go there and look up and ask, "Why?" (Why is it so big, so rude, so bright, so striving, so meager, so right? Why is it so?), the answer will be: "the process." When planners announce they've patched the city, when activists crow or give one last growl, when an architect cites some midnight inspiration, the truth will be the process *fecit*. And when the politicians line up to cut their ribbons, whatever shades the dais that day will be at once stranger and more fitting than anything they had imagined when they set about to govern its birth. In a way it will be perfect.

1

FIRST RESPONDERS

FRANK GEHRY, perhaps the most famous non-acting, non-directing, nonathletic son of Los Angeles, was in Manhattan on September 11, 2001. He was in town for the opening, the night before, of an Issey Miyake boutique in Tribeca, just ten latte-soaked blocks north of the World Trade Center. The architect had contributed a signature cloud of folded sheet metal for the store's interior, and his son Alejandro, an artist, had drawn several murals. The next morning his son went back downtown for a meeting, and Gehry couldn't contact him as he watched the neighborhood smothered on TV. "I was in *shreck*," he said. Stuck in town with the airlines grounded, he would go down to the site later that week to take a look—"around the edge, as close as you could get." Because he toured the perimeter with his patron, Thomas Krens, director of the Guggenheim Museum, it was soon rumored that the two had designs on the place. Though Gehry's interest was undeniable, and he played a longer game than any of his colleagues, he would sit out most of the ensuing follies—the projection onto the site of hysterical, inappropriate visions that sought to bring to Ground Zero, in the sneering words of the *New York Post*'s indispensable real estate reporter Steve Cuozzo, "truth, beauty, and Architecture-with-a-capital-A."[1]

The site was a magnet for all, but for architects—always thinking big—it was irresistible. They could see in the devastation a clean slate, a chance at greatness, a reprieve, at least, from another decade of museums and Miyake. Or Prada. Rem Koolhaas was probably the most influential architect in the world at the moment of the attack. In the summer of 2000, a *New York Times Magazine* cover story had helped take him out of the design studios, where he was a hero without peer, and into the public eye, revealing for mass consumption his stable open marriage and his jet-set ennui, but also his passion for expanding architecture's ambit and his odd, piercing insights into our fallen world: public space is dead; shopping is our civic religion; the future of the city is elsewhere.[2] His claim on New York City's attentions in the years before September 11 was a flagship store he was designing for Miuccia Prada in Soho. After a long drama—during which the whims of the architect and the forbearance of his client turned the commission into an arts-and-crafts playtime that more than one observer thought would "revolutionize" retail—in 2001 the store was nearing completion at last, having dallied through the city's boom.

On September 11, Koolhaas was in Chicago, at a meeting for a stalled project there. He had flown in from New York that morning to find himself stuck with clients who decided that the end of the world would not delay their business. He could catch only glimpses of the event on television. After a day of indecision and appeals to travel agents (and, yes, a trip to a local Prada store), Koolhaas hired the cab driver he had been using, a Syrian man, and a second driver from Egypt, to take him and an associate back east. The trip through the flag-draped heartland would be salted with assertions of Israeli complicity and Osama bin Laden's innocence, and overshadowed by the passengers' fears for their drivers' safety in late-night Pennsylvania truck stops. When they pulled up to a Manhattan hotel in the very early morning of September 14, police standing guard rushed the car. Like Gehry, Koolhaas stayed in town and made his pilgrimages to the cauldron, often at night.

Star architects were far from the only ones drawn by the allure of Ground Zero. In the first hours after the calamity, as every newly essential construction worker headed for the wreckage, less burly sorts were struggling to assess their place in a world that had gone from decadent to defenseless in a span of a hundred minutes. In that utilitarian moment, those whose contributions to the crisis would by nature remain more abstract were already at work to forestall their irrelevance. A rush was on to stake a claim, to put sneakers and loafers *down there* with the boots on the ground. Poets flooded the zone with images, theorists with ideas; theater and fashion critics, asserting the pertinence of their criticism, assessed the collateral damage on Broadway (as actors started to pitch in at the support center at Chelsea Piers) and on Seventh Avenue (as model Heidi Klum volunteered incognito at a supply depot). Fashion designer Michael Kors spun the attack as an opportunity for couture in a statement released at his runway show the week after: "Life continues on, but it is an unavoidable truth that life is also irrevocably changed. We must remember that fashion and the fashion community have always been receptive to change. . . . I know we will all be able to move forward in these trying times."[3] David Bouley, star chef and owner of several restaurants near the site, opened a franchise—it came to be called Green Tarp—in a ruined deli hard by the pile on Liberty Street. David Byrne and Candice Bergen served stew to the workers there.

Though physically Ground Zero resembled nothing that had been visited on this country before, from the beginning its culture looked just like America. There was, of course, that descent on the site by volunteers from all points, that salutary wave of *giving* at a scale the United States had never seen. But there was also, beyond the papers, a larger, more colorful, less useful descent, exhibiting in spots the full measure of prime-time narcissism. Depending on one's threshold for tolerating the absurd, this might have been an abomination or a hopeful reclamation—"Life victorious," as Daniel Libeskind, the World Trade Center site's eventual master plan architect, would repeat in later years. Either way, it was clear to all, especially to the audience at home—removed from what one volunteer referred to as the "tomato sauce and vomit" stench—that this disaster area, in its recovery and its redevelopment, would play by limelight rules. The parade of stars preceded in some cases visits by prominent politicians: Susan Sarandon circled the pile hawking donated pizza from the back of a pickup truck; John Travolta visited with volunteer ministers of the Church of Scientology, ready to offer succor in the form of "nerve assists." Product placement was not far behind: Campbell's Soup, Starbucks, McDonald's. The place was not without humor—workers called one tent, designated for R&R, "Ground Zero's"—or, naturally, a reflection of the politics that began there; invoking the nation's preferred emotional solvent, another tent was named "Freedom Café."

It was the curse of culture makers to get a handle, each as his métier allowed. Actors could get by just by putting their bodies at the site; Hollywood would not attempt a September 11 movie right away. Others had to represent with their ideas. And in tapping the sensibilities of the day before to make sense of the aftermath, it became clear what every effort shared: a culture of surfaces had left its artists poorly equipped for depth. "Make no mistake," one poet wrote in an introduction to a large collection published in 2002, "our arts have thrived on remoteness, deflection, over-the-shoulder innuendo, a myriad of aesthetic dispensations, and have (have they?) disdained the masses in need of their sustenance."[4]

Every artist drawn to Ground Zero faced the same problem—adapting the frivolity of his practice to the horror of what smoldered before him—but it was the architects who revealed just how perilous the new normal would be. On Sunday, September 16, 2001, the *New York Times* posted online the text of the next week's magazine section, in which architects first aired their ideas about the site. Under the title "To Rebuild or Not: Architects Respond," the editors arranged remarks from nine local opinion makers. The reporting for that story, the would-you-care-to-comment calls, took place within one or two days of the attack, in a week that most New Yorkers remember as progressively more harrowing, as fright overtook shock and—forgetting that al Qaeda takes its time between attacks—the city waited for the second shoe to drop.

Most of those interviewed called for a defiant, though not identical, rebuilding; one proposed a national vote: "Maybe it's not just our decision."[5] But the standout response came from Elizabeth Diller and Ricardo Scofidio, the husband-and-wife team whose theory-rich investigations at the intersection of technology and space had earned them architecture's first MacArthur Foundation genius grant. They struck one of the most regrettable notes of the too-soon thereafter: "What's most poignant now is that the identity of the skyline has been lost. We would say, Let's not build something that would mend the skyline, it is more powerful to leave it void. We believe it would be tragic to erase the erasure."[6] No other early comment showed quite how far architecture's intelligentsia were from the grit of the event, or how ill prepared were the profession's fashion-addled thinkers even to answer some of the top-line questions posed by the attack: Why do we gather in cities? What does it mean to build to the sky? How can more building—mere building—make sense of all this?

Architects found themselves in an awkward position: to exercise their professional expertise would be crass, yet all the time the public clamored for it, filling the letters columns of the papers and the open lines of radio chat shows. Rebuild to complement "the lovely lady in the harbor, the Statue of Liberty," one public radio caller urged in late September. "So we have here now another torch that is at the center of the old ruins." The columnist Liz Smith, on the same show to discuss the future of gossip, weighed in on the future of the site as well. "I think the spirit of the Phoenix will rise," she said, favoring the reconstruction of the Twin Towers.[7] Ed Koch, the irrepressible former mayor, was also an early advocate for building copies. "We have the plans," he said.[8] (At the time of its construction, he had decried the World Trade Center as "a conspiracy by people who think they know what is best for New York City.")[9] Donald Trump, the taste-deprived developer, also piped up for the cause of reconstruction, with the caveats that any rebuilt Twins should have a touch more finesse about them, and must once again be the tallest in the world.[10]

From the earliest days after the attack there was a near-universal belief that a building at Ground Zero could give meaning to what had taken place there, and that architecture's "best minds," despite such a long, long vacation from pathos, could create such a thing. But hubris was producing the wrong questions and the wrong answers: the response to the attack was not an architectural problem. "In my shock I want to rebuild it," a New York architect wrote on September 13. "That's all I can say because of the thousands of lives we cannot rebuild."[11] How can a building stand in for a life? Even the Taj Mahal, built by a shah as a tomb for his favorite wife, could not succeed in reviving her. And that is a building serving no other purpose than memory. Ground Zero would have to be rebuilt with office buildings, and expressing vengeance and grief are not things that office buildings do; they may rise from a graveyard but they do not redeem it; they may fill a site but they do not heal it. The attempt to make of commercial construction an emotional balm would leave architecture's emperors standing naked over and over in the following years. But the public was so hungry. On October 2, Richard Meier, among the most famous architects in New York City, appeared on television with Barbara Walters. He had not been shy about his ideas for the World Trade Center site—the *Times* had interviewed him twice, and twice he favored rebuilding grandly—but to his credit, Meier declined to bring a sketch when, incredibly, he was asked.

Shortly after his return to Los Angeles from New York, Frank Gehry, certainly high on any short list of best minds, was approached from all sides with requests for a therapeutic image. He demurred: "I just said no comment, no comment, no comment."[12] Though it was an inexact parallel—the pickup-sticks chaos of the pile might have been more accurately compared with the work of the so-called deconstructivist architects—a consensus soon emerged, codified in November by *New York Times* architecture critic Herbert Muschamp, that the ruins were somehow Gehryesque.[13] Everyone was searching for a solving name, and words were stretched to fit. "When the two towers collapsed," Jean Baudrillard wrote, "you had the impression that they were responding to the suicide of the suicide-planes with their own suicides."[14] One Dutch critic saw the buildings as "a death-collecting sandwich. Millefeuille, the horror of concrete puff pastry filled with bodies."[15] "Somebody burned down the Christmas tree," a homesick ex–New Yorker wrote the week of the attack. "Burned it all the way to the ground."[16] On September 12, a reporter for a local radio station described her push into the site and the emergence of one severed wisp of the towers through the still-thick smoke. It looked like "modern art," she said. And then there was Ada Louise Huxtable, the grande dame of American architecture criticism, who quickly established herself as one of a very few unshakably sane voices in the process. Asked by a magazine to contribute to yet another platform for pundits, she filed this rebuke: "It's a very large, tough subject, and there's too much static out there, too much talk and not enough thought. . . . I frankly wish everyone would just shut up for a while."

Robert A. M. Stern was another whose voice rose above the noise. A week and a day after September 11, the architect delivered a lecture for the Friends of the Upper East Side Historic Districts, one of the few Manhattan civic organizations that would not retool to address the crisis downtown. Stern is a diminutive man with perpetually arched eyebrows and a wry cock to his voice. He is also invariably the smartest architect in the room, a fact noted by Philip Johnson, his teacher at Yale, to whose mastery of the politics of the profession Stern is the only heir. The lecture was delivered as scheduled—Stern insisted—but he had adapted the speech to circumstance with poetic results.

"The toll in human lives is vast and the impact tragic," Stern said that day with characteristic sureness over his first slide, a connoisseur's view of the Twin Towers from the west in sideways light. "The political and economic implications are only beginning to be understood. Architects and investors are beginning to consider the future of the skyscraper building type. I am not proposing to enter into that discussion now, but simply to point out that whatever its shortcomings as a work of architecture, the World Trade Center was a powerful symbol of our city. It was a landmark. Oh, the tricks history plays on our aesthetic senses; how we now miss this imperfect monument. Landmarks are important— buildings bear silent witness to what we do, what we believe. They are our immortality on this earth. And when a landmark is torn down we lose witness to our humanity. Buildings are at once silent witnesses and yet they speak."[17]

That maximal take on the function of buildings would become a fixture of the American Pop understanding of the new cultural hot spot of Ground Zero. At that moment, the usually architecture-averse public was ready to buy into such a remedy: not buildings, architecture; not construction, not containers, not merely the largest of our business machines, but art, bearers of meaning, *transcendence*. The larger architecture firms in town sidestepped this new calling, or burden, carrying on as they had before with only practical problems in their sights; a week after the attack, the biggest of them held a summit to plan a coordinated response to the loss of 10 percent of the city's class-A office space. For the academic elite—the artsier wing of the profession that is assumed to be better equipped to conjure symbols—there could be no such out; to dodge the ugly questions of sanctity would have been to embrace obsolescence.

One wet night in the summer of 2003, almost two years after the attack, a wild-haired, forty-something woman from New Jersey was wandering the south rim of the site, lost under the mercury vapor. She had come down after sitting through a nearby hearing on the impending memorial competition (the rebuilt site was to include a memorial to be chosen from the submissions in an open competition). Staring through the tall fences, she was not sure exactly where the site was. The space was so clean and clear then, looking nothing like it had, either as built or in the iconic images of the aftermath. She was looking for the footprints, the offset squares where the towers had stood—everyone was—but the sawed-off nubs of the perimeter columns, the last on-site remains of the structures themselves, were buried under a layer of mud on the bedrock at the bottom of the pit. She was thrown off by the construction of the temporary PATH commuter rail station along one side of that seven-story depression, known as "the bathtub," and by the remains of the color-coded parking garage still wedged into the far end—a speck of the ruins about the height of the Murrah Federal Building in Oklahoma City, and resembling its bombed state in the rag of its exposed layers. She described her vision for the memorial, as she would have to anyone who came too close: there would be 2,792 angels—the death count had stabilized at that number, though it would soon fall again by forty—rendered in bronze, wings spread, looking down on the pit from the top of its concrete retaining walls. "Is there enough room?" she asked. "Can I fit all my angels here?"

As time passed, it became clear that the scale of the site was elusive. In New York City, value is measured in square feet, and every apartment is a measuring stick. No one knows how big an acre is. As the papers came out with the first exhaustive reminders of the Twin Towers' giganticism (forty thousand doorknobs), we learned that each of them occupied one acre—and, because they lacked the decorous setbacks of older buildings, one acre per floor, a square roughly two hundred feet per side. There's safety in numbers, a kind of *accounting* that is impossible any other way. In the fall of 2001, a professor at one of the elite East Coast architecture schools asked her students to imagine accessible ways to represent the center's lost space; it would equal 261 football fields, one student found, stretching from the site up to the middle of the Bronx; another calculated the number of cups of coffee that could fill both twins. Journalists cast about for hooks—As much office space as downtown St. Louis! Twenty Toledos! A thousand Peorias!—before defaulting to that anodyne measure: sixteen acres, sometimes seventeen, when the area of the rubble on surrounding streets was thrown in. It was a confident assessment for a mundane city. But it left the site's capacity for the sacred undefined. How many angels can dance on the edge of the pit? Like everything else in town, that would have to be quantified before it could be sold.

Faced with the unknown, Washington and New York reacted in concert by returning to first principles: New York would not forget its wallet, and the capital would not forget that Americans, with little else to bind them, love their flag. This should have been a comfort, one of few in that terrible season. We don't want to see the act against a city that would change its ways; we don't want to see a devastation so complete that those native rules of engagement are thrown out. No one had witnessed such destruction outside of a movie theater, but it would become very clear that the events of September 11 were not a big enough hit to make a new ethic stick. They were not a big enough hit in Washington to change one of that city's signal habits: exploiting tragedy for political gain. What those sixteen acres could do, how they could be put to partisan work even as they burned, was first grasped by beltway politicians, with Republicans out in front of Democrats by a mile.

After what seemed in the warped time of that first week like an interminable delay, George W. Bush arrived at Ground Zero on the morning of Friday, September 14. Here he found a stage-prop elderly fireman, not too tall to hook a consoling arm around, and also a convenient mound from which he addressed the workers through a bullhorn. As one of his sharpest critics had already noted, Bush tends to belligerence anyway when speaking without benefit of a teleprompter. So it was no surprise that, answering a call from the crowd—"We can't hear you!"—he would bellow one of the defining lines of his presidency: "I can hear you, the rest of the world hears you, and the people who knocked these buildings down will hear from all of us soon!" The hard hats responded with "U.S.A.! U.S.A.!" and—the perils of live television—some off-color anti-Arab remarks, behind the camera but audible, quickly squelched by cooler heads. Bush wouldn't directly invoke rebuilding until a speech the following Thursday, but this first statement set the tone. As translated into the popular imagination, it sanctioned the distinctive tenor of the early response and inspired the first widely seen proposals for the site.

Juliet McIntyre, a twenty-year-old Scientologist from Manhattan, helped run the commandeered showers at Stuyvesant High School for the first three weeks after the attack. Her job put her in constant contact with recovery workers on break, looking to talk, and they found a receptive audience in the young volunteer under a stars-and-stripes hard hat (a coveted trophy on the pile). In an enthusiastic account of her time at Ground Zero—she wrote a chapter chronicling the many visits by celebrities—McIntyre recorded, somewhat scandalized, the earliest architectural stirrings of the culture of retribution at the site.

"When we asked the guys how the area should be rebuilt, half the men thought the Towers should not be rebuilt and the area should be turned into a memorial park," she wrote. "The next few answers I got were a little more radical. Quite a few workers thought the Towers should be rebuilt a story taller and at the top they should have a giant statue of a hand flipping off the terrorists. The next one was similar but even more extravagant. These rescue workers thought we should build five buildings, also forming the shape of a hand with the middle finger extended. Two short ones on either side, then two a little higher, and finally the middle building sticking high into the air. I'm not sure whether that one is going to be the most popular."[18]

In fact, it remained among the most popular and durable ideas for the site. Within days of the attack, a crude Photoshop doctoring of the Twin Towers—cut, multiplied, and pasted back on the pre-eleventh skyline—was making the rounds on the nation's jangling e-mail nerves. This was the first scheme many people saw—*FUCK YOU!*—the first essay at making meaning through construction at Ground Zero. In this case it was an emotion that architecture, wielded in the spirit of a broadside snipe, could successfully express. It was also the closest that architecture would ever come through the long campaign to reinventing itself as a medium of popular mass communication. In time there were at least three versions, all unsigned, two of which found their way to an online shop where they were available on T-shirts, boxer shorts, mugs, and the inevitable mouse pads.[19]

It was clear in the language that grew up instantly around the event, in the ferment at the site, that there would have to be a shrine to the civic religion of the United States—"we hold these truths to be self-evident," etc.—as well as to the swashbuckling variant that had been reborn that day in force; within hours of the attack, someone had scratched "An eye for an eye, Semper Fi" into the ash on a window of a Brooks Brothers store that was being used as a makeshift morgue. No corner of New York had been asked to celebrate America—not New York's glory—since the statue, a gift from the French, was assembled on Liberty Island in 1886. Now, beyond replacing the offices and shops and train stations—things it could do and, by local standards, do well—the city's peculiar development culture would have to produce that other much more slippery thing. The national audience, and particularly their representatives in Washington, needed a new symbol raised, as sure a sign that the nation was fighting back as an unqualified victory in Afghanistan (or later Iraq) and the capture of Osama bin Laden (or later Saddam Hussein). The patriotic pressure on the site only intensified. Rebuilding Ground Zero was the only response to September 11 that America could achieve without the cooperation of her enemies.

But New York is not exactly the homeland. That was demonstrated spectacularly in the summer of 2001 by George Bush himself. On July 10, he visited the famous screening station on Ellis Island to announce plans to streamline immigration policy. ("New arrivals should be greeted not with suspicion and resentment, but with openness and courtesy.") As he posed for a photograph with the harbor and the elapsing downtown skyline as a backdrop, a reporter asked him what he thought of New York City. "It's a beautiful day," he snapped, and his hosts, Governor Pataki and Mayor Giuliani, squirmed. Bush had visited thirty-two other states before he made it to New York, and to his country's most important city, the one he did admit later that day was "the capital of the world."[20]

New York is at once the most and least American city, and its repatriation would not be simple. Many New Yorkers were probably surprised to learn that their home was the nation's first capital, as was repeated so often when Congress rolled into town on September 9, 2002, for a special session a few blocks from Ground Zero. They met at Federal Hall, the Greek Revival block built over the site of George Washington's inauguration and the drafting of the Bill of Rights, a building occasionally sought out by tourists but known to natives only because its steep steps make an inviting seat for lunch on the Wall Street corner it shares with the New York Stock Exchange.

And then New Yorkers are averse to flags. The most prominent public building after the Pentagon that represents all four branches of the armed forces is a little recruiting station perched on a narrow traffic island in Times Square. In 1998, it was rebuilt by a young local firm. They had struggled to find an expression for it that would please their feuding warrior clients. Finally, out of options, they proposed to ornament the building with the American flag—one on each long side, rendered in colored fluorescent tubes—an on-the-nose gesture they, or any New York sophisticate, would never have made except under duress. The military men loved it, and, as it was lost in the swirl of the other Times

Square signs, the architects went along. So it was something new when the city followed the country and hoisted the colors in the fall of 2001—along every avenue in Manhattan, the boroughs veering more to hand-painted tricolor lampposts and Old Glory fire hydrants. In some of the more predictably dissenting neighborhoods around town, from the same windows where posters had promoted Ralph Nader's candidacy for president the year before, another strange new symbol appeared: a banner with fields of white, Dutch orange, and ocean blue (colors familiar to fans of the Mets and Knicks), an Indian standing in for trade, and a windmill for industry—the seldom-seen flag of New York City.

Those two flags flanked Rudy Giuliani at the secret command center he set up on September 11 at the Police Academy, and for a time he would bridge the distance between them: "America's Mayor." But as he found later when he began to argue for making the whole site a memorial, Giuliani was powerless to change the people who build his city. In New York, an acre is as an acre does. And as the smoke cleared in those very early days, those sixteen acres downtown were being asked to do the impossible: to make sense of the senseless; to extol the dead even as they were being exhumed; to transform victims into heroes and heroes into gods; to find meaning in the squalor of real-time mass murder. This last task was of particular interest to the largest group of stakeholders, looking on from near and very far: witnesses beyond number. As the redevelopment process rolled forward, they would be there to demand an architectural object onto which all could project their confusion and have it returned to them as resolve—pain soothed, bloodlust sanitized. The flag and the wars and the site itself would only be a stopgap until the burghers and bureaucrats of Manhattan could serve up something more.

"What is the response to the event?" architect Daniel Libeskind asked in the summer of 2003, gesturing at a paper model of his master plan in his new office near Ground Zero. "It is what we build here. That is the response."[21]

2

OUR BUILDINGS, OURSELVES

MINORU YAMASAKI was born in Seattle in 1912. He grew up without plumbing, washing once a week in a galvanized tub. When he was young, his father took him along on weekends to help clean a chocolate factory but would not allow him a single bite. His mother imagined him a pianist. She dressed her little boy with the result that the kids at school called him "sissy." Visiting Japan in 1933, he got drunk for the first time and was propositioned by a cousin. (He was so rattled he couldn't sleep.) Yamasaki weathered the Depression working at salmon canneries in Alaska. He stole from the owners' larder to prepare a Fourth of July feast for the other nisei workers, breaking their starvation diet of rice and beans. One day an overseer on the cannery line told him to work faster, and Yamasaki—a small man, at that moment holding a long steel spike—knocked the boss, in his Sunday best, into a bin of rotting fish. It was, Yamasaki later wrote, "the most violent situation I have ever experienced."[1]

We know these things because, like many of the prominent architects in the decades after World War II—perhaps following the lead of that grand narcissist Frank Lloyd Wright, in whose shadow they worked even then—Minoru Yamasaki recorded his life in an ambling memoir. His *A Life in Architecture*, published in 1979, also tells us that as an architecture student at the University of Washington in the 1930s, he "had no drawing skills" and "no aptitude for sculpture." He asked a professor if he should drop out and was told he would become one of the best architects ever to pass through the school. He rallied, graduated, and went to New York City, where he bounced between the top firms. When World War II came, he studied the design of air-raid shelters, then moved upstate to build a naval training station on Seneca Lake, having satisfied military inquisitors that his marriage, on December 5, 1941, had not been timed to beat the Zeros to Pearl Harbor.

Yamasaki's Alaskan indenture made him determined to live life "more beautifully," he wrote, "not solely a material life, but one in which aesthetics and gentility were much more involved,"[2] and his work as an architect would be characterized by an attempt to weld a sort of sissy finesse to the broad shoulders of American commerce. To him the result was grace; the best of modern technology and the best of proven decorative forms. In the 1950s and 1960s, when Mies van der Rohe was a living and then a recently deceased god, and his "less is more" a drafting-room mantra, Yamasaki's buildings, at once gracile and fussy, gently dissented. His detractors labeled him a "cosmetician," an "exterior decorator," a "romantic,"[3] a "kitsch-monger;"[4] an ally called him an "Oriental enigma."[5] The World Trade Center—particularly the Twin Towers, with their Moorish filigree top and bottom—was the mature expression of Yamasaki's style, developed earlier, among other places, in a synagogue outside of Chicago and an airport in Saudi Arabia.

In the noise that followed their destruction, Yamasaki's two towers were made to mean many things. They became symbols of commerce, symbols of American strength or diversity, even, though they looked like cages, symbols of freedom. But few of the ex post facto caption writers, assigning intent to the fallen giants to leverage one agenda or another, would have dared before to apply the meaning that their architect had fancied for them. To Yamasaki, the Twins were aspirational. "I am happy I was able to design these very large buildings with the proper scale relationship so necessary to man," he wrote in his memoirs. "They are intended to give him a soaring feeling, imparting pride and a sense of nobility in his environment."[6] That aspiration was to evoke a still higher frame of mind; when people stood under the towers, their thoughts would not turn to shipping rates or the difficulty of their commutes, but to the abstraction that the buildings were somehow to represent. Beyond bringing dignity to office workers, Yamasaki had another aim. Prejudice had shaped his life in Alaska and Washington—his parents had moved in with him in New York to avoid internment during the war—and, he thought, his defiance of it had shaped his World Trade Center into a "physical expression of the universal effort of men to seek and achieve world peace."[7]

When that physical expression was brought down by the specific efforts of ten hate-crazed ideologues, it was clear what had been lost in human terms; Giuliani said it that first week: "more than any of us can bear." But the value of the towers in architectural terms was an unknowable quantity. Were they "sheer bombast" soured by "a dose of hubris," as *Newsweek* had claimed when they were built?[8] Were they "the ultimate Disneyland," an example of "pure schmaltz," or "General Motors Gothic,"[9] as Ada Louise Huxtable, then the *New York Times'* enormously influential architecture critic, had decided? Lewis Mumford, perhaps the only critic whose words held more sway, had argued that, like all tall buildings, they were the product of "outmoded . . . Victorian" thinking: "The World Trade Center's fate is to be ripped down as nonsensical."[10] For all the millions in the area who had looked to them as a thrilling anchor on the skyline—for the millions more who had visited to experience their particular frisson—a cadre of elite opinion had fixed the idea: the buildings were just plain bad.

One result of this long consensus was the ease with which, breathtakingly close to the event itself, unreconstructed critics could openly express no regret over the loss of the buildings, as if their inability to satisfy the vogues of new eras had rendered them disposable. Nearly every other now-beloved symbol in town had gotten off on the wrong foot: the Chrysler Building had been dismissed as an advertising stunt, the Empire State had been dubbed the "Empty State"; even the towers of Rockefeller Center, long the gold standard of responsible, inventive urbanism, had been welcomed with vitriolic ink. The Twin Towers' disgrace was certainly a temporary state; younger New Yorkers who had never known the city without them—the same generations that had made the 1970s and even the 1980s cool—would have laundered their reputation in time. But the drumbeat that had started before they topped out continued as they burned. Why was it so easy for one observer to share his first thought after watching the towers fall: "Thank goodness. At least it's not the Chrysler Building or the Empire State Building"?[11] One tradition-minded architect, just a touch blunter than most, said, "If you could have lost the World Trade Center without loss of life it would have been an incredible victory."[12]

There were other responses. One came loud and clear out of many of the miniature obituaries written by the *New York Times* for its monumental "Portraits of Grief" project: people loved those buildings, they always had, even the ones who had to work there.[13]

Jonathan Hakala worked in the north tower, where the company he ran, Threshold Capital Management, had its office. His best friend died twenty-five floors above, at Cantor Fitzgerald, the tragic firm where no one who had come to work that day survived. Hakala did, but like many people, he couldn't leave the buildings behind. "The seventy-seventh floor of One World Trade Center was not my apartment, but it was my home," he said on one occasion. Hakala was the spokesman for Team Twin Towers, a group that formed in the spring of 2002 to represent the interests of those whose adoration of the towers, mixed with fury at the manner of their loss, had brought them to advocate what was always among the most popular and least politically correct options for the site: reconstruction. Their message had an appealing simplicity, one that Hakala spelled out in all its vengeance: "We will rebuild at least a hundred and ten stories of *occupied* height and we *will* go back."

Team Twin Towers was not pushing for direct copies—that was a cause for less sophisticated groups—but it was insistent that a wounded America had to draw a line in the sky at 110 stories, twice, and not retreat from it. Again, the message was moral clarity simple. "This is a site that was destroyed in an act of war," said Bill Hough, another Team Member (as they called themselves). "The regular rules should not apply." It was about pride: two towers went up, two came down, two should go back up—higher. Amiad Finkelthal, the Team's publicist, put it even more plainly: "It's time for New York to kick some ass!"

It was about pride, but also about the ancient urge to dominate that architecture, when extremely tall, can still express so well. Louis Epstein, founder of the World Trade Center Restoration Movement—an allied group—is a pale and studious man, tall but stoop shouldered, with an amazing red Gandalf beard that reaches nearly to his waist. He knew what to do when a great tower fell. At one public hearing on the redevelopment, when a local resident said, "I encourage you to build as low as possible," Epstein, seated, put his chin down on his chest, clamped his brow and shook his head—his beard so long it took a beat to catch up—before, silently, in a kind of ecstatic rage, he shot twin fists, twin thumbs raised, high in the auditorium air. *Build up! Build up!*

The idea of returning the world's tallest building to the site was around from day one—some of those early middle-finger proposals appeared to be at least three hundred stories high—but the advocacy of Team Twin Towers helped keep it alive. The group articulated a rotating list of rationales to fit the season, pride-based arguments segueing into practical ones—tall buildings would preserve more space on the ground for parks or a memorial—as the blood slowly left people's heads. More than once reporters chose to make news from Jon Hakala's words, leading to headlines such as "At Hearing: A Resolve to Rebuild Twin Towers"[14] in the *Times* or this front pager in the *Post:* "Half of New York Wants the Twin Towers REBUILT."[15]

Though it would always run at least 50 percent in scientific polls (online it did much better), the idea of replacing the Twins never really had a fair trial. It was a victim of the hobbling assumptions the process gathered. Team Twin Towers addressed this in its 2002 annual report: "Many people have given up hope that the Twin Towers will be rebuilt, largely because of 'conventional wisdoms' such as: 'the process has already been decided,' 'no one will work or rent there,' 'the victims' families won't permit it.' [The Team's] massive publicity campaign will rouse this silent majority to action . . ."

In the Sunday-after survey of architects in the *New York Times Magazine*, Richard Meier said, "We need office space, though we don't want to build the same towers—they were designed in 1966 and now we live in 2001."[16] Others would invoke the environmental impact—sewage, shadows, crowded sidewalks. But, in the end, the argument could not be so handily dismissed without recourse to taste, elite taste: that three-decade-long litany of critical invective. And what could be more arbitrary? There would have been no question what to do had the Brooklyn Bridge been attacked. But what of a structure of such middling iconic status as the Flatiron Building, a building that to admire is really to celebrate the anomalies of the Manhattan grid? If it were to go, well-heeled nostalgists would have it rebuilt in a New York minute. That was part of what fired the Team Twin Towers activists, a secondary anger that would carry them through the years spent on the crowded margins: the sense that they were on the losing side of an undeclared class war.

Like the best underdogs, they never acknowledged the perfection of the powers they tilted against—Larry Silverstein, whose bombproof lease decreed exactly how much office space would have to be rebuilt; the combined will of local, state, and national government; even the silent majority, stoked by grief and whipsawed by received wisdom, happy enough to accept a less literal defiance. Hakala, for one, never countenanced that his battle could be lost before it had begun; long after the process had taken another course and the possibility of new Twins on the skyline was nil, he confided, "We're working behind the scenes to build the coalition we're going to need to bring this whole house of cards tumbling down." At one hearing, where his teammates attempted to forge an unlikely alliance-of-the-powerless with some of the victims' family groups, Hakala stood at a microphone in a near-empty auditorium. (The room would have been empty but for the diligence of the rebuild-'em warriors, one of whom had flown in from Germany to say, "Allowing terrorists to permanently destroy the Twin Towers is like allowing them to remove a star or a stripe from the flag.")[17] Elegant and forlorn, he closed out the meeting. "Where is everybody?" he asked, pointing to the unfilled seats. "Where's the public input for the most important architecture project in the world?"

The mistake made by Jon Hakala and his fellow travelers was to believe that the World Trade Center meant all that its architect had said it did. Though architecture can speak, it does not do so with the certainties of a Hakala or a Yamasaki. Great architecture sings, but it does so wordlessly, not so much by telling us this or that, than by triggering some nameless emotion (and the more nameless the better). As anyone traversing the contemporary sprawl knows, most buildings just sit there mute, declaring themselves in desperate pantomime. Or they stammer: *gas, food, lodging; HoJo, Wawa, Hess.* In cities, having endured a thousand insults from the drafting board to the site, there is usually little more for a building to say than *I stand, and it was a damn hard slog to get here.*

For modern buildings, this problem is acute. Stripped of the cues of history, often rejecting the powerful, stone-simple tools of hierarchy and symmetry and, crucially, ornament—which can so easily bridge the distance between an architect's intentions and the beholder's response—what is left? New York's old Customs House at Bowling Green, built in 1907 with all the opulent vigor of the *École des Beaux-Arts*, announces its nature from afar with heavy columns and arches and a broad central stair; its function, intrinsic to its meaning, becomes clear closer up, conveyed effortlessly by the four sculptures set before it—allegorical figures of Asia, Africa, Europe, and America swathed in their respective bounties. Grotesque busts ringing the building depict the tribes of the world that trade through this entrepôt would reach and ennoble.

Three parts racist, one part comical, it's not a message anyone would endorse today. But the task for modern architects—one that the pioneers of the movement set out for themselves in the 1910s and 1920s—was not to refute old messages or communicate none, but to forge vehicles for conveying new ones, appropriate to new times, new people, in new forms, propelled by advances in materials and techniques. The architecture of New York's next Customs House, the irregular black hulk of 6 World Trade Center, could be endlessly interpreted—a bastard child of greed and expedience, an avatar of bureaucracy—but as we have seen, its designer had imagined a very specific symbolic life for it, and for its neighbors. In reality, though, tucked into the corner of the site, indistinguishable from buildings 4 and 5, trumped by the towers, the Customs House could be identified only by signage. And when a sign tells you what a public building is because its architecture can't even grunt a hint, something's wrong.

That gap, between architect's intention and building's effect, would have to be closed before any design could satisfy the prodigious public craving for a meaningful architecture at Ground Zero. But how does modern architecture mean anything? We know what traditional columns and arches and domes and such are supposed to be telling us when they are stacked by convention this way or that to make temples and palaces according to laws set by arbiters of decorum in some lost age. Thanks to the tenacity of cultural readings, they mostly still do mean those things—dignity, splendor, order, permanence—when they are repurposed for government buildings or banks or mansions, even if at times their context, the real world of today, soaks the whole affair in irony.

Classical architects, of which there seems to be an increasing (and increasingly well-organized) number, limit themselves to the rearrangement of their proven Greco-Roman syllabary to get new words for the old senses they want to convey. God bless them, but it's a pursuit with all the ambition of an undertaker's. Collectively, modern architects pursued a much more audacious project—the invention of a language. But having long before cast aside the meanings that clung to classical forms—the ones that people actually *get*—they never succeeded in that next brave step, to make their buildings speak or, failing that, an even braver step: to accept that they need not speak at all.

The modern movement was young when the question of how to transmit civic meaning through new forms and symbols—in short, how to make monuments—was taken up. Eventually codified under the rubric "The New Monumentality," the quest would remain modern architecture's great unfinished project, its Achilles' heel.

In the beginning, in Europe, with the modern style primarily deployed for private buildings—factories, villas, shops—there was less of a need to project anything beyond the obvious; set within aging stone cities, it was clear by contrast what white walls and pilotis and plate glass stood for: mental hygiene, material progress. But after World War II, when it displaced a lingering classicism in public construction, modern architecture had to expand its palette. It faced then the challenge of all victorious revolutions: proving that its ideas could really work to make a better world.

Theorists had been preparing for this day. In 1943, modern architecture's master polemicist, Siegfried Giedion, wrote one of his more influential manifestos, *Nine Points on Monumentality*. In his first point, Giedion defined monuments broadly as "human land-marks which men have created as symbols for their ideals, for their aims, and for their actions."[18] The eighth point—one repercussion of which was the World Trade Center's grand plaza—suggested that, after the war, it would be necessary to raze entire quarters of cities to create "vast open spaces" in which "monumental archi-tecture will find its appropriate setting which does not now exist." In his final point, Giedion got down to the nitty-gritty, listing the means that modern architects had at hand to achieve the legibility and presence of a monument: "light metal structures; curved, laminated wooden arches; panels of different textures, colors and sizes. . . . Mobile elements can constantly vary the aspect of the buildings . . . changing positions and casting different shadows when acted upon by wind or machinery. . . . During night hours, color and forms can be projected on vast surfaces . . . for purposes of publicity or propaganda."[19]

That it was not architecture but advertising that picked up Giedion's thread confirms how lost the monumental project be-came in the years after the war. The editors of *Architectural Review*, the leading trade journal in the United Kingdom, saw it coming. In 1948, they published the proceedings of a symposium, "In Search of a New Monumentality." In their introduction, they antici-pated, from the economic shambles of the immediate postwar years, the approach of a crisis at the moment when prosperity re-turned to demand the construction of nonutilitarian buildings: "Before long, representational buildings, those in which the com-munity requires some kind of monumental gesture, will be re-quired again: town halls, cinemas, sports arenas, public libraries." If, at that time, modern architecture had failed to develop the "richer vocabulary required," then, the editors argued, it would "strengthen the hands" of the movement's foes.[20]

That crisis did arrive, and its residue is all around us. You can see it in aging modern public schools, where roadside signs and flags have had to be brought in to augment the symbolic shortcomings of strip windows, yellow brick, and plastic panels. You can see it in modern city halls, where concrete eruptions or perforated metal screens promote some idea of civic life far too cryptic to discern. It is particularly easy to gauge modern architecture's distance from easy reading in the great wave of churches and synagogues that were built in the United States in the 1950s and 1960s. Meant to convey the messages of their faith, they more often confound with a rain of symbols decipherable only by that elect class of high priests, their architects.

Most cities, and all university campuses, have examples of monumental modern buildings so far from comprehensibility that they generate their own shadow histories: *The architect was drunk. He lost the plans. He ran out of money for windows. He built it upside down.* But it was not drink, not carelessness that brought these buildings low; it was the attempt—noble, really—of their architects to make them say grand things in an untested, immature style that did not anyway lend itself, even in the hands of a genius, to projecting society's dreams. (How does a nonrepresentational art *represent?*) Maybe a dozen buildings worldwide got it right, and two in New York: The spinning drum of Frank Lloyd Wright's Guggenheim Museum on Fifth Avenue clearly says, *There is another world in here*, and must have said it even more clearly when it first took shape in the late 1950s. Eero Saarinen's wingspread concrete Trans World Airlines terminal certainly said, *Come fly with me into the future* in a way that the first departing passengers in 1962 could understand, even if, having been built for propeller planes, its functionality was soon challenged by the jet.

It is the birthright of modern architects to reinvent the wheel; successful precedent was rarely followed, and had it been, it would have been attacked as derivative. During the postwar building boom, architects galloped off in all directions as they searched for ways to create a new language for civic monuments, as they tried to realize in modern form Giedion's "human landmarks." In the process, buildings of nearly every type, whether they merited such treatment or not, were reimagined as vectors for communication, symbols for societies' ideals, aims, and actions. This undisciplined, unsuccessful monumentalizing—and the heavy-handed urban planning that cleared the way for it—is responsible for much of the forbidding look of cities redeveloped at mid-century: rows of obscure, self-important buildings set on their own plazas or podiums, aloof from the street, oppressing, not connecting with, passersby.

The search for a modern monumentality contributed to a proliferation of styles, opening up a dizzying array of new directions for architects. By 1960, those American architects who had grown used to modernist dogma were in a self-declared state of emergency. Philip Johnson, typically insouciant, fanned the flames that year in an article titled, "Where Are We At?" "We are going through a foggy chaos," the man who would later be known as the Dean of American Architecture wrote. "Let us enjoy the multiplicity of it all. Let the students have a new hero every year. Maybe it is good for them."[21] In 1961, *Progressive Architecture* published a three-part series surveying the state of architecture in what the magazine had decided to call "the Period of Chaoticism."[22] Yamasaki, as sure a cause of the chaos as any architect, piled on the next year. "There is no question about the existence of such confusion," he wrote in *Art in America*, not long after he was selected from a group of forty firms to design the World Trade Center. "Its evidence is in the explosion of architectural ideas that have indiscriminately gushed forth to fill the streets of our cities. . . . Today we have a kind of anarchy in architecture. . . . Without the discipline and inspiration which can be provided by a clear understanding of purpose, we will not be able to accomplish the gigantic job of framing modern man in his proper environment."[23]

Architects had rebuilt the public landscape with the intention of making it comprehensible to the public, but no one on the street could read the good intentions embedded in the bad urbanism all around. Even the architects themselves were forced to assess the crop of new monuments with head scratching and a collective "oops." Had the moderns thrown out the baby with the Beaux Arts bathwater?

Enter postmodernism. Despite his role in popularizing modern architecture in America—his 1932 show at the Museum of Modern Art had given birth to the International Style—Philip Johnson's permissiveness and, profoundly, his high-profile turn back to historical precedent in his buildings of the 1960s did more than anything to prepare the ground for modernism's successor. A widespread rebellion against the dysfunctional urban environment that modern architecture and planning had created in the service of monumentality—the windswept plazas, the dead streets, the lonely towers—signaled the end of modernism. Yamasaki's own Pruitt-Igoe public housing project in St. Louis—meant, like all his buildings, to aggrandize its occupants—became such a breeding ground for crime and anomie soon after it opened that it had to be evacuated and condemned; order-seeking architectural historians have long used the moment of the project's controlled implosion in 1972 to mark the dawn of the postmodern period. More than anything, postmodernism—a style in which architects once again played the classical canon (if now reveling in the ironies of their play)—was a testament to the failure of the New Monumentality, a measure of how far modern architects had come from making modern buildings speak to and for modern culture, and a rebuke of the mess they had made trying, a mess that for many was nowhere more conspicuous than in Yamasaki's inscrutable, inhospitable Twins.

"All architecture is what you do to it when you look upon it," Walt Whitman wrote in "A Song for Occupations." "(Did you think it was in the white or gray stone? or the lines of the arches and cornices?)" Like most buildings, the towers were, as they appeared, a blank. On the skyline, at their best, they offered only the meanings of minimalist sculpture: there is light here, at dusk it is orange. There is a surface; there is an edge. This is solid, this is air— qualities teased out of the complex in 1977 when the artist Robert Irwin, installing one in a series of interventions around the city, stretched two wires across the main gate to the plaza in what he said was an attempt to amplify the center's subtleties.

Its architect having failed to communicate a specific vision, the World Trade Center invited everyone's. To a single busy critic writing in 1976, the Twin Towers were "mysterious, tombstone-like monoliths," "a pair of giant cigarette cartons," "a standing monument to architectural boredom," "an aluminum-sided disaster."[24] Ever-popular, too, were the cynicisms of a socio-economic reading: the towers as the very maw of Mammon. Undeniably, there were humans shelved tier upon rentable tier in the World Trade Center. But it was never quite clear how that common condition brought with it a collective facelessness—any more than does Manhattan in aggregate—as if to work in the towers or gaze upon them would confer an irrevocable loss of humanity.

Like nearly every architect of his day who is now accused of making our cities unlivable, Yamasaki preached humanism. "The concept of an architecture for all people instead of a select few is only possible through the adherence to a humanist philosophy— one which is consistent with the ideals we seek," he wrote in 1962. "Proportion, elegance of detail and nobility exist in the wonderful European buildings of the past. Though they must be translated into our own idioms, we can be much inspired by the expression of these qualities in great examples of architecture."[25]

Humanism for Yamasaki—as it was for his peers who came to be called the New Brutalists—was a humanism for consenting adults, unafraid of the bracing *grand geste*. The Twin Towers, above all, were pitched to those willing to face the true scale of modern technical achievement. When, during the planning for those buildings, his colleagues began to think that the effect might be something other than uplifting, Yamasaki sent them to walk around the base of the Empire State Building: "They came back convinced, as I was, that there was no diminution of the soul, no antlike feelings in the face of such a large object. Man had made it and man could comprehend it."[26] To join Yamasaki in that take, one had to bring an equal appreciation of the man-made sublime, the thing that moves people to be near the Hoover Dam or the Golden Gate Bridge or, when it stood, the World Trade Center. Those marvelers know why the wonders of the world are so wonderful: "Man had made it," just plain folks (the man who made the Twin Towers liked "rumble seat necking,"[27] went wild for azaleas, and was for a time addicted to morphine), and to appreciate the work, it doesn't matter what shape it comes in.

In the mixed-up world of politics, architectural history, and blood that the attack begot, the breadth of interpretations of the towers' meaning was reflected in the breadth of theories about Osama bin Laden's motivations. Though Washington claimed that the events of September 11 were intended to strike a blow against "freedom," there is very little in Bin Laden's statements before or since to suggest this. Was it about money? Al Qaeda may not have been behind the elaborately stoked greed that led some unknown master of the universe to short-sell futures for the airlines whose planes were hijacked just days before the attack—an investigation into that corruption was inconclusive—but there is anecdotal evidence that past business slights may have played a role: when American builders and architects (Yamasaki among them) flocked to Saudi Arabia in the 1960s and 1970s to bring modern roads and plants and ports to the desert kingdom, the bin Ladens' construction company (in which Osama then worked) was bypassed for foreign firms.

And then, writing for *Slate*, Laurie Kerr detailed the debt to Islamic architecture in Yamasaki's failed symbolic program for the trade center. Her article included the assertion that the plan, with its icons distributed around a central open space, might be seen to blithely mimic the arrangement of the holy places in Mecca—suggesting that Osama bin Laden's hatred for the towers was based in part in aesthetic critique. "Having rejected modernism and the Saudi royal family, it's no surprise that Bin Laden would turn against Yamasaki's work in particular," she wrote. "He must have seen how Yamasaki had clothed the World Trade Center, a monument of Western capitalism, in the raiment of Islamic spirituality."[28] It would be less of a stretch to look for such motives in Mohammed Atta, the terrorist assumed to have piloted the first plane into the north tower that day. At the Technical University of Hamburg-Harburg, Atta had studied urban planning—he had already trained as an architect in Cairo—with a slant toward the anti-modern; his thesis on the souk in Aleppo, Syria (which has been embargoed by the school's library), is said to have argued for traditional development as a means to resist Western influence on Arab cities. He was especially disturbed by skyscrapers. Thus the inevitable joke in architecture circles: Atta merely acted out the will of the towers' many critics.

The anti-modern impulse was also evident in one of the first well-publicized visions for the site. The Manhattan Institute, a conservative think tank, invited the classical architecture firm Franck Lohsen McCrery and the Scottish sculptor Alexander Stoddart to conceive a design that would "correct the errors" of Yamasaki's World Trade Center. The results were published in the November 2001 issue of the institute's magazine, *City Journal*. ("Part of the U.S. triumph over its attackers should be the swift rebuilding of the site where the massacre occurred, constructing something even prouder and more splendid than the vanished Twin Towers," the editors wrote.)[29] The plan proposed to reintroduce all the streets through the superblock that the trade center had occupied, with a long plaza, "Liberty Square," located at its core and approached through triumphal arches. The architects were careful to operate within the limits of the informal mandate—

big buildings, a train station, a memorial—that conventional wisdom had already so effectively established. On the south end of the square, they sited "Liberty Station," to the north, a defiant skyscraper, "One Liberty Square." In front of each iconic building, they proposed that old standby, representational sculpture on a monumental scale: statues of firemen and police in front of the station and, opposite—under what would be the world's tallest building—allegorical monuments "thrice life-size" that would translate the event into the comforts of the civic record: "Two great pylons are surmounted by History, who directs one's gaze to her tablet, and Memory, who bears her always-illuminating torch aloft, directly above the draped catafalque—the resting place for the deceased, many of whom have no other grave but this."[30]

All the buildings in the Manhattan Institute plan, with their urbanistically correct setbacks and matching cornice lines, were rendered in a kind of stripped Art Deco—the style that many classical architects had resorted to at mid-century in an effort to counter the threat of the ascendant modern alternative. As the process wore on, the reductive simplicity of this plan, and its faith in timeworn markers, made it attractive. At least it was urbane, and comprehensible, which is more than can be said of the less hidebound architectural deluge that would follow.

A sister reaction to the classical retreat to statues and arches was to glory in the profundity of the ruins. Again, through the intellectual heritage of the West, we are all supposed to know what ruins mean: romance, principally, a confrontation with the weight of history, pining for great cultures lost. There were also, among architects, more recent referents: the work of trendy designers in the "blob" or "decon" modes, whose forms aped the chaos of contemporary ruins. As images of the lean-to wreckage were broadcast to all points, it was only a matter of time before the ruins would be fetishized—by those seeking comfort in dusty Romantic tropes and by those in that high architectural stratum where eyes are tuned to fragmentation and minds are trained to distrust order.

When Philippe de Montebello, director of the Metropolitan Museum of Art, approached the scenic pile soon after the attack, he must have had Goethe in mind, bracingly looking out over some tomb-strewn Italian field, or perhaps he was channeling the ecstasy of Schliemann discovering Troy. Certainly he found what he saw quite moving; a few days later, he took quill in hand to draft a plea for the preservation of the ruins, which was published in the *New York Times* on September 25. He summarized some of the ideas then in the air—buildings? a park?—then made his case for the ancient meaning hidden in the brand-new monstrosity. "But no matter what form the reconstruction of the site takes, New York should make a commitment now to preserving the searing fragment of the ruin already so frequently photographed and televised that it has become nearly as familiar to us as the buildings that once stood there," de Montebello wrote. "This is the huge, skeletal and jagged steel fragment of the World Trade Center and its facade that still stubbornly stands in the midst of the utter destruction of ground zero." After citing some precedents—"Coventry enshrined its blitzed cathedral"—he got down to connoisseurship: "A relic of destruction, it could become a testament to renewal. As a symbol of survival, it is already, in its own way, a masterpiece."[31] A masterpiece. This only two weeks after the planes hit and the fireballs burst and the jumpers jumped and, from their burning offices, the soon-to-be-dead left their last words by cell phone on their answering machines back home.

De Montebello might have been uniquely tasteless, but in his love for the ruins he was not at all alone. Exactly two months after the attack, the *Times* architecture critic Herbert Muschamp wrote an article—"Commemorating the Beauty of Tragic Wreckage"—in which he described his evening on September 10. Muschamp had been with Frank Gehry, Alejandro Gehry, and Issey Miyake that fateful night, getting a sneak peek at the Miyake boutique in Tribeca, the important new work the three had contributed to the patrimony of New York retail. He mentioned his dinner at a high-end sushi place nearby, and then offered this: "It was raining heavily, but during dinner the downpour stopped. When we left the restaurant, a little before midnight, the twin towers reared up to infinity through tumbling, gray Wagnerian clouds. It was a good last look." The spirit of his outing carried through to color Muschamp's view of what was left on the ground the next day. Referring to the same peel of one tower's facade that de Montebello had celebrated, Muschamp applied the other, more contemporary rationalization to a defense of the ruins, which he had decided should be called "the Walls." "The bending, folding, curving shapes of the World Trade Center wreckage echo the neo-Baroque contortions of blob architecture as practiced by Greg Lynn, Ben van Berkel and others," Muschamp wrote, mentioning a style he had helped to promote and listing two of his favorite architects. "As a result of my experience, the Walls remind me of Miyake's pleated clothes, and of peaceful times."[32]

The last upright ruins—a ten-story piece of the south tower known to workers as "the shroud"—were pulled down on December 15, 2001. But the possibility of appropriating the ruins was by no means lost, even when the final column was removed, with fallen-hero's honors on a flag-draped bier, the following spring. As the first truckloads of debris left the burning site in the darkest days of the cleanup, an architect hired by the Port Authority was on hand to tag those pieces of morbid steel that were judged in passing to have aesthetic worth. The resulting collection, intended for use in a future memorial, was brought to an unlikely holding area: Hangar 17 at New York's John F. Kennedy International Airport. The Port also saved "the shroud" there—cut into thirty-one pieces and labeled for reassembly—along with dozens of crushed cars, a fire truck or two, and, for a time—until it was installed as a temporary memorial in Battery Park in 2002—the charred and dented *Sphere*, the nearly thirty-foot-high monument to world peace that had been the focal point of the trade center's vanished plaza.

The meaning of that abstract work, like the meaning of the buildings that had surrounded and overshadowed it, was known only because the artist had announced his intentions. But in the towers' absence, a new meaning was, for the first time, organically evolving toward consensus. Perhaps the earliest to codify it was Vincent Scully, a charismatic art history professor at Yale who has enthralled generations of students with his excitable accounts of architecture's expressive potential. Scully had been in the trenches of the later debates over the New Monumentality; in his short and therefore widely read book *Modern Architecture*, published in 1961, he had specifically directed younger architects to try to express modern values through the "tenaciously physical force of the Western architectural tradition."[33] But that was many enthusiasms ago; recognizing, as the world did, that the experiment had monumentally failed, he became an early champion of the initial wave of postmodern architects—many of whom were his students and colleagues at Yale—and, later, a key champion of the New Urbanism, the style's anti-modern urban planning wing.

On September 11, Scully gave a lecture that, in one of those haunting twists that seem so common, was planned to conclude with slides of the World Trade Center. There, and again at a symposium at Yale days later, he announced the new religion: the towers were now human symbols. "As you know, very few of us really liked the World Trade towers," he said in an interview soon thereafter. "They seemed too big, dumb and inarticulate. When they got hit, all the associations changed. All of a sudden, instead of looking inordinately tall, they looked heartbreaking. Now I love them."[34]

Popular culture was right there with Scully. Taking advantage of their twinning, the towers were used as stand-ins for the heroes of the day. Everywhere, artists arrived at the same brainstorm, depicting the towers as a firefighter and a policeman—"Standing Tall Together," as the bumper stickers had it—adding stars-and-stripes bunting to match the national mood. The image was also made into clumsy desktop sculptures, the bodies of the rescue workers morphing out of square tower stumps. Factories in China were soon receiving orders to update the products they made for sale at the Trade Center's gift shops: key chains, money clips, laser-etched plastic-block paperweights, all now with the dates "1973–2001" affixed. And there were new products, among them snow globes with fire trucks parked under the towers— underscoring the obvious, hideous memories that the falling glitter evoked—some mounted on music boxes playing "God Bless America."

These wares now found their way to lines of folding card tables set up on Broadway, and, when the construction fences moved back, to the edge of the pit itself. The trade in kitsch was brisk; repeated attempts to suppress it in response to the victims' families' complaints came to nothing, with each well-publicized purge undone by the vendors' limitless supply and the buyers' insatiable demand. Pilgrims to Ground Zero could find the souvenirs they needed, and bring them home to add to the store of images in their magazines and books, on their hard drives, and recurring whenever possible on the incorrigible news.

In their distribution to the four winds and the far corners of the earth, the buildings attained the kind of immortality that Victor Hugo once credited only to books. And it is in the way we revere them now, tamed in keepsake form, that Yamasaki's towers finally mean what he thought they always did: "The World Trade Center should, because of its importance, become a living representation of man's belief in humanity, his need for individual dignity, his belief in the cooperation of men, and through this cooperation his ability to find greatness."[35]

3

THE COOPERATION OF MEN

HAD SEPTEMBER 11 never happened, the big story through the fall of 2001 would have been the weather: warm and dry, day after day, with more of that clean, clear, dreadful deep blue sky. The long Indian summer was a boon to the recovery efforts, operating around the clock (at first under floodlights borrowed from a film production company) in a miracle of coordinated labor that would clear the site to bedrock months ahead of the best predictions. By late October, about one-quarter of the rubble—estimated at an incomprehensible 1.2 million tons—had been removed. Except for the steel pretzel twists archived at JFK—and similar trophies doled out for the asking to quickie memorial builders from Oak Ridge, Tennessee, to Fountain Valley, California—major pieces of structural steel were floated across the Hudson to scrap dealers in New Jersey, who bought the lot for about ninety dollars a ton. World trade, indeed: the manager of the yard handling the majority of the 285,000 tons of recyclable steel suggested it would be exported, smelted, and poured into everything from toasters to Toyotas. And, he told the *New York Times* three weeks after the attack, new beams and columns: "Hopefully, it will be made into a series of towers that are as proud as the ones that came down."[1]

The other destination for the wreckage was the unfortunately named Fresh Kills Landfill on Staten Island, fabled as the largest in the world and, with the Great Wall of China, very often said to be the only man-made object visible from space. At highway speeds, it takes about three minutes to wind between the landfill's five or six ersatz drumlins, separating the web of creeks (in Dutch: *kills*) from which it takes its name. On the highest point of the highest hill, a rounded crown with a clear view of the emasculated skyline of Lower Manhattan, a vast triage area was established immediately after the attack. If the pile downtown was the domain of machines— the grapplers and diggers whose clumsiness enraged firemen looking for their lost brothers—then Fresh Kills was the last preserve of handicraft. Workers attacked the barge- and truckloads with rakes and sifting screens, separating out Holocaust-evoking piles of watches and wallets from the roughly nine hundred thousand tons carted there. They also found twelve hundred wrecked vehicles and about twenty-nine hundred human body parts.[2]

Efforts were made to reunite the collected items with the families of the dead, and any recognizable remains found were sent to join the rest in the refrigerated trailers set up behind the city morgue at Bellevue. But in the infinity of the carnage, there was more than even the best efforts could count, and more than any agency would admit to; what was gently described as the "ashen remains," tons of it—enough to fill two stories of one twin, floor to the ceiling—were interred right there at Fresh Kills. A late-coming organization, WTC Families for Proper Burial, was born to right that wrong. "We didn't know it had happened until last year," said Diane Horning, cofounder with her husband, Kurt, in 2003. "I think it's outrageous. When we find a mass grave in Iraq, we all say, 'Oh my god!'" She had with her a photograph of the puddle-covered dump, as much the final resting place of her son Matthew, she felt, as the place where he died and was never found. At a meeting with the Hornings, Mayor Bloomberg told them, "I intend to leave my body to science, so that doesn't really worry me."[3]

There was some hope early on that the development powers would bend to the sobering context—that the Port Authority, which had built and owned the World Trade Center; Larry Silverstein who had just leased it; the politicians who sought to shape

the project; and the interest groups that had formed to thwart it
would, at the very least, engage under a flag of truce. How could
they possibly not? Few observers were as jaded (or, it would turn
out, as prescient) as Ada Louise Huxtable, when, just six days after
the attack, the *Wall Street Journal* published her first assessment of
the state of play:

> . . . one can almost predict what the New York process
> will be. This city can show its compassion, and its resolve,
> as it is doing now, but it is also a city incapable of the
> large, appropriate gesture in the public interest if it costs
> too much. . . . What are our values? How do we count the
> cost of those lives? Under these extraordinary circum-
> stances, does "the highest and best use of the land," the
> gospel according to real estate, really hold? Traditionally,
> that has meant filling the land to the maximum permitted
> by law, for the greatest return, while ignoring every social
> or human factor.
>
> If the usual scenario is followed, the debate will lead to
> a "solution" in which principle is lost and an epic oppor-
> tunity squandered. With the best intentions the Munici-
> pal Art Society, a conscientious watchdog of the city's
> urban quality, will announce a competition to determine
> what should be done with the site. The results will make a
> nice little exhibition, and discussions and lectures will be
> held. All this will be ignored by the movers and shakers
> making big building plans under the expedient banner of
> physical and symbolic reconstruction. There will be a fuss
> in the press, with letters to the editor, pro and con. City
> Hall, in a split political decision between greed and glory,
> will come out for the builders and a memorial—a monu-
> ment or a small park, something financially inoffensive in
> the larger scheme of things. This is The Compromise. Or
> the tradeoff, to put it more bluntly. A properly pious,

meaningless gesture that everyone can buy without loss of face or obvious shame.[4]

Huxtable was right; though it would be writ very large, the wrangling that followed mostly differed only in degree from New York City's everyday planning battles. The usual tribes that take part in the ritual of construction immediately re-formed in caricature; though the Municipal Art Society considered a competition, it decided not to sponsor one, but that group did conduct a massive "visioning" outreach—open sessions where New Yorkers were encouraged to draw their own plans—discussed at an emergency board meeting within days of the attack and launched big the following spring. But one thing Huxtable could not have foreseen was just how little power the mayor would have over the development of this site, three short blocks from City Hall.

The state capital in Albany is about 130 miles from Ground Zero, and Governor Pataki's Manhattan headquarters is seventy blocks north of the site. The distance could have been a lot shorter; one of the first decisions made by the governor when he was elected, in 1994, was to move the state offices out of the World Trade Center, where they had made up a large part of the public occupation of the Twin Towers (fifty floors of Tower 2) that amounted to a de facto subsidy for the center in the twenty-five years before it began to stand on its own with private tenants.

Being in New York, capital city of culture and money and its own self-regard, it is sometimes hard to remember the great swath of land that shares its name. But there was a third flag in the TV camera's frame as Giuliani spoke to the world in those first days: the flag of New York State. Usually, too, there was Pataki himself standing behind the mayor, saying nothing more often than not, but towering over him with his broad, made-for-politics build: the man behind the man, and the one who in this game would hold all the cards.

Unlike Queens-born Mario Cuomo, whom he succeeded as governor, George Pataki was never seen as much of a friend of the city. His power base was in Peekskill, where he had been mayor, only an hour up the Hudson but already well into the oblivion that city residents wave off as "upstate." New York City tilts overwhelmingly to Democrats, so as a Republican it was in the vast, depressed country stretching up to Canada that Pataki had found his backing for higher office, and it was there that he lavished his attention and the state's resources, even with fellow Republican Giuliani (and then nominal Republican Michael Bloomberg) in control of City Hall, even after September 11. (Somehow, part of the $20 billion in disaster aid that was strong-armed out of the Bush Administration by New York's two Democratic senators later found itself earmarked for upstate transportation projects, an overreach that did not survive its exposure in the press.)

The line on Pataki has been that he invites underestimation, playing up his invented folksiness, drawling a warm, soft drawl with no provenance, hoping that the blank look he puts on his face will divert attention from the hard look in his eyes. People close to him point out that he has never lost an election. Pataki's stewardship of the redevelopment of Ground Zero would reflect his politics of public quiet and private force—long, critically assailed stretches of safe silence interrupted by terrain-shifting decrees—and all the while those taking the heat were serving at his pleasure.

New York's governors have often played a role in the city's largest real estate projects—Nelson Rockefeller's backing was essential to realizing the World Trade Center—but the extent to which George Pataki took control of the redevelopment went well beyond the norm. He arrogated all power to himself and wrote his opponents right out of the script. Pataki's first move at the site was to create the Lower Manhattan Development Corporation (LMDC), lawyered into existence with Giuliani's help and announced on November 2, 2001, the Friday before the mayoral election. Bloomberg's victory that next Tuesday was a surprise; polls running up to the vote had favored Mark Green, a fixture of the city's Democratic in-crowd and a constant critic of Giuliani in the latter's less sensitive pre-attack incarnation. The outgoing mayor, having failed in a democracy-bending attempt to extend his term, wanted to limit Green's control over the agency that was being put in place to manage the redevelopment and channel its federal funding; the governor wanted to eliminate any role for the state's Democrats. Hence the rush to bring the LMDC to life, with its board of directors weighted heavily toward Pataki appointees. Assembly Speaker Sheldon Silver, the most powerful Democrat in Albany, complained publicly that the Republicans were "worried about Mark Green being elected mayor and they don't want him to have any input." Those were his last words in the process: Silver, whose district encompasses Ground Zero, would himself be sidelined. "Clearly partisan," he said, and then he disappeared.

The mayoral election set a precedent: the process would be shaped by a series of elections, stepping neatly up the rungs of power from City Hall to the White House. Throughout 2002, the rhythms of the redevelopment were set by that year's race for governor, and Pataki would use his full control of the LMDC, and his effective control of the Port Authority, to speed or slow or, in one case, stop the proceedings as suited his campaign for a third term; by the time he had won the race, the shadow of the 2004 presidential election was already falling on the site. It had long been assumed that Pataki had ambitions in Washington; as a passably popular moderate governor from a large northeastern state, he seemed tailor-made to someday balance a Republican ticket headed by, say, a candidate from Texas. Managing the creation of a national symbol at Ground Zero would be Pataki's chance to shine, particularly after it was announced that the Republican National Convention would be coming to Manhattan just days before the third anniversary of the attack. It was the governor himself who gave the name Freedom Tower to the 1,776-foot-high spire that would ultimately be chosen for the site. As one *New York Post* reader noted so perfectly, for Pataki "the building will be nothing more than a perch for staring off in the direction of the White House."[5]

For the first few weeks of its existence, the Lower Manhattan Development Corporation did business as the Lower Manhattan Redevelopment Corporation. Like every other aspect of this instant bureaucracy, the name was scrutinized. The reconstruction advocates theorized that the prefix quickly disappeared because the agency did not want to imply that the Twin Towers themselves could be rebuilt. But the LMDC did not arrive at the table with an architectural agenda; as the conduit for the federal aid, the LMDC came with deep pockets, and, empowered to take property by eminent domain, a big stick. As Pataki's principal check on the process, it was charged with the heavy political lifting: the job of the LMDC was to make sure something got done and nothing went wrong.

The chairman of the board, and for several formative months the lone high-level appointee, was John Whitehead, seventy-nine, a former leading partner at Goldman Sachs. He was there first as a symbol, to calm the world of banking—his world—at a time when a wholesale exodus to safer, cheaper New Jersey seemed imminent. Beyond overseeing the redevelopment of the World Trade Center site—about which he caused a flap early on by saying he didn't know what to do—Whitehead's mandate was to kick-start the economy of what came to be called the LMDC's "mission area": everything south of Houston Street, a zone only about ten kernels up the corn cob of Manhattan but larger than many large cities. While it shepherded the players at Ground Zero, the LMDC also tended to that hinterland, coordinating grant programs to reward residents and businesses that moved in or stayed put, pursuing scoundrels who filed false claims of victimhood, mapping traffic patterns, studying the gentrification of gritty Fulton Street, reopening a popular farmers' market, setting up (after much discussion) an information kiosk, and, later, publishing a guidebook intended to draw New Yorkers back to the still-struggling restaurants downtown.

At least officially, John Whitehead did not report directly to the governor. In another quiet power move, Pataki had conceived the

LMDC as a subsidiary of the Empire State Development Corporation (ESDC), a business-promoting public agency he controlled and that he had used, among other things, to bully the honky-tonk off Forty-second Street. The ESDC is run by Charles Gargano, a Pataki loyalist, fund-raising chair of his 2002 campaign, and vice-chairman of the Port Authority—a man whose merciless politicking had earned him the sarcastic nickname "Ambassador of Love." Gargano and Whitehead clashed from the beginning. Almost as soon as Whitehead was in, there were reports that he was out, reports that spiked a year after he was appointed when, boldly snubbing Gargano and the governor, he traveled to Washington in secret for a private meeting with the president.

Paternal and inoffensive, frequently speaking off message and out of turn (he was a favorite call for reporters), John Whitehead represented the older Republican mode of more measured plutocratic action that had fallen out of favor nationally with the rise of George Bush. In the years before he was named to head the LMDC, Whitehead had given nearly $400,000 to the party. In the Reagan administration, he had served as deputy secretary of state; early on, Whitehead made a point of mentioning to the press, reportedly with condescension, that he had sworn in Gargano when Reagan had rewarded that loyal Republican with the ambassadorship to Trinidad and Tobago.

In part because Whitehead was so independent, power at the LMDC would be vested instead in its executive director, first Lou Tomson, the managing partner at Pataki's old Peekskill law firm, and then, in early 2003, Kevin Rampe, former senior counsel to the governor, head of a state regulatory agency, and son of an upstate Pataki ally. Bloomberg, whose ties to the state Republican machine were only as old as his ambition to be mayor, fought that appointment for months. His failure to stop it was yet another example of City Hall's impotence at the site. Though Bloomberg would eventually even the city/state balance on the LMDC board and name his own people, it sometimes seemed that the city's power in the

process rested entirely on the ability of one of them—Dan Doctoroff, the smiling deputy mayor for economic development—to
charm his new colleagues. (It never seemed to matter much that
Bloomberg's girlfriend, the elegant Diana Taylor, worked as a top
Pataki aide, even when she came to represent the governor at the
crucial negotiations leading up to the selection of a master plan for
the site.)

Neither Bloomberg's closeted-Democrat pragmatism nor the
gracious eastern Republicanism of John Whitehead would get
much traction at the LMDC; it bent instead toward a more fashionable neocon passion for subterfuge, personified by Matt Higgins, the twenty-something powerhouse who served from the start
as the agency's communications guru and later, also, its chief operating officer. Higgins, a whip-smart player, winning, wicked on his
BlackBerry, watched over his gaggle of regular press with quick
eyes and a relaxed, catch-me-if-you-can smile. In Giuliani's City
Hall, where he had served as press secretary before hopping to the
LMDC, Higgins had earned a reputation for brutal, Rudy-esque
effectiveness that carried over to his new hot-seat job. Early in the
life of the LMDC, a coworker dubbed him "Baby Satan," an intra-
office joke run amok that the beat reporters cheerfully threw back
at him and that he just as cheerfully embraced.

The world into which the governor inserted the LMDC is as
cranky and convoluted as any in the city. The development of New
York has always been a team effort, and this new entity, though
loaded with Washington dollars and Albany juice, was superim-
posed on a dirty game of stickball already in progress. With so
much novelty in the air in the fall of 2001—Americans were at that
moment learning to cope with postal anthrax—the old ways were
mostly the order of the day in the redevelopment of Ground Zero.
Protesters would still protest; the various civic organizations—
advocates for inspired public space known to their detractors as
the "goo-goos"—would still try to do their good; developers and
politicians would still jostle and receive supplicants seeking to

persuade, though these now ranged in delicacy from Team Twin Towers' passionate rabble to such redoubts of high-mindedness as the Regional Plan Association—an eighty-year-old think tank on the future of the city, doing business after September 11 as the lead component of an advocacy group called the Civic Alliance.

The driving principles of New York real estate are not only "location, location, location"—the site in question has all three—but also "get it done, get it done cheap, and get it done fast." Or try to; the economic expedience of the city has its opposite: activists who activate each time the visible hand of increase comes near. Plans are unveiled and pilloried. Voices are raised and silenced. Suits are filed and countered. Deals are brokered and abrogated. And out the other end comes a building. In 1987, in an act of civic disobedience arranged by the Municipal Art Society, hundreds of protesters opened black umbrellas in Central Park to dramatize the extent of the shadow to be cast by a skyscraper planned for Columbus Circle, bringing unwanted scrutiny in the press and helping to stall the project for nearly twenty years. When a senior LMDC official remarked that "the whole point of the LMDC is to make something happen that would not happen otherwise," this was the otherwise he meant.

In New York City, all development protest is local. And local in the case of Ground Zero meant two cans of worms: Tribeca and Battery Park City. Tribeca is one of those cast-off commercial neighborhoods that got its new name from newspapers and real estate brokers—viz Soho, Dumbo—when artists, their galleries, cafés for the gallery crowd, and finally the art buyers themselves moved in. By 2001 it was well into its second decade as elegant stroller country. The area had been known as the Washington Market, the city's wholesale food district before the grocers got packed off to the Bronx, and sometimes also as the Lower West Side, a flank of the island that has been missing on maps since Tribeca got its new name and the World Trade Center stamped out its sister neighborhood just to the south—the much-nostalgized Radio Row.

Battery Park City is a very different beast—much closer to the attack itself and, as a bedroom community for Wall Street, coming out of the events with very different concerns. It owes its existence to the World Trade Center, having been built up out of the Hudson with fill from the two-block-wide, four-block-long hole in the ground—the bathtub—that Port Authority engineers devised to find clear bedrock for the Twin Towers' foundations. It was the creation of this ninety-two-acre annex to Manhattan, in a kind of land-for-streets deal, that smoothed the way for the Port to close five city-controlled thoroughfares and assemble the sixteen-acre superblock that the authority's fiscal and monumental dreams required. But as the city pondered and rounds of master planning dragged on, the land lay empty in the river.

The decidedly postmodern plan that was finally implemented—with streets continuing Manhattan's uneven downtown grid and apartment towers meant to evoke the best of uptown grandeur—was chosen only in 1979 and not substantially built out until the early 1990s. The plan called for two residential neighborhoods, north and south, framing, opposite the Twins, a festive riverside commercial zone that became the World Financial Center. At the time of the attack, the southern enclave had nearly completed its Manhattan mimicry, though in its sterility it felt like another world; the northern area was still mostly vacant, with the exception of Stuyvesant High School and a scattered half dozen apartment towers.

Bordered on three sides by the river and on the fourth by eight-lane West Street, Battery Park City is an island, and the residents of its mostly posh towers like to keep it that way. It is not so bad, many people find, to be isolated by choice in New York City; the first murder recorded on Roosevelt Island, a crowded strip of apartment complexes in the East River, came soon after a subway station opened there. Cherishing their near-private domain, and putting them at odds with their neighbors in Tribeca, the several groups that formed to represent the residents of Battery

Park City called early and often for leaving the highway-wide rift of West Street as is. Their specific statements concerned the inconvenience that burying it or bridging it could bring—something that everyone else (Silverstein, the goo-goos, the governor) endorsed—but the argument was always the same: *please, we've suffered enough.*

Though they opposed one another on some issues, the residents of Battery Park City and Tribeca were united in their demands that the commercial resources of the World Trade Center's mall not be lost in any redevelopment. The primary patrons of that space may have been the sixty-five thousand office workers spat each morning out of the center's commuter rail station, but it was also well used by nearby residents; at the public hearings called to solicit comment on the use of the site, hundreds rose to reminisce about the big Borders bookstore there, and the important role that the suburban fixture had played in downtown life. Even the World Trade Center plaza, a place that critics would have us believe was darkness itself, was sung by locals for what it was: one of the largest open spaces anywhere near their crowded home.

What the residents did not want at the site was, as so many of them put it for the record, "a graveyard." Certainly they were victims too; these were, after all, people who had been locked out of their homes and returned to find them polluted, left to breathe the air that the Environmental Protection Agency said was safe when it wasn't, people whose stories of discovering this or that unutterable object on their balconies would dribble out as a steady B-theme in the press. But downtown the attack also brought a New Yorker's perfect emotional storm: well-earned post-traumatic stress, victimhood to wield, and then, with those barely mellowed, the return in force of the city's rampant not-in-my-backyard self-concern.

The task of making that brew palatable in negotiations involving the day's other living victims fell to Madelyn Wils. The sole downtown resident on the LMDC board, Wils was the voice of her cosmopolite neighbors as they squared off with the families, many of whom, married to commuters, lived in very different neighborhoods far away. From the perspective of her constituents, she was an effective leader. Before Pataki appointed her to the LMDC, as chair of her local community board Wils had racked up an impressive record of inducing change in the slow-to-change city: protecting her fragile Tribeca through rezoning, forcing the Battery Park City development bureaucracy to relinquish one vacant block to local Little Leaguers. But she was not ideally suited to the subtle work of speaking to the strident mourners who came to represent the survivors of the World Trade Center's dead.

Madelyn Wils brought to that work some of the intractability that had allowed her family's egg-and-cheese wholesale firm, Harry Wils & Co., to survive as the last holdout of the old Washington Market, its yellow trucks persisting so long among Tribeca's boutiques and bakeries that, before the warehouse itself was converted to loft apartments, they had started to look like a tourist attraction. In early 2002, Wils more or less single-handedly kept the victims' families from installing the World Trade Center's *Sphere* as a memorial in the Tribeca park that was their first choice—the neighborhood's only park (one so overrun by nannies it is known as "Baby Park")—before settling on the less convenient site at the Battery. Monica Iken, a trader's widow who founded the group September's Mission as a vehicle for her very prominent advocacy, was Wils's primary opponent. Both tall, chemically blond, and exceedingly ornery, they were well matched. At one contentious meeting of Wils's community board, Tribecan after Tribecan rose to tell Iken and a friend, in some of the most direct language leveled at any World Trade Center widow, that they would never roll over for the *Sphere*. "Don't underestimate us," one woman said, threatening open war. Not long after, Iken told a documentary film crew, "It was very discouraging to see how the residents don't take any consideration to the fact that we need to honor those people who were murdered on national TV, and now we have to worry about the fact that the Borders bookstore is not there and they don't have a bookstore to go to?"[6]

The face of her neighbors' intransigence, Wils was vilified by the families and threatened repeatedly—in several letters with death, as if anyone needed more of that—for her impiously direct calls for streets free of pilgrims' tour buses and parks for local kids; the heart of her job, though it could not be spoken, was to resist the sanctification of Ground Zero that would make it the graveyard she and her neighbors feared. One day in 2003, as he stood at the very edge of the sacred pit, a representative of another advocacy group, the Coalition of 9/11 Families, said that "Madelyn Wils will burn in hell," and he said it at the mere mention of her name.

During the supercharged early years of the process, the loudest among the residents and the families accomplished something extraordinary: through their bad behavior, they managed to lose much of the sympathy that the tragedy had generated for them. Improbably, Larry Silverstein came away from the attack a certified victim. But unable to set aside the habits formed by a lifetime in New York development, he too squandered that asset, in record time.

Only six weeks before the attack, Silverstein had closed on his agreement with the Port Authority, signing a ninety-nine-year lease on the World Trade Center's ten million square feet of office space. He had lusted after the property; his acquisition of it was only the last act of a decades-long play, beginning in the late 1980s when he built the only post-Yamasaki adjunct to the complex, 7 World Trade Center, which collapsed in a footnote on the afternoon of September 11. "Here I was with this beautiful 47-story, two-million-square-foot building," Silverstein told the *New York Times*, "but when I walked outside I realized it was totally eclipsed by the towers and thought, 'Wouldn't it be wonderful to own that, too?' It was a compulsion with me."[7] In the April 2001 press release announcing the Port's preliminary approval of his bid, he was quoted as saying, "This is a dream come true."

The catastrophic dashing of his dream might have given Silverstein the impetus to pause and retool, perhaps even to find a way to exploit his special status among the victims. But those were new tricks this old developer could not learn. At his moment of greatest sympathy, Silverstein was very publicly working to secure his investment. Despite a flurry of communication in the early hours with his insurers and his architects, he failed to grasp that the demands on the reconstruction had moved far beyond the usual developer impulse—"filling the land to the maximum permitted by law, for the greatest return, while ignoring every social or human factor," as Ada Louise Huxtable wrote.[8] "It would be the tragedy of tragedies not to rebuild," Silverstein told the *Wall Street Journal* two days after the attack, going on to stress that he had a "moral obligation" to replace the World Trade Center.[9] But he also had a legal obligation (the lease, as he and his landlords interpreted it, *required* him to rebuild) and a financial obligation (he still had to pay the Port Authority about $10 million a month in rent), and a proposal for the site that he presented nine days after the attack showed that those bottom-line concerns still ruled. It was a marvel of the developer mind-set: four towers, each at fifty-five stories, or half the height of one twin, surrounding a central space for a memorial but replacing the lost square footage to the inch.

Skidmore, Owings and Merrill (SOM), the most powerful architecture firm in the city, had been working with Silverstein just before September 11 on plans to renovate and expand parts of the complex. Though they were in close contact and already discussing the future, the developer managed to describe his four-towers plan to the press before his architects had heard of it. If they had no hand in Silverstein's ill-received first scheme, it would be their last passive moment. As the developer's public relations firm—

Rubinstein Associates, the best—took on the salvage of their client's image, his architects embarked on the education of Larry Silverstein, public patron, city father, stakeholder in the mental health of a nation. A reporter who spoke to him the week of September 11 heard the unvarnished voice of a New York developer citing numbers; when she called back three weeks later, Silverstein was suddenly "talking the talk": there would be new streets, grand public spaces, and an appropriately soaring memorial.

But by then it was too late. Silverstein was already being described with that tenacious epithet: "typical New York developer." It was just too hard not to make the central-casting connection. With his shiny shoulder-padded suits, his shiny cuff links, his shiny ties, he looks like someone you're not supposed to trust (although many certainly had, enough to allow him to grow the purchase of a single property in 1956 into an empire of twenty million square feet). And he sounds like one too: Silverstein speaks with an antic delivery that can run from hatred to ingratiation— the mouth grimacing, the brows charging—within the space of a single hastily meted syllable. There is an uncanny sense of speed about him—even at seventy, his age when his towers fell, even with no visible neck, even after the crushed pelvis he suffered in 2001 as he was preparing his final bid to the Port. (A much-told story has him ordering his doctor to cut his morphine so he could continue negotiating with a clear head.) "For a developer, nothing can move fast enough," he said a few months after the attack. "And so the private sector always says, 'move it, move it, move it'—time is precious. Public sector is somewhat different."[10]

Despite the best efforts of his handlers, Silverstein played the role of typical developer with ease. A typical developer would have come out too early with an inadequate scheme that insulted the grieving public (as Silverstein did); a typical developer would not have been satisfied with the prospect of a $3.6 billion insurance payout (as Silverstein was not); a typical developer would have filed suit against his insurers to get double that amount, claiming that the coordinated two-prong attack on his holdings represented two discrete "occurrences" (as Silverstein alleged, though no one else, judges and juries included, seemed to agree); a typical New York developer might then have clogged the courts for years with this hopeful lawsuit and, when he seemed set to lose, tried to smother the news with a meaningless announcement that three more marquee architects had been selected to design buildings for which there was at that moment no tenant, no money, and no lot.

To a city always ready to loathe its developers—unfairly, of course, since without them there would be no city—Silverstein confirmed the stereotype. Fate had given him the opportunity to be a tragic figure, but a developer has a job to do. "Poor Larry came in with this big shit-eating grin on his face, and the gods were cruel," said Jack Robertson, an architect who worked with him just after the attack. "They gave, and very quickly they took away."

Like Silverstein, when given the chance to change its ways, the Port Authority reverted to form. New York City is blessed with what may be the planet's largest and best-situated natural harbor, and the Port Authority of New York and New Jersey was created in 1921 to increase that harbor's potential for trade. The Port's earliest projects, many unrealized, focused directly on that goal. But as it matured, guided by its monarchal director Austin Tobin, the Port expanded into other areas—managing the Holland Tunnel and building the George Washington Bridge, running the city's airports and bus stations—all of which enriched it with a constant flow of money from fees and tolls. In addition, the Port Compact, the authority's charter—approved by the state legislatures of New York and New Jersey with an eye to harmonizing the operation of their shared waterways—gave the agency the power to float its own bonds. This ensured a ready stream of revenue for its increasingly grand projects and allowed an autonomy that immunized the Port from political oversight. The Port's financial freedom led to the growth of a forceful entity, a kind of Vatican in the metropolis: secretive, impenetrable, and prone to putting its own interests above those of the city it was meant to serve. The construction of the World Trade Center was the apogee of the agency's extracurricular search for power and money, and the Port was not about to lose either in the course of the towers' replacement.

September 11 was a very personal tragedy for the usually faceless Port Authority; with the thirty-seven officers from its private police force and fifty other employees, the dead included Neil Leven, the popular director, who was at a breakfast meeting at Windows on the World, the storied restaurant at the top of Tower 1, when the first plane hit. The Port Authority also lost its headquarters, its history, and—for an institution run by engineers—its pride and joy. But throughout the cutthroat redevelopment of the site, the tragedy never seemed to have shaken the agency's core—the private, corporate culture of a deep bureaucracy insulated by arcane legislation and protected by its enormous, regenerating wealth. The Port is a creature of the governments of two states but beholden to the citizens of none. As we were reminded when the cause of the collapse was investigated, its dual-state status even exempted it from observing New York City's strict highrise codes. The Twin Towers symbolized nothing so much as the power of their legal framework; they could never have existed without it.

Though it had built two of the largest buildings in the world, the Port Authority was not supposed to be in the real estate game; its charter even forbade certain types of development. Theodore Kheel, a celebrated labor lawyer and the Port's foremost critic at the time the towers were planned and built, liked to remind the agency's leaders of this fact. He dogged the Port with his refrain that the World Trade Center was "socialism at its worst,"[11] and grabbed space in the papers covering the dedication on April 4, 1973, when he called for its immediate sale to private enterprise.

A wiry man nearing ninety, Kheel resurfaced after the attack to press his favorite point: that the Port had pursued the development of the World Trade Center in order to launder the windfalls it was getting from bridge and tunnel tolls, before a public clamor could be made to redirect the money for the public good—to fund mass transit, for example. Kheel also raised new questions. Why did the Port's lease with Larry Silverstein dictate that he should not only continue to pay rent on the property but fund the rebuilding as well? Why would the Port want to depart so far from traditional practice, where, in the case of catastrophic property loss, rent is abated and the insurance proceeds default to the landlord? (Such normative language would have had Silverstein out of the process in a trice. But there he was, in the fall of 2001, holding fast to his brick-thick lease.) Mostly, Kheel railed against the rapacious history he saw repeating itself. In 1976, *New York* magazine had quoted him interrupting a meal of sushi and Chablis at Windows on the World to announce, "The ghost of Austin Tobin stalks these halls saying, 'Thou shalt not do a goddamned thing for mass transportation because there's not any money in it.' "[12] In a letter he was circulating in 2002, Kheel wrote—referring again to the powerful director who built the towers—"The ghost of Austin Tobin is now stalking Ground Zero saying, 'Thou shalt not do a goddamned thing that doesn't turn Ground Zero into a massive real estate opportunity.' "[13]

With the public poised from the first days for a healing renewal, construction afterward could not exclusively be the practical kind at which the Port Authority excelled. But its executives never seemed to get past their essential, honest view of the World Trade Center as real estate, an architectural mechanism for turning tossed coins and floated bonds into leasable floor plates, a train station, a mall. After the attack, one Port Authority spokesman reminisced that the wide bank of escalators bringing people up to the shopping concourse from the center's commuter rail station had been lovingly known to insiders as "the human hose."[14] The temporary replacement station for the Port Authority Trans-Hudson trains would use the same incline for its escalators—it was the only place to come up from below without disturbing an intruding subway line—though only eight escalators were installed, in place of the original nine. "There are fewer people now," explained Peter Rinaldi, the site engineer and a force in the recovery, as he surveyed the construction. He had a look in his eye and a drop in his voice that said all is not quite as it once was at the Port.

What bureaucracy or businessman has ever succeeded in solving emotional riddles? The players who assembled to influence the use of the World Trade Center site were well primed to conduct an ugly New York real estate battle, but they were largely at sea regarding the redevelopment's special conundrums. Missing from the process as it took shape was a state-sanctioned voice that could rally all of the necessary characters into collective, tonic action, pushing from the direction of art. The LMDC, once it got its footing, did this to a point. But despite the talents of Alex Garvin, director of planning, and his successor, Andrew Winters, the LMDC—as its top officers freely admitted—didn't know from art. And it was art, of course, that the public demanded, and art that, in the form of a nationally relevant resurrection, Ground Zero's *capo di tutti capi*, George Pataki, was obliged to deliver.

Luckily, for the sake of the redevelopment, there were others—many, many others—willing to provide that vision thing. As the governor wound up his toys and watched them spin, as the LMDC tested its muscle, as Silverstein rallied his lawyers, as the Port grieved in its curious way, as the goo-goos brewed their remedies, as the families and the residents learned how to spar, and as the recovery workers carried on through the night—because like any deep wound, Ground Zero had to heal from the bottom up—a new class of process participants was approaching the problem top down, from the clouds.

4

AMATEUR HOUR

ON THE Friday after the attack, as George Bush preached revenge at Ground Zero, Ethan Ernest was out of earshot across the pile, finishing his seventeenth straight hour as a volunteer link in a bucket chain. Dressed in yesterday's night-out clothes under his borrowed rescuer's gear, Ernest, forty-four, stout, a woodworker by trade, looked like many of the men drawn to purge themselves of the tragedy by direct action. That day he was probably not exhibiting his best trait: boyish enthusiasm and energy; Ethan Ernest is one of those people who retain their youth simply by never growing up.

In inexperienced hands, a design epiphany is a dangerous thing. Hit with that first flood of images—that moment when, after dwelling on a problem, you find a solution as if from nowhere—many are fooled into thinking that what has come to them is not an idea but *the* idea. Ernest had some experience—he had studied architecture one summer at Harvard; he had developed a process to press laminated wood into fine corrugated panels—but still, in the intensity of that September, the order his mind conceived for the site took over his life.

The morning of September 11 Ernest was planning to go to an Ashtanga yoga clinic at Chelsea Piers, a popular recreation complex not far from the backyard carriage house on West Nineteenth Street where he had lived and worked for twenty-three years. He

heard the roar from the first plane as it zeroed in on the north
tower—"I remember thinking, 'Wow, that was really low'"—but
he didn't tune in to the event until a friend called from Chicago:
Turn on the TV. With the momentum that carried so many forward,
he went over to Chelsea Piers as planned. In the company of three
hundred-odd other limberists, Ernest watched the event play out
forty blocks away through the south-facing windows of the club.

So I saw them go down and the rest of that day was sort of
a dream. I had a friend flying in from Brazil who was stuck
at the airport—she was actually one of the last people to
see the buildings still up from the air. She didn't get out of
Kennedy for like two days. And then I had dinner with her
and another friend on Thursday. Somewhere on the Lower
East Side. And they went home, and I was just—you
know, those couple days were just like this sort of sublime, awestruck daze. And I ended up wandering around.
And I all of a sudden just got it into my head that I'd walk
down there—I was in pretty good clothes—and I kept
walking downtown.

That night there was lightning. It hadn't started to
rain yet, but there was this lightning over Brooklyn. And
there were these papers all around. I saved one scrap of paper. It was the only souvenir I took at all, this scrap of paper from the ground—I got it somewhere—that showed it
was from the World Trade Center.

I had a chocolate bar with me, and there was a cop car
that came by once and told me to go back, and I gave them
the chocolate bar, and after they were gone I just kept going south. It was a very strange perspective. It was like being on a hiking trail in the wilderness. When I got down to
the Battery, there were some National Guard guys who
were guarding one of the buildings. They said, "What are

you doing here?" and I said, "Well I'm walking down to the site," and they said, "Well you really can't go." And it started to rain.

I ended up just hanging out talking to those guys for about an hour and a half, in the rain. We were just talking about what happened. Then after the rain let up I walked basically right toward the buildings. I arrived at Liberty Plaza, and there was a little depot right there. By that time the rain was starting to come down again, and I walked to the supply depot, and they said, "What do you need?" And within literally minutes I had the boots, I had a raincoat, I had all the things you'd need. And I was at the top of the pile doing buckets.

Ernest stayed at Ground Zero through the next day and into the night—he won't say what he saw—and then, after missing Bush's speech and crashing with the other workers for a while at St. Paul's Chapel, he went home. He wasn't done doing what had drawn him down there, but he thought he could return the next morning and get through the many security lines—at Canal Street, at Chambers Street, at the perimeter—with a Transit Authority pass he had picked up from a fast friend on the pile. But the frontiers had been formalized for the presidential tour, and Ground Zero did not return to its previous level of useful anarchy. "It was locked down, you couldn't get in, but for me there was still the catharsis of those couple of days. There was the physical wave of the vibrations of the buildings falling, and the psychic or mental waves of the event."

Those waves and vibrations would coalesce in a suite of ideas for the World Trade Center site that Ernest called "Ripple Effects." It was not a specific design but a collection of palliative allusions (to Revolutionary and transcendentalist and New Age America) and generous attitudes (collaborative, "open source") that he presented as an ever-growing file of collaged tearsheets bound into handmade and lovingly oiled wooden binders. Ernest had made those binders years earlier, in an edition of 343—by chance the number of firefighters killed on September 11—and that kismet became for him a validation of the project.

He called his book *Themes for Building as Memorial* and gave it an archaic subtitle befitting a man with his name: "Including the Rescue Worker and Architectural Toolmaker's Drawing-Book with appearances by (in alphabetical order) Sails, Scallops, Schist, Serpents, Spirals, Stars, Stars & Stripes, with annotations on ALL OF THE ABOVE for friends everywhere." One sheet had a photograph of two sailboats pulled by spinnakers over this quote from Ralph Waldo Emerson: "We want a ship in these billows we inhabit. An angular, dogmatic house would be rent to chips and splinters in this storm of many elements. No, it must be tight, and fit to the form of man, to live at all; as a shell must dictate the architecture of a house founded on the sea." Another, with a portrait pulled from a hundred-dollar bill, included Benjamin Franklin's 1775 ruminations on the rattlesnake as a symbol of America, and his cartoon of the colonies as a severed snake: "Join or Die." On other pages were Ernest's thoughts on high-rise escape (slides), Manhattan's enabling bedrock ("Schist Happened"), and the relevance of the Continental Army's "Don't Tread on Me" rattlesnake flag (printed on scraps of fabric with burned edges that resembled pieces of World Trade Center fallout). As Ernest explained, "The snake is a symbol of healing in almost every culture and a symbol of America, and Moses nailed the snake to the cross with a golden spike to heal the whole world, and Moses was revered by Muslims, Jews, and Christians—so then you have this litany of metaphors at work for people."

Ernest is open to the mystical. Finding himself from time to time, he had discovered and returned to Arcosanti, the utopian camp established by the checked-out architect Paolo Soleri in Arizona, just off the shoulder of I-17 north of Phoenix. Students spend their days there casting the bronze wind chimes that stock

the gift shop and keep the enterprise afloat as they work sporadi-
cally to complete the megastructural monuments—"Arcologies"—
that had come to their guru with the force of a life-altering vision
in the late 1950s. "Ripple Effects" emerged from a vision Ernest
had a week after September 11.

> I was lying in my bed and I started to think about what
> they were going to do. First thing, I was thinking about
> the smoke. And there were a bunch of things that came
> together immediately. One was to build along the long
> axis of the site, from the northwest to the southeast, be-
> cause that way you'd be able to maximize the space. And
> I thought about the corrugated form. And I thought
> about how it paralleled the smoke, sort of blowing in the
> same direction, and it all came together very quickly. I
> didn't say, "Build a building that looks like a flag." I dis-
> covered a flag in the building. I think that if you were
> looking at this from the outside, you'd say, "Oh yeah, a
> building that looks like a flag. That makes a lot of sense."
> But I actually found the form completely the other way
> around.
>
> In one crystalline moment everything came together—
> the whole idea that the building itself should be the me-
> morial. Because having been in New York all my life I
> knew all the fights that were going to take place, and I
> said, "This is going to solve a lot of problems for a lot of
> people." There was one basic emotion—dread—which
> was why the fuck do you have to have this idea? Why did
> *you* have to get this idea? I got cursed with having a form
> that was workable right away.

Ethan Ernest was not alone; beginning the very moment of the
attack, thousands across the country and around the world were
compelled to take on the job of imagining the future of Ground

Zero. Some were architects moonlighting from less important work, but most were amateurs, in that older, truer sense of the word that still points to love. Not all of them would be as pitch-perfect as the angry wags behind the anonymous five-fingered fuck-you towers that made the e-mail rounds. But they all drank deep of the same intoxicating fiction: in the vacuum left by the buildings, the right idea could be found that, given a fulcrum, would move the world. Some just drew for themselves. Others drew their vision for the site and then believed—*Why not? This is America!*—that it could be brought to the attention of the right powers, catch fire, get built.

It was sometimes hard to see the grandiose intentions of the amateurs through the humble presentation of their schemes. Scores of pointy towers, vague domes, and world's tallest ziggu-rats were posted on storefronts and construction fences all over Lower Manhattan, often with an e-mail address: *If you see what I see, get in touch*. But this new folk architecture was not just a local phe-nomenon. As the flood reached a high point near the first anniver-sary, dozens of websites collected thousands of images, including a vast archive posted by CNN.[1] *Newsday* had a similar rogues' gallery, supplemented with a simple drawing program, a DIY me-morial generator: surfers could click and drag little cartoon icons to arrange towers and parks and plaques and fountains into that one elusive, solving constellation that would make the site, and the makers, whole again.

The serious volunteer visionaries were not content to post their pearls, lost among thousands, at some out-of-the-way URL. They sent them to the top. Barbara Wagtskjold, a nurse from Ed-ina, Minnesota, was an industrious promoter of her scheme, which she called "Raphael Remembrance: A Healing Memorial for the WTC." Her plan also evolved from a vision: "It popped into my head, thinking about the pile of rubble," she said. "The pile of rubble slowly turned into a glass dome of faceted glass, like a dia-mond." She developed the plan with the help of local artists and an architect and then, when it was all clearly drawn—with a hissing fountain, a gold eagle nesting on the dome, a ring of memorial sculptures (including a firefighter in bronze carrying a child made of glass)—she sent it off to her congressman, Jim Ramstad, a long-serving Republican with a seat on the powerful Ways and Means Committee. Ramstad peppered official New York and Washington with correspondence on behalf of his constituent, sending a letter to Mayor Bloomberg ("I am proud to forward to you this spectacular and truly fitting design . . ."), but not before he tried his hand at the White House. A letter from Ramstad was sent to Nicholas Calio, George Bush's senior adviser for congressional affairs. "I would greatly appreciate it if you could pass her design on to the appropriate officials and the President for their consideration," Ramstad wrote, going well beyond his obligation by adding in longhand at the bottom: "Nick, This truly has merit, and I trust you will see that it gets serious consideration. Thanks, Jim." Reporting back to Wagtskjold the next day, Ramstad wrote, "I know the President will react the same way I have to your remarkable design."

Every public figure was targeted by a thousand Barbara Wagtskjolds. Proposals were typically sent in multiples, with Governor Pataki, Larry Silverstein, and Mayors Giuliani and Bloomberg topping the list of recipients. Some of the most ambitious, Ethan Ernest among them, also made their cases at public hearings and sent care packages to participating architects, local architecture critics, and influential unelected officials. In this way, Ernest generated his own ripple effects; he was told that the book he had delivered to Roland Betts—the developer of Chelsea Piers and the most powerful person on the LMDC board—ended up in the hands of George Bush himself, when Betts went down to Camp David to visit his old Yale fraternity brother.

Most submissions found a much less exalted audience. Or none at all; those sent to New York politicians typically ended up at the Lower Manhattan Development Corporation. The submissions, classified as "unsolicited designs," were processed, labeled, and forgotten in the warrens of that young bureaucracy. In one locked storage room, the designs fill seven white cardboard boxes sitting on a gray plastic mail cart.

That storage room is but a small corner of the LMDC offices, which occupy half of the twentieth floor of 1 Liberty Plaza, a fifty-four-story tower across the street from Ground Zero. Before it became well known as a backdrop in photographs of the site, 1 Liberty had a short, dark career in Hollywood. In *The Siege*, the 1998 film that imagined the debut of suicide terrorism in New York City, the FBI had its offices there and the tower was blown up by a truck bomb in the second reel. Bruce Willis had seen enough: he rounded up all of Brooklyn's Arab men and boys and detained them in a hasty Camp X-ray set up on an island in the East River.

The LMDC offices are a typically Dilbert tableau of wood-trimmed cubicles under will-sapping fluorescent lights, much more middle management than civil service in feel. Visitors are greeted by framed photographs of Governor Pataki and Mayor Bloomberg and, on the wall behind the receptionist—every other call to whom seems to be a question about residential assistance grants—the LMDC's polemical logo: the words "Remember, Renew, Rebuild" next to a graphic that resembles a stepped pyramid. Around the corner, past the galley kitchen where the regular press soon learned to cadge free coffee (you get what you pay for), the cubicles and little offices begin; beyond is the locked storage room, the graveyard of amateur dreams.

The tubes and portfolios kept there represent only about one-eighth of the official collection. In the space of two years, the LMDC received about four thousand unsolicited designs. Half of those came in via e-mail and never made it to a printer. The great majority of the old-fashioned works on paper are stored elsewhere, in a different limbo; in response to each submission, the LMDC sent a letter informing the designer that he or she had twenty-one days to return a form waiving intellectual property rights and claims to compensation or "your design will be placed in the files of the Legal Department, where no LMDC staff member or third persons will have access to it." A giant lime green Post-it found on one submission—"See oversized parcel stand in vacant 'Legal Dept.' office"—testified to the bureaucratic obscurity of the reception of these offerings: a once-over from the planning department, an entry in a database, a letter of receipt (and would you please cede all rights to your work?), then on to storage.

That didn't slow anyone down. Designs came in from a Hackensack lawyer, a Bronx doctor, a Yonkers nun; six people named Anderson, ten Browns, four Cohens; Mohs Seaplane Corporation in Verona, Wisconsin; the Guild of Carillonneurs in Evanston, Illinois; the Little Thinkers Day School, in Dallas; something called "Freedom's Flame" in Rancho Cucamonga, California; the Copiague Beautification Society, on Long Island; and the Boston Visionary Cell. (The force behind the last is an artist who said his first word—"Constantinople"—at six months old and, much later, found an alien implant in his brain.) The LMDC also logged designs from Nicholas Scoppetta, New York City's Fire Commissioner, and from the Department of City Planning in Detroit. The United States Embassy in Pretoria sent an idea. A proposal was prepared by one Oulad Hadj Youcef Abdelhamid, of Ghardaia, Algeria, and another by Martha Masako Yamasaki (no relation to the architect) of Harlem. A retired army major in Ohio proposed a one-hundred-story stainless steel pylon lit with "lazer lights." A submission from a group of philosophers in Ljubljana reminded us that "the two annihilated skyscrapers are the orientation point of nothingness, the gap that the great ideas of humanity swirl into," before going on to describe the "Restaurants of the Five Continents" that their two steel-cage replacement towers would include: "The selection of world cuisines symbolically emphasizes the mission of the former World Trade Center. The VIP restaurant located in the southern tower will welcome the most demanding customers." George Bush, a retired physicist from Lexington, Virginia, was "thinking about the state of the world" in early 2002 when a dome popped into his head. He sketched it out and mailed it off.

The cache of unsolicited designs was a great equalizer; if you were not specifically responding to one of the LMDC's sanctioned requests for proposals (or working directly as a consultant for that agency, the Port Authority, or Larry Silverstein), in went your best intentions. Even Tom Bernstein, Roland Betts's partner at Chelsea Piers and the entrepreneur behind the politically popular plan to build a Museum of Freedom at the site, earned a place in the growing pile. A submission from Michael Sorkin, one of several that the perennially insurgent New York architecture critic would release, was listed in the official database between Rita Soproni of Kent, Washington, and Terry Souders of Gilbertsville, Pennsylvania. An architect at the Chicago office of Skidmore, Owings and Merrill got no more play than Peter Aitken of Syosset, New York—"I am neither architect nor artist"—who, in March 2002, sent Governor Pataki a drawing of a park with four symbolic entrances: "St. Nicholas Gate" (to honor the tiny Greek Orthodox church that was crushed in the collapse of the south tower); "Mychal's Gate" (in memory of Father Mychal Judge, the beloved Fire Department chaplain listed as the first official fatality); "Giuliani's Gate" ("in recognition of the mayor's leadership and comfort"); and, to the north, from where they would presumably come to pay their respects at this modest memorial, the "Loved One's Gate." That same month, David Mariano of Brooklyn located the other end of the sacred/secular spectrum when he proposed a detailed and perfectly plausible office complex of 12,192,240 square feet—close to the original area of the World Trade Center. "The skyline has a huge hole in it and needs desperately to be restored," he wrote in a hand-lettered note on his old-fashioned blueprints. "We are ALL so lonely without the TOWERS' PRESENCE."

Loneliness may have been one motivation to take this project on; among the new folk architects, civic-minded eccentrics of the daily-letter-to-the-editor variety were well represented. And there were certainly those among the group who needed to answer to the charge of having too much time on their hands. But this deluge of optimistic visions was heartfelt. "I was consumed by this undertaking," Barbara Wagtskjold wrote, "thinking about it, praying about it, planning, drawing, crying, hashing, re-hashing, redesigning, etc., etc., etc., until the day I finally sent it in."[2] Still, the amateurs' work was somehow at once civic, spiritual, generous, and selfish, with personal healing as a goal, as if a sixth stage—design—had been tucked into Elisabeth Kübler-Ross's five stages of grief.

Perhaps participating in the process—seeking, in effect, to control it—was a way to restore sense to the unraveling universe. Predictably, many of the unsolicited designers were attracted to more or less arbitrary systems of order, particularly the numerology of the event. Barbara Wagtskjold had six representative angels (when her vision came, she thought the dead numbered six thousand); Arnold Goldstein, a Manhattan sculptor, based his "Cathedral of Hands" on the secret meanings of the number five: "There are five points on the American star in our nation's flag. There are five wings in the Pentagon, also attacked." John Buenz, a Chicago architect, proposed a seventy-nine-story tower. Why seventy-nine and not, say, eighty? "It's indivisible," he said. "Nothing goes into seventy-nine. Not even an airplane."

Another indivisible number—eleven—had its fans. Coupled with nine, it appeared somewhere in every imaginable measure of a building; a man from Staten Island proposed towers in the shape of those numbers, standing side by side. Here the amateur architects were following the cues of a wider culture of order-seekers that blossomed after the attack. One adept in extreme numerology, a Wiccan, posted this analysis online:

The towers of the World Trade Center stood out like a giant number "11" in the skyline of New York. The event took place on the 11th day of the 9th month, or 9-11, and $9 + 1 + 1 = 11$. Have you ever wondered why 911 was chosen for the emergency number, just as "Mayday" is a distress call? May Day, or May 1, is the high sabbath of Beltaine and witchcraft. We also know that September 11 is the 254th day of the year, and $2 + 5 + 4 = 11$. This leaves 111 days left in the year, which are side-by-side 11's. The words "New York City" have a total of 11 letters. The word "Afghanistan" has 11 letters. New York was the 11th state to join the union. Flight 11 was the first plane to hit the towers. One flight had 65 passengers, $6 + 5 = 11$. The other flight had 92 passengers, $9 + 2 = 11$. The number 119 is the area code for Iran and Iraq, $1 + 1 + 9 = 11$. The words "The Pentagon" have 11 letters. President Bush ordered the American flags to be flown at half staff for 11 days, and 11 days after the 11th is the 22nd, which is the witches' sabbath of the autumnal equinox or first day of autumn.[3]

The next most popular number was *phi*—the Golden Proportion, 1:1.618—a place where a great many designers were finding comfort and seeking to share it. It is a device architects often default to when seeking to address their creations to higher circumstance; its variations, the Golden Rectangle and the Golden Spiral, show up all over the Acropolis, as well as in the proportions of the Boeing 747 and everything, anywhere that grows. One amateur supplicant from South Bend, Indiana, described his plan for the World Trade Center site as:

> The Indomitable Spirit
> of Mankind Soaring Inexorably
> Into Eternity Anchored in

the Immutable Curves of
Nature's Golden Spiral

The particulars of each design might not have stirred much passion among the politicians and bureaucrats to whom they were sent, but in the aggregate the considerable influx of oversize, mail room–clogging material served as a constant reminder that there was ferocious public interest in the site, its symbolic contents most of all. And in the early climate of possibility, the license of the amateurs was infectious. Every pundit had a plan in his pocket, and every politician, too. In his farewell speech on December 27, 2001, Rudy Giuliani called for a "soaring, beautiful memorial" covering the entire site. "I really believe we shouldn't think about this site as a site for economic development," the outgoing mayor said from the pulpit of St. Paul's Chapel, across the street from the pile. "You can do the office space in a lot of different places." The poker-faced George Pataki broke his tactical silence to get in on the act. "I've had visions of a soaring arch that rises above a hundred and ten stories," the governor said. "On the other hand, just reflecting pools, quiet knolls." Bloomberg offered a similar visionary ambivalence: "It may be tall. Maybe it will go down rather than up. I don't know."[4]

The quality and content varied enormously among the LMDC's unsolicited designs, from sketches in crayon to bound volumes of measured, computer-drawn, contractor-ready plans. But the path taken by their designers varied not at all: the experience of the tragedy, followed by the revelation of the idea (frequently from God), its depiction and transmission to worldly powers, and then the long, lonely wait for the world to catch up. A certain *certainty* was a distinguishing feature. From a letter accompanying a proposal by Avi Adler of Brooklyn: "My hope is that everyone who will be part of the rebuilding process will have an opportunity to take a look at it. It is the answer." Or this, from a letter to Mayor Bloomberg: "Even though I am merely a furniture designer from Oregon, cut off from decision-makers in New York, a feeling of certitude compelled me to take my vision this far. It is a sense of confidence that comes from knowing in my heart and soul that the vision I have is quite possibly the best solution out there."[5]

Despite the insane variety, as one LMDC staffer who had handled the submissions noted, the designs fell easily into only a few categories. There were the mystics (Ethan Ernest among them), the healers (Nurse Wagtskjold, certainly), the God-fearing (there's a plan in the LMDC files for towers in the shape of a Christian cross and a Star of David), the developers (John Buenz proposed a complete trains-to-mall complex under his indivisible tower), the redevelopers (the many after Team Twin Towers' heart), and, for lack of a better term, the screaming eagles. Amped-up nationalism being the approved mode of relief from day one, the last was by far the largest group: amateurs who promoted a screaming new World Trade Center as a vector for the screaming new patriotism.

Michael Howard McDonald, the confident Oregon furniture designer, produced one of the most visible designs in that last mode, one that became a favorite of the LMDC. The LMDC distributed images to the *New York Post*, *Artforum*, and other publications, and included it in a display of unsolicited designs that was part of a breezy exhibition of the process timeline mounted in the spring of 2003. The favored image, appearing in all three places, was an aerial view looking down on the World Trade Center site. Everything is as it was before—buildings 4, 5, and 6 are standing again; the North Bridge still crosses West Street—but the towers, while retaining their height, have taken a new form. "Imagine [two stacks] of poker chips, but instead of being round chips they are in the shape of stars," McDonald wrote in the project description he circulated far and wide. "The phrase we are hearing so much of these days, 'United We Stand,' would literally be expressed in the new shape of the Twin Towers. As one would stand in the new plaza, they could gaze up and see the silhouette of the stars against the blue sky, a vision that would echo the stars on the American flag."

In this way, the production of the nation's new folk architects was ahead of its pedigreed architects and in step with public sentiment and the needs and tastes of officialdom; it would be over a year after McDonald's plan, or Ethan Ernest's more subtle synthesis of Americana, before a prominent architect dared to wave the flag in a similar manner. Indeed, every idea that came from approved channels had its facsimile in the files of the LMDC. Avi Adler was right when he wrote of his plan, "It is the answer." His design was one of dozens, maybe hundreds, that proposed a tower with offices only up to about the seventieth floor—a limit that Larry Silverstein announced as a safe maximum for stress-free leasing—with open construction above reaching for the greater heights that pride demanded.

A very similar solution would be part of Daniel Libeskind's commission-winning master plan: a seventy-story office building next to a 1,776-foot-tall spike, the ensemble that came to be called Freedom Tower. The same hi-lo logic was shaping a tower that David Childs, lead partner of Skidmore, Owings and Merrill's New York office, was developing in secret for Silverstein. As revealed by the *New York Observer*, the tower would go up to the sixty-fifth or seventieth floor and then be capped by an unoccupied superstructure serving as a memorial. "It kind of opens up, like a latticework," one source told the paper, "and gets more and more open—more and more ethereal—until it disappears into the sky."[6] Eighteen months later the final design for Freedom Tower was unveiled in a flag-draped, camera-ready ceremony at Federal Hall, Governor Pataki presiding. It looked a lot like Avi Adler's answer.

5

CIRCUS MAXIMUS

"Tonight, the eagerness to heal after the September 11th attacks seemed evident in the hundreds of people packed shoulder to shoulder inside the Max Protetch Gallery and lining the street out the door. All waiting to see what could become the new World Trade Center . . ." (WCBS)

Architecture made all the local newscasts on the night of January 17, 2002. After weeks of the heaviest PR drum roll anyone could remember for an exhibition of high-concept fantasies, at six o'clock the doors were thrown open at the Max Protetch Gallery on the main drag of Manhattan's Chelsea art ghetto. The space was mobbed immediately, making the decision to hire a plus-size bouncer look less like a hype-fanning affectation. Even the red-velvet ropes—another unusual prop for a gallery dealing in architectural drawings—were put to good use, helping to channel the ever-growing crowd into a wide, unruly queue that spilled down West Twenty-second Street and around the corner for another block, up to a gas station on Tenth Avenue. The crowd had gathered to see the work of fifty-eight architects and firms invited by the gallery to illustrate their "what if" ideas for rebuilding Ground Zero. But the big story that night was the line; in it, for the first time, the touching faith in building as a healing art was given a physical presence on the ground.

". . . Through sketches, models, and videos, dozens of architects shared what they envision at Ground Zero. Some practical, some not so . . ."

There was as yet no official program for the site—no specific to-do list—so the only check on self-indulgence was what the market in vanity would bear. And at that point, only a few short years and one catastrophe from the bursting Internet-bubble era that had so affected the profession, it would still bear quite a lot.

To scan the offerings from this grand, eclectic assembly of poobahs, insurgents, and unknowns—something that became possible only when the crowds thinned well into the show's monthlong run—was to witness the fracturing of architecture as a profession and the limits of architecture as a communicative medium. Here were the experimenters, young and aging—Asymptote, LOT/EK, NOX—shouting their pretensions from their shingles. Here was the California bad boy Thom Mayne, with a shattered-glass mimesis of the aftermath. Mixed in were some standbys from the New York establishment: Fox & Fowle, architects of the new Times Square; Hugh Hardy, go-to designer for correct restorations; Tod Williams and Billie Tsien, designers of the American Folk Art Museum, in their second and last volunteered proposal for the site before Tsien was tapped by Mayor Bloomberg for a spot on the LMDC board. They shared the white walls with designs from Michael Sorkin and Joseph Giovannini, architecture critic for *New York* magazine, courting conflict of interest by dabbling in the process. Then there were the stray icons: Frei Otto, revered pioneer of lightweight structures, proposing a burial mound and "ponds of memory" in a park set with domes and minarets; Paolo Soleri, Ethan Ernest's guru, submitting the "Babelnoah Arcology"—a towering iteration of Soleri's recurring eco-apocalyptic daydream—despite having been overlooked on the long invitation list; and, from left field, Vito Acconci, an infamous New York performance art pioneer, reborn as an architect in the late 1990s and here proposing a Swiss-cheese massif of "pre-exploded towers." Finally, there was a dusting of stars, among them the Iraqi jet-setter Zaha Hadid, perhaps the most important female architect in history; Steven Holl, famous for presenting his concepts in watercolors; and Daniel Libeskind, making his first formal appearance in the fuss with an idea for a bifurcated tower that resembled a pair of rusty pruning shears—a fearsome image nonetheless wrapped in the language of healing.

It was an international, intergenerational, and interstylistic sampling of the profession that might have pleased a pollster. And what did the adepts bring? Distraction, mostly: "Nano-Towers" and "weeping towers"; 220-story aviaries and 911-foot-deep memorial pits; "a total transformation, a place where human experience and aesthetic sensibilities are interwoven in total freedom"; notes toward an "E-Motive Architecture"; "Twin Twins"; and "The Tower of Babel Revisited." That last title was given to an entry submitted by the venerable Viennese avant-gardist partnership Coop Himmelb(l)au, which they described as "reversed towers, built upside down, [to] provide multifunctional signs for the future of architecture."

". . . The ideas are getting mixed reviews: 'It doesn't seem like they're really addressing the program as they are throwing out these forms.'"[1]

The bespectacled student who offered the above on-camera critique had clearly come from the architecture world, in which *form* has a very specific meaning. There is the usual, neutral usage—something plastic, evolved in three dimensions—but more often the term takes a negative sense, implying the sacrifice of everything else: empty *form*; *form* for *form*'s sake; *form* as a truncated form of the epithet *formalism; form* as an intimation of that dreaded title *formalist*, one for whom substance follows surface, and function, if it comes, comes last.

Given some of the headlines from the weeks before the show—"Downtowners Worried Sick,"[2] "Job Loss from September 11 to Impact for Years,"[3] "Still Digging for Lost Sons after a Million Tons

of Pain"[4] (and that was just the local news)—the public relief at
finding this diversion was easy to understand. Not so the motivation for the more flippant submissions. Foreign Office Architects, a
young London duo at the edge of fame, sent a smug note with their
"Bundle Tower," a sheaf of eight wriggling, 110-story garden
hoses. "Let's not even consider remembering . . . What for?" they
wrote. "We have a great site in a great city and the opportunity to
have the world's tallest building back in New York." That was the
most visible faux pas in the show, but the exercise itself struck a
callous note. Was it—could it ever be—too early for form?

It is not obvious from his name, but Max Protetch is an actual person, not a German synth pop band or an artsy Rotterdam atelier.
He is a tall, strangely serene man under tight graying curls, a self-
described "sixties guy" from the Midwest but with definite Northern California finer-things-in-life airs. He can also be a flamboyant
character—he named his dog Zaha, after the architect—and his
showman's instincts have for decades made his gallery an important nexus for architectural tastemaking. Studying political science at Georgetown in the early 1970s, Protetch set up his first
gallery there, giving per-formance artist Vito Acconci his Washington, D.C., debut—a sort of sexed-up, pre–reality television
dare called "Broad Jump": if you could jump farther than the artist
over his two girlfriends, you got to take them home. "I bought the
piece for a hundred dollars and I sold it for a thousand," Max said
one night in 2003 at a Chelsea bar a block from his gallery. "That
tells you how long ago it was."

The idea for the show—"A New World Trade Center"—came
to Protetch very soon after September 11. His goal was opposi-
tional. "The whole thing was awful because I just know how the
city operates, and it's been such a sad scene in terms of contemporary architecture here," he said. "This is the center of the world—
the Western cultural world, the financial world—and we have at

best mediocre architecture. So I started doing this show and I thought, 'I have no choice.' I was suffering—we all were suffering—and it sounds a little trite now, you know what I mean: us New Yorkers, we're all so jaundiced and sophisticated."

In architecture circles after the attack, you could sometimes find people engaging in pitiful closer-than-thou pissing matches, as if one's proximity to the towers that day were a qualification to design their replacement. (SOM, the firm that ultimately designed the first new buildings for the site, had to evacuate its Wall Street offices and lost several employees, so maybe there's something to it.) By that measure, Protetch, though not a designer himself, should certainly be part of the team. That morning he had just dropped his nine-year-old son off at P.S. 234 on Chambers Street, a brand-new schoolhouse, the pride of Tribeca, just four blocks north of Tower One. He had driven south to the edge of the World Trade Center when he heard "a sonic boom" right above. "So I pulled over and I was talking to this guy and he said 'Hey, a plane just went into that building,'" Protetch recalled.

And there was the outline of a plane in the World Trade Center. And I was thinking I had a show of a guy called Gregory Green a few years ago, an artist who pushed all of my buttons, and one of the things he did was this most gorgeous perfect little atomic bomb—perfect except it didn't have enriched plutonium. The point is, if an artist like Gregory, who's a bright guy but an artist, can make an atomic bomb, anyone can. He had also made a little missile that I bought, put on my roof, and I aimed it at the World Trade Center. It was 1996, maybe 1995. So when I saw this, I thought, 'Okay, that little indentation in the building is from a little rocket.' I had this argument with this guy. He said, 'No, no. It was a big plane.' So I thought, 'Oh, you know: they bombed this building again.' I wasn't even worried about my kids because I also knew about the

building, that it was designed to withstand an airplane flying into it. I didn't know enough to know about the fuel.

Like many of his classmates at P.S. 234—corralled in school and
then sent out into the dust—Protetch's son had a hard time afterward. To get away, the family, sans Max, relocated immediately to
Ottawa, where Protetch's then wife had grown up. Protetch spent
much of the balance of that September driving to Canada and back,
and it was on those drives, on the phone with his right hand, Stuart
Krimko, that the idea for the show developed. Larry Silverstein's
four-towers plan was a catalyst. "I was shocked at Silverstein's lack
of vision, his lack of understanding of the enormity of this and of
his own position in the world," Protetch said. "Here's this
seventy-year-old guy who's got a zillion dollars who didn't understand he could leave a great legacy. It shocked me. I was so positive
it was going to be a disaster I thought, 'I have to do something.'"

What he did was barrage his Rolodex, calling on architects to
contribute designs. He had lunch with Philip Johnson. He con-
tacted Oscar Niemeyer, the ninety-year-old modern master, at his
home above Rio. He leaned on Peter Eisenman, bully king of the
theory-headed, formalist corner of New York architecture. He
sent out 125 letters, thinking he would get fifty designers for the
show. But it wasn't that easy. "I had legitimate objections from
everybody, which I really respected," Protetch said, "and then I
beat on them." The beating took the form of a very persuasive argument, one that had been apparent to many architects since the
day of the attack: "I said, 'Look, you either do something or you're
acquiescent.'"

Still, despite vigorous arm-twisting all through that fall, many
of the highest-profile architects—Johnson, Niemeyer, I. M. Pei—
refused to participate. The most famous New York architects—
Charles Gwathmey, Richard Meier—were no-shows. Peter Eisenman
told Protetch he was too busy. ("You know, it was just Peter bull-
shit," Protetch said. "And I was very comfortable telling him I

thought he was chicken.") Frank Gehry wanted no part of it: "I got sent a thing inviting me and I threw it away." Robert Stern thought it was "too soon and too ghoulish." Rem Koolhaas also stayed away, though it is hard to know whether he and others were conscientious objectors or were merely banking their professional capital hoping for the chance at a less risky play.

A perilous middle way was attempted by a handful of architects who signed on, then used their projects to critique the undertaking. Brad Cloepfil, who leads the Portland, Oregon, firm Allied Works, tempered his "room in the sky" with this disclaimer: "Let others create new towers to repair the skyline more spectacularly than we can imagine. . . . Just not here. Not now." Marwan Al-Sayed, a budding critical darling practicing in Phoenix, made a case for beauty ("Beauty and Creation Overcome Death"), drew five wavering, beautiful towers on the site, and then noted that the questions of the rebuilding "will not be put to rest by this exhibition." The New York firm Weiss/Manfredi sketched the empty skyline with the towers still reflected in the waters of the Hudson, an image that inspired an ad by Kmart that ran in local papers on the first anniversary.

Tokyo-based Shigeru Ban, an incomparable talent, sent a small paper-wire-and-wood model that he had made immediately after September 11, "without having been asked by anyone." It may be the most humble proposal conceived before or since: a round tempietto, about two stories high and twenty feet across, within which, up two steps, behind a curtain, there would be a single slab of stone, appropriately inscribed. Maybe ten people could fit inside at once, an implicit rebuke to the cyclopean scale that had quickly become a driving assumption among his colleagues, and in all but the quirkiest amateur designs. Ban's shrine was small, cheap, and frankly ephemeral. Like the shelters he had developed for survivors of the Kobe earthquake, and later, via the United Nations, for refugee camps in Africa, the structure would be made from recycled cardboard tubes. In the catalog for the Protetch show, Ban titled his project "A Departure from the Ego," adding in his text, "I cannot imagine designing another high-rise building to indicate 'the EGO.' "[5]

Since the great legions of the unsolicited were already doing quite a good job at providing sugar-plum visions, it didn't seem like too much of a stretch to expect architects to apply other, harder-won aspects of their expertise to the problem. Such skills include less photogenic but necessary specialties: navigating a complex political landscape or managing an ambiguous client structure. One firm, Della Valle and Bernheimer Design, resisted grandiosity, and form, while trying to steer discussion in precisely this practical direction, where it might have done some good.

Though both barely out of school—infants by architecture's age-weighted standards—Jared Della Valle and Andy Bernheimer had some experience in these areas. Their breakout project, a job they had won through an open competition in 1996, was a public plaza doubling as a truck-bomb buffer in front of a federal building in San Francisco. Their design, an angular challenge to the four-square block it fronted, was perfectly à la mode and it was published far and wide. What they took to the Max Protetch Gallery were that project's extra-formal lessons. They presented there a long box of plastic cubes, each representing one of about eighty process players they'd identified, each sized to reflect that entity's relative power—"a device for the study of currently indeterminate relationships," they wrote. "A physical metaphor for the complex dialogue required by the task of rebuilding."[6]

The proportions of Della Valle and Bernheimer's cubes provide a snapshot of public perceptions in the early months of the process. Reflecting the success of his vigorous courting of the press, Larry Silverstein was given one of the two largest blocks—larger than all the family and public advocacy groups put together. The Port Authority got the other one, equal in size to the Empire State Development Corporation, the U.S. Congress, the president of the

United States, and the LMDC combined. That was a fair assessment at the time; the LMDC was then in the throes of its birth
and had not yet shown its teeth publicly. More striking in retro-
spect is the small role implied by the block labeled "Office of the
Governor." It was the same size as those representing the Department of City Planning (which would have zero role), the Metropolitan Transit Authority (which would have a tiny one), and the
9/11 Widows and Victims' Families Association (ditto). The governor was only one-sixth as potent, Della Valle and Bernheimer
thought, as Silverstein or the Port; it was a sign that Pataki's pup-
peteer strategy was working. Had they been able to see through the
veils at that moment, the designers might have proposed scattered
grains of sand around a monolith inscribed "George Pataki."

The number of architects choosing to highlight this necessary
engagement of their craft in the world of the real—one project
out of fifty-eight—reflects the shrift such things are given in the
artsier offices. It is strange that more architects don't try to grap-
ple with the more everyday aspects of their work, to understand,
exploit, and even revel in them. These mundane forces are, after
all, the arena where architects spend most of their time, and from
which they get most of their money. But a mastery of public process or a feel for pleasing bureaucracies dazzles few posh clients, or
critics, and makes poor fodder for a magazine spread.

Situated where purpose and inspiration cross paths, architecture at all times finds itself pulled between the glamour of the
other arts and the grit of engineering. But the prejudices of high-
profile designers skew the profession toward art, a limited expression of its potential. One reason architecture is interesting, and
ultimately important, is that it is so compound by nature. Is it an
art? Yes. A science? Often. A business? Always. Denying this com-
plexity makes of architecture a curio; embracing it allows architecture to do what it still does better than the other arts: shape
the world.

Not surprisingly, considering the venue, nearly all the architects in the Max Protetch show chose to hew close to the limited but critically acclaimed model of the artiste provocateur. Too early for form? Never. Most ran with the opportunity to chip in and sound off, to deploy a shape or two, to take the soapbox given them.

Among these was Greg Lynn (who calls his firm FORM), an ever-rising star who cut his wisdom teeth in Peter Eisenman's office before discovering the computer and becoming a proponent of blobism—the vapid, digit-driven chic of the late 1990s that Herbert Muschamp had seen in the World Trade Center wreckage. From his office in Los Angeles, Lynn phoned in an unremarkable design—a collection of jagged, low-resolution renderings showing twinned, pustulous towers in battleship gray—which he explained in an extraordinary bit of wall text. Over a line drawing of a German bunker on the Normandy coast, a reference that had been fashionable in architecture for some time, Lynn wrote, "The siting and design of the surrounding public space and the form of the skyscraper will be designed to avoid and repel attack." A longer caption explained why: "The attack and collapse of both towers of the World Trade Center marks the lack of distinction between military and urban space. The use of commercial aircraft as weapons and the targeting of office towers both represent the collapse of boundaries between global military conflict and everyday life. There is no return once these distinctions disappear. From now on, new skyscrapers, whose size, location, and design make them significant targets of terrorism, will need to incorporate defensive military design and technology."

It was this prospect—that our buildings must become fortifications—that seemed to excite Lynn, looking to the carnage for a new intellectual hook. Though it was hard to tell from the accompanying graphic (and, to be fair, many designers contributed to the show on very short notice), he seemed to be proposing a structure that would, somehow—possibly through the use of intelligent, animate materials not yet known—actively protect those within. But his text made it clear that public survival came second to artistic possibility:

> This return to medieval and renaissance architectural and urban design—when defensibility and resistance to siege were primary design factors which forced architects to study trajectories of projectiles, maneuverability of troops, and resistance of materials—will significantly affect the design of buildings and cities today. The transfer of military thinking into daily life is inevitable and any true security is futile.[7]

There was of course nothing in Lynn's revelations or the design they inspired that would get anyone even an inch closer to making a safer tower. And we already knew what the dangers were. But more than just being hollow, Lynn's spiel underscored an old structural problem within the profession—the practitioners who build don't get anything from the theorists who talk about building—and another that was highlighted anew by the response to the attack: architecture's fatal distance from public need. The class of problems that Lynn and his thinker ilk take on are invariably too conjectural, too personal, too obscure, too sensational, or, as in this case, too all of the above to be of much use when utility comes calling. And it was very much calling after September 11, 2001. The issues facing tall buildings—fire, gravity, life, death— could not have been more real, and the larger, corporate firms of the type scorned by architecture's divas were busy grappling with them. In the wake of the attack, as architecture found itself more often in the limelight, what could have been written off before as a backstage spat was beginning to exert itself on the process. The public—edgy, engaged, clamoring for answers—was for once, God help and bless them, knocking on architecture's front door. Which architects—the glossy preeners or the boring, competent professionals—would answer?

Rising out of the "chaoticism" at mid-century and the postmodern pastiche that replaced it, a putative avant-garde, led largely by Peter Eisenman, had for decades tried to bring other frames of reference to architecture: turning into rigorous formal manipulations and then out, first to the joys of French linguistic theory and later to concepts stolen from the sciences. These efforts succeeded only in severing the head of the profession from its body, a split that may be irreparable. The critique is not at all new; since at least World War II, and probably as far back as Vitruvius, architects have worried openly about the uneasy coexistence of artists and practitioners in the field. But, jazzed by the possibilities of the computer, and supported by a star-struck press and an increasingly accommodating academy, in the 1980s and 1990s this divide widened.

Sociologists and architects took on the problem in a string of books, pointing out the ways that an elite, a practice within a practice, was a drag on the profession. But by the time of the attack, the thinkers had become more than just a drag. There is, of course, nothing wrong with not building; like any art, architecture needs its unshackled muses. But one hopes that those designers with the luxury not to build—the academics and self-supporting visionaries about whom the press makes the most fuss—would use their time to inspire something of substance. Or, better, to blaze a trail that others might actually follow. Shouldn't a self-styled avant-garde architect act in some way for the greater good of the grand army he ostensibly serves? For whom, otherwise, is he scouting over that next hill?

Every architecture project starts with an infinity of possibilities. And that has its own terror. On one side, there's the physical world in all its unruly grace—space, climate, the land—and the thorny trappings of human society—money, politics, use. Then there's history, weighing on this unformed thing, and taste, and clients, and time. Some of these factors can be listed neatly as fixed specifics in a program brief, but that does not strip them of their caprice. As an architect first faces a design, the competing forces arrange themselves into fleeting orders that collapse and collapse again as they are tested by an equally volatile set of priorities and goals. To commit this roiling mess to form is necessarily daunting. In May 2002, Ed Wyatt, Ground Zero beat reporter for the *New York Times*, described the predicament well when he wrote that the multiple design decisions at the World Trade Center site were "so intertwined as to be essentially one decision, whose many parts will have to be made almost simultaneously."[8]

This is true of all building, everywhere. But there is usually a reprieve: when an architect commits to an exclusive ideological or formal strategy—be it Beaux Arts or blob—one path through that thicket is marked. That is a great relief, the comfort of style, and seeking it is one reason why, looking at the methods promoted by leading architects, we see so many fixed forms, universal ideas, and gimcrack gimmicks applied to widely differing architectural dilemmas. Indeed, much of what is known generally today as architecture culture—the sort of formal and textual crutches seen in such maddening array at the Max Protech show—are symptoms of individual maneuvers around the fear of a blank slate.

Few practicing architects have the luxury to think outside the parameters of their last built box. It's hard enough to keep track of new materials and methods, to do business. So for direction, some still look to the profession's thinkers. They turn to the magazines to see what their celebrated colleagues are up to, or to the fancier journals, where they might hope to discover a missive from on high. And what do they find there? Not a log of current thinking—an assessment or summary of research that might be put to use, practical or poetic—but generally a collection of private indulgences, products of the blank-slate fear, skewed heavily to the glamorous. Those who occupy the place where, in a healthier profession, one might find a research wing—a proper avant-garde—cleave only to the rules of the retail marketplace. What is sexy? What is new? What is *dangerous*? What can I do to spotlight my work, my myth, my glory?

This antic stance can lead to notoriety—on the newsstands, in bookstores, in galleries, in schools—which in turn leads to influence in the narrow world of architecture culture and in the greater toiling practice beyond, eventually rattling through the machine to become a fact on the everyday ground. In this formula, buildings become by-products of the star architect's need for exposure. Their quest for notoriety influences practicing architects who, through the filter of commerce, shape the world.

You can read in Greg Lynn's statement the excesses of the young, look-at-me starlet. But you can also read in it a kind of yearning for substance—taking the disaster as an opportunity to bring back to architecture some of the gravity lost in the lightness of the preceding years. And in New York those years were very light. Just as no great monuments were raised, the late 1990s were marked by an increase in theoretical babble and unbuildable but eminently publishable propositions. Usually architecture thrives on paper in the bust, and boom times bring a return to the kind of thinking that might lead to construction. But in those years, as architecture got caught up in the wider evolution of the design world as a whole, the usual rhythms were reversed. Design achieved a new currency in the culture and the marketplace, returning to glamorous prominence in the form of the candy-striped iMac and the New Beetle and a thousand other objects that were beginning to fill the shelves with signature forms. To keep up, architects had to work in media much more nimble than buildings and all the messiness that comes with them.

The problems of architects at that moment were compounded by their love affair with the computer, a recent revolution they had not yet assimilated. The new three-dimensional modeling software allowed architects to wrap their designs in photorealistic materiality, bathe them in seductive ray-traced light, and fly through them in a way that even the most obtuse client had to understand. But the tool was pushing the hand. Morris Lapidus, the great apostate of American modernism, designer of many free-form

Miami Beach hotels, was resurrected just before his death in 2001 to lecture at Columbia University, his alma mater and a school deep in the thrall of new technologies. Before his talk, Lapidus walked through the studios, usually a joyous scene of piled drawings and models, and he was disappointed by their starkness. He asked where all the work was, and someone introduced him to the computers. His reaction: "They're wrong if they think those machines are going to do the thinking for them. You can't ask a machine to give you an idea."

Of course, that is precisely what architects most often ask of their machines. But like so much in computing, it's a case of garbage in, garbage out. Tom Kovac, an Australian architect, sent Max Protetch an excellent example of the use of the computer as a surrogate author: a series of digital manipulations that resulted in images of a lacy, banded extrusion that looked something like a twisted jockstrap—a marvel of digital production, but the task at hand was to design a new building to stand at the site where three thousand odd had recently been killed. "Using software in unprecedented ways, we interrogated the organizational relationships within the complex, mapping the connections and representing them in space as an efficiency web," Kovac wrote in his project description.

> The traffic of people between these "attractors" was known, and we represented this in tubules with a thickness to scale. The volumes of space used in the old towers were then located as spheres. All this data was maximized for efficiency in space, the software pushing and pulling everything until it was in the optimum relationship to everything else. An envelope for this calculation was derived from a median topological mapping of the upper surface of Manhattan Island. And the footprint of the site was held integral. Then we programmed a surface into the interstices between the data, using the rule that the surface be

trapped in the cage of the data, but never touch it. This formed the chassis for the design.[9]

The architects playing in their sandbox when the World Trade Center fell were hardly qualified to become overnight experts in poignance. Michael Graves, one of the leaders of the postmodern classical revolt, spent the height of the boom years designing designerly products for Target, at one point sketching 365 items in as many days. For "A New World Trade Center," Graves prepared a kind of palimpsest map of Lower Manhattan. "We can never erase the memory of the tragic events of September 11, which will without a doubt require a central formal monument of some kind, whose form is as yet unknown to us," he wrote. "I feel, however, that the most meaningful way to memorialize the innocent victims . . . would be a marker within a restored context of layered urban pattern on the site."[10] Or, in English: the architectural answer to all that recent death was to bring the street grid back through the graveyard. Graves's teapots and slotted spoons had made him rusty.

Not everyone had joined the yahoo chorus. In New York, there was a distinct countercurrent, made up of younger firms and buoyed by a hopeful interest in fundamentals among students who were years away from practice. These architects wanted to build. They wanted to exploit those properties of architecture—how its materials work in real gravity, how its spaces work in real life—that were not favored in the flashing orgy of digitalia. An academic attempt was made in 2000 to align this energy with the thinking of American Pragmatism, but, true to that philosophy's resistance to dogma, it never took. In 1987 Michael Benedikt, an architecture professor in Texas, had written what should have been the mantra of this new way: "In our media-saturated times it falls to architecture to have the direct esthetic experience of the real at the center of its concerns."[11]

Architects brought to the problem of Ground Zero all their

new toys, none of which offered a way forward as promising as Benedikt's credo. Chris Strom, a veteran of many of the city's larger architecture firms, updated that idea neatly for the redevelopment. "What has architecture been doing for the last ten years? Looking for conflict," he said in the spring of 2002. "Now that there's conflict everywhere, can't architecture return to its role of affirming permanence?"

Perhaps, but not at this time, in this place. Caught up in the public's search for solace, the Max Protetch show was a juggernaut. Protetch himself was everywhere in the national press, and when the show traveled to the National Building Museum in Washington in April 2002, it broke all attendance records. The show also took on a political dimension; it represented the United States at the Venice Biennale the following September, and was later accessioned into the permanent collection of the Library of Congress. Thanks to the curators there, the value of "A New World Trade Center" was fixed. The value to the profession may have been zero. The value to some of the architects making their process debut was incalculable. But we know for certain now the value to the federal government of a collection of fifty-eight hypothetical responses to a national tragedy: $408,140, payable to its organizer.

"I haven't had anything worth fighting for in a long time," Protetch said, reminiscing at the bar near his gallery. "I mean, how hard can you fight for Al Gore, you know? The things that I believe in now, it's very hard to put body and soul behind them. And at this particular moment in time, I really needed something that I could be behind one hundred percent. Here was a moment where I could really do something. So I had to give it a shot."[12]

6

LISTENING MODE

AS PUBLIC officials got busy fixing the sixteen-acre lot down-town, the public itself got busy making noise. Armed with an unprecedented sense of entitlement to shape the site, New York-ers rose as one to growl (with apologies to George Bush), "The people who will put these buildings back up will hear from all of us soon!" Responding to the overwhelming ferment, seeking to con-trol it, in early 2002 John Whitehead announced that the LMDC would spend the next several months in "listening mode."[1] Begin-ning that January, you could take a seat in a packed high school or community college auditorium, observe a moment of silence, then step up to the microphone—from your lips to the governor's ears—to have your opinions fed through the stenographer to the limbo of the permanent record. Dissent that might have spilled onto the streets in the time-honored tradition of New York de-velopment was channeled instead into rounds of formal meet-ings; dozens of open hearings were held to generate consensus on the goals of the redevelopment—the two largest were given the grandiose name "Listening to the City"—but the public at large was provided the opportunity to vent only under the watchful eye of the LMDC. The effect was to create the illusion of power. As one disgruntled participant remarked, "This is the story of a thousand people drinking Shirley Temples and smoking candy cig-arettes, and they all think they're in a back room with their Scotch and cigars."

Each meeting was prefaced by a long recitation of the rules of engagement: keep to the time limit (heed the lights and bells) and don't ask questions of the panelists (they were there to *listen*, not to indulge in give-and-take). That barely kept the circus in check. In the lobbies, as the hearings dragged on, pamphleteers from various pressure groups would mingle with amateurs hawking their designs, all in the glare of documentarians' cameras—for this was history—sometimes eddying around the beat reporters phoning stories in when the meetings ran late, as they always did, for there was so much to say, so much hurt to convey, so much passion caught up in the act of venting. And for many, it seemed, speaking, not building, was the best possible response to September 11: gearing up with statements and evidence—at one meeting a woman concerned about lingering dust brought in and brandished a clogged air filter—then heading out to the show.

Bernard Goetz, the controversial subway vigilante who had reinvented himself as a fringe mayoral candidate and a protector of pet weasels, was not the only eccentric who found a new home in the process. Mixed liberally with the devastating (survivors' testimonials) and the mundane (*"We want our Borders back!"*), the absurd was well represented. In about the fourth hour of one meeting—when most of the audience and even the press had fled, exhausted—Abe Hirschfeld, a former owner of the *New York Post*, not long before convicted and jailed for plotting to assassinate a business partner, took the mike to argue that the memorial should adopt the form of his first love and the source of his fortune: a parking garage. More than once, a local representative of the Audubon Society braved universal scorn to make his impassioned, statistics-rich plea that any new buildings must be "avian-friendly." Those with weightier concerns got no special treatment; at one meeting, the bird man spoke just after Sally Regenhard had gotten up to make another of her righteous calls for bringing the Port Authority and the site under the rule of New York City's building codes, a campaign launched to avenge the death of her firefighter son, his picture, as was by then the custom for the activist mourners, hanging on a heavy disk around her neck.

The first public meeting to solicit community input on the redevelopment was convened on the summery evening of January 29, 2002. It was held at Stuyvesant High School, just north of the site, in an auditorium that would only later be cleaned of all the toxic dust that had settled there. The meeting was organized by Manhattan Borough President C. Virginia Fields, an elected Democrat making a rare appearance in the process, and Madelyn Wils, in her capacity as chair of Community Board 1. They were joined by fourteen others, including Lou Tomson, recently appointed director of the LMDC; Bob Yaro, head of the Regional Plan Association; and Liz Thompson, the executive director of the Lower Manhattan Cultural Council, a venerable arts group, who one sunny morning four months before had taken the last elevator down from Windows on the World.

The first speaker at that first meeting was our very own Ethan Ernest: "I was born, raised, and educated here in New York City," he said. "I believe the entire site should function as a memorial." Then he hit them with the vision that his time as a Ground Zero volunteer had inspired: Emerson and Franklin, flags and snakes. The cameras found the presentation board he held—they must have been glad for the unexpected eye candy—and with that exposure on the news, Ernest's "Ripple Effects" had one of its short days in the sun. Albert Capsuto, owner of a nearby restaurant, came with an idea to share the love by "decentralizing" the debris throughout the city. Others offered more banal suggestions: a library, a hospital, a school, or, the most popular position, nothing at all.

Roger Ebert, the thumbs-up film critic for the *Chicago Sun-Times*, may have been the very first to call for a memorial park. "Let it be a green field, with trees and flowers," Ebert wrote in an article—"Make It Green"—published three days after the attack. "Let there be paths that wind through the shade. Put out park benches where old people can sun in the summertime, and a pond where children can skate in the winter."[2] The artist Ellsworth Kelly ambled in with the same idea just before the second anniversary, having glued a single green piece of paper onto an aerial shot of the site that appeared in the *New York Times*. This he sent off to Herbert Muschamp, who, despite having by then offered up many architecture-intensive responses himself, was smitten. He framed an article around Kelly's vision, explaining that an anonymous donor had appeared—Kelly's collage was apparently not a gift to the critic or the city—and the important new work had been purchased by the Whitney Museum.[3] But of course "just a park" was never an option; there could never be a no-construction alternative at Ground Zero. "Do not build again on this place," Ebert had written. "No building, no statue, no column, no arch, no symbol, no name, no date, no statement." Some of those things could— and, in the case of symbols, should—be omitted. But there had to be building; without it, there would only be the site's raw depressions—two stories deep to the east and seven stories deep to the west—and no surface at all on which to plant green grass. Or, in Ebert's case, patriotic corn: "Let students . . . plant a crop there. Perhaps corn, our native grain."[4]

Just as that first hearing brought about an airing of all the ideas that became perennial, it also brought together many of the characters who went on to become the usual process suspects. Ron Devito, an electric company systems analyst, rose, red-faced, to demand that the buildings be replaced; three months later he joined with a backer to found Team Twin Towers. Sudhir Jain, a resident of Battery Park City who tirelessly relayed to the LMDC the concerns of his neighbors, was there that night; not far from him was one of those neighbors, a large, wheelchair-bound woman whose cause was the return of the convenient mall. Monica Iken, the prominent activist widow, made a statement like a hundred others she would make through the year, trying to temper the enthusiasm for commerce rising from the ashes. "Those towers are

gone," she said, standing at her aisle seat in the high school auditorium. "They're done. They're not here. They're not coming
back. That is a burial site. Most of us will never get any remains
found."[5] Not long before she had issued one of her many public
threats to ring Ground Zero with widows in a human chain. "The
world is watching," she reminded the hearing (as Madelyn Wils
eyed her skeptically from the dais). "How are we going to honor
those like my husband who died? How can we build on top of their
souls that are crying? We have to send a strong message that this is
not about money."[6]

In truth, it was not all about money. It was also about turf, as
Iken and her allies discovered when they tangled with Tribeca—
and lost resoundingly—over placing the World Trade Center's or-
phaned *Sphere* in the neighborhood's only park. That fight with the
residents revealed one of the redevelopment's hard truths: there
never was a families veto. Particularly after Giuliani aligned himself with the whole-site-as-memorial camp, the families seemed in-
vincible. What politician or panel could resist them? Wouldn't a
single hero-invoking turn at the microphone dull any designer's ex-
cess or magnate's greed? But the residents were only the first to
test the families' power and prevail; 2002 was, after all, the year
those mourners lost all but two of their sacred acres.

Their biggest foe was not another Ground Zero faction, it was
an idea: opportunity. In *A New Deal for New York*, a quick, thorough
book on the process, historian Mike Wallace wrote at length about
the possibilities for improved transportation and public space that
had opened for New York City on September 11. "The opposite
side of disaster is opportunity,"[7] he concluded. Away from the
fastness of the families, that idea became a rare common bond.
The goo-goos, particularly those folded into the industrious Civic
Alliance, an umbrella group for dozens of organizations, were ex-
pressly looking to improve the city—that was their job before and
after the attack—and they always had the attention of government and the press. "The opinions sought and listened to in the

formative stages of the official process were far from representative," reconstruction advocate Louis Epstein complained in the insightful tract history of the process, "Anatomy of a Disgrace," that he printed out and distributed at public hearings. "They involved pre-existing lobby groups that had an intrinsic bias toward making the city different than it had been."[8] That January night at Stuyvesant, one local resident summed up the already fixed idea: "We have a blank slate, why not make it better?" Lee Ielpi, who had lost his son, stood at the back and told the room, "Good luck."

The opportunity crowd would need luck—for the slate, of course, was not quite blank. From the families' perspective, it was worse than blank; from Larry Silverstein's, it was just blank enough. His lease and all his partners' paperwork still described a full buildout of all that had been there before, in the ground and in the sky: ten million square feet of office space (97 percent occupied on the day it disappeared), six hundred thousand square feet for a hotel, six hundred thousand square feet of shopping mall (with an option, later exercised, to go up to one million). The need to fit all that space—under Silverstein's self-imposed seventy-story height limit and minus the acreage of the increasingly sacred tower footprints—proscribed the future of the site in a way that nothing else would; all the democracy in the world was not going to change those numbers or the conditions they dictated. It was for good urbanistic reasons that Minoru Yamasaki, after considering 105 possibilities, had chosen to pack the office space into two fat towers; with that square footage spread out among lower, more slender buildings, there would have been next to nothing left of the site—little room for the five-acre plaza the architect thought his modern monuments required, or, in the site's second life, little space for a "soaring memorial" or the items on dusted-off wish lists: parks, plazas, shops, museums, concert halls, and the replacement PATH commuter rail station that everyone was calling "a Downtown Grand Central Terminal."

Silverstein's case for a full-bore rebuilding—for hanging on at all—always came back to the terms of his agreement with the Port Authority. But the relevant language in the lease was ambiguous. In section 15 of the ominous document, the Port dictated that if the property were destroyed by "fire, the elements, the public enemy or other casualty," the lessee, Silverstein, "shall remove all debris resulting from such damage or destruction, and shall rebuild, restore, repair and replace the Premises . . . to the extent feasible, prudent and commercially reasonable, with the plans and specifications for the same as they existed prior to such damage or destruction or with the consent in writing of the Port Authority, which consent shall not be unreasonably withheld, conditioned or delayed, make such other repairs, replacements, changes or alterations as is mutually agreed by the Port Authority and the Lessee."[9]

Okay: rebuild it or, with the Port's approval, make it better. The next paragraph allowed that if the destruction of the property occurred in the final fifteen years of the lease—any time after 2085—whoever then held the lease had the option to terminate it (if the mortgage was paid off) by a simple letter delivered to the ageless Port within sixty days of the calamity. But even in the first years, subject to the passage above, both parties had an out: "to the extent feasible, prudent and commercially reasonable." Such language seems designed to relieve the pressures on the site after September 11. The feasibility of returning ten million square feet of office space could certainly have been questioned—except for a few vengeful pledges, there was zero tenant interest. The prudence of rebuilding was considered in the press from day one—would it be safe to work there?—and then tacitly when Silverstein imposed his seventy-story cap, but higher powers never called for the developer to sacrifice his entire investment to fear. That last point—"commercially reasonable"—was the green light Silverstein needed: too much valuable real estate had been lost, and the mechanism for its resurrection was so close at hand, immortal in filing cabinets, signed with schoolgirl delicacy by Cherrie Nanninga, representing the Port, and with a quick three-stroke slash, a deal-makers' mark, by Silverstein himself. *Move it, move it, move it—time is precious.*

The burden of that commercial square footage was something the public process was never able to touch. But there were other limits on the redevelopment that were coming closer to codification at each meeting: a body of managed assumptions that passed for consensus, allowing the public and private arbiters of the site to act under the umbrella of conventional wisdom as they navigated the minefield of unconventional dispute.

Those assumptions framed the discussion at the first "Listening to the City" meeting, organized by the Civic Alliance and held just ten days after the players had gathered at the inaugural public hearing at Stuyvesant High School. The venue was a food court dining hall in South Street Seaport, a vintage festival marketplace that had fallen on hard times and then fallen harder after September 11. It was a gray day—the Brooklyn Bridge looked particularly brooding just outside—but the mood inside was upbeat, perhaps picking up on the floor-length Technicolor dreamcoat that the day's moderator, the commanding Carolyn Lukensmeyer, wore to increase her visibility at such events.

The presence of Lukensmeyer was another reminder that this local tempest was playing out in the national teapot. The Washington, D.C.–based nonprofit she founded, AmericaSpeaks ("America" in blue, "Speaks" in red), organizes "21st Century Town Meetings™"[10] in which statistically representative microcosms hash through civic problems face-to-face (in the tradition of a New England town meeting, she writes) with the aid of networked computers, trained "facilitators," corporate sponsorship, "groupware," and a handy remote control–like device that the virtually empowered citizens themselves can key to voice their assent or criticism of the agenda at hand as preselected questions and multiple-choice answers are posted on giant screens. A sketch artist is sometimes present to interpret the issues and conclusions in jolly hues as they are beamed in, vetted by a "theme team," and then announced from the stage by the bright and calming Lukens-meyer. At South Street Seaport that day, the artist filled roll after roll of white paper with Magic Marker doodles: a policeman riding a rainbow; a figure standing on a globe balancing "HEALING" in one hand and in the other, predictably, "REBUILDING," the word itself blurring into a Lower Manhattan skyline thick with smoke and flames and little red hearts.

The AmericaSpeaks Web site opens with a quote from Aris-totle: "A citizen is one who participates in power."[11] But the expe-rience offered at the two "Listening to the City" gatherings America-Speaks ran—the first with six hundred participating, the second, five months later, with forty-five hundred—was to see powerlessness conferred in real time. As Lukensmeyer, her facilita-tors, and her enabling technologies honed the incoming opinions to a fine, conflict-free, Middle American politesse, diversity and dissent went missing. This suited the LMDC, which, abetted by the sponsoring Civic Alliance, had formed all the questions and framed the debate. The booklet handed out to citizens arriving at the first "Listening to the City" session began with an aggrandiz-ing assertion—"This day-long event provides people who live and work in the metropolitan region with a chance to influence the re-building of Downtown New York"—but then channeled the feed-back to come into the few narrow issues that, five months after the attack, had become the sole accepted currency in the strange new polity of the process:

> How do we create a healthy, diverse, and sustainable mix of commercial and residential development in Lower Manhattan?

> How can we maintain a critical mass in financial services and other business activities?

> How can we improve and expand the subways, transporta-tion systems, and streets that will be rebuilt?

Should we restore the historic street grid?

How do we balance the need to remember those who lost
their lives with the need to restore Lower Manhattan?

The leading nature of the questions is obvious—no one would
have been talking about the street grid were it not consonant with
voguish urban planning dogma—and many of the answers had already been determined elsewhere by those controlling the discussion. At the second, much larger "Listening to the City" confab,
the designing critic Michael Sorkin took a seat at one of the five
hundred tables laid out in Manhattan's vast Javits Convention
Center. Reporting on the day, Sorkin noted his growing frustra-
tions with Lukensmeyer ("who combined many of the more an-
noying aspects of Oprah and Kim Il Sung") and the faux
democracy she was conducting: "My own strained ability to participate in well-behaved Nielson-family fashion finally evaporated
when Lukensmeyer ('give yourselves a nice round of applause')
embellished her script with a brief pep talk on how the meeting
was democratic as all get out because, 'in democracy, the people
have a chance to speak!' Seizing upon this right, I rose to my feet
to shout 'Buuuullllllshiiiit! Democracy means the people have the
power to choose!' "[12]

Sorkin's outburst "attracted a smattering of applause from
nearby tables," he wrote, but no notice from the stage. Elsewhere
in that hall, a young architect and downtown resident who de-
scribes herself as a "committed urbanist" (and who had shown her
commitment after September 11 by moving even closer to the site)
had given up her Saturday to play this game. When she introduced
herself and ticked off her credentials, one of the two firefighters'
moms sharing the table dismissed her with, "Yes, but you didn't
lose anybody."

That sort of ugly exchange didn't make it into the facilitators'
laptops and across the network to pop up as progress in an agreeable

graphic splashed on the hanging projection screens; no extremes did. Passion and anger were very much forbidden at these happy, compromising sessions. Though some outlying views, if charmingly and pithily put, did make it into the final reports, the goal—the "deliverable" that AmericaSpeaks had been hired to produce—was pastel harmony. Not surprisingly, the public's opinions, as processed, made few waves. In the final report for the first "Listening to the City," later presented with fanfare to what Lukensmeyer called "decision makers," charts tallied votes on such things as "Most Important Vision Elements" ("a vibrant, 24-hour mixed-use community," the darling of conventional wisdom, was the most popular of the limited visions offered) or "Vision Elements Most Likely to Occur" ("incorporate affordable housing" lost that vote, though one speaker's mention of it had generated the only spontaneous applause of the day). Not everyone leaving the Seaport had been fooled into thinking they had just effected change. A pie chart in the final report showed that only 11 percent of participants had high or very high "confidence that this forum will make a difference"; nearly half knew it would not.

But by then the event had served its purpose: the participants' views had been digested into a passably official document that affirmed the preexisting assumptions of the powerful. Build offices and stores and cultural facilities? Certainly. Build a big train station? Definitely. The grid? Yes, bring it back. The World Trade Center's street-closing superblock had been one of the most ridiculed urban gestures of the 1960s. The unthinking embrace of streets-for-streets'-sake is a pendulum-swing chestnut of contemporary urban planning. But the grid idea owed its easy traction to more than a love of New Urbanist theory. It was a win-win move for development: the new streets would increase retail frontage and the prestige of individual buildings while erasing Ground Zero's iconic perimeter, an inconvenient aide-mémoire. And having broken the sanctity of the-site-as-it-was, the decision led neatly to the final question, about honoring the dead, in the "Listening to the City" booklet: all mourners please proceed to the footprints in an orderly fashion.

How the tower footprints evolved into holy ground, how any of the working assumptions acquired their tenacious hold, owes far less to planning, or even urban trend, than to accident, ego, and the race for governor. On April 17, 2002, the second day of his campaign, Andrew Cuomo, challenging Pataki for the office his father had held for three terms, invited the press onto his campaign bus for an informal, straight-talk bull session. Not long into the ride, he volunteered a critique of the performance of his opponent after September 11. "He stood behind the leader," Cuomo said, referring to Giuliani. "He held the leader's coat. He was a great assistant to the leader. But he was not a leader."[13] September 11 had by then been thoroughly politicized, but rarely with so little craft, and Cuomo's strategy backfired instantly. The Democratic candidate's comment caused a predictable slow-news-day uproar—"Cuomo's Criticism of Pataki's Role After 9/11 Sets Off Furor," the *Times* blared—and, digging out in the following days, as the press turned on him, Cuomo shifted his attack to the governor's handling of the redevelopment, a change in tactics that would prove consequential.

There had been a lot of rumblings of discontent through the winter of 2001–2002, but most of the complaints were focused on the LMDC and its slow start: formed in November, a director in place only in January, then "listening" for months as the board was appointed. "No one's home over there," a source told the *Post* in February. Shortly before Cuomo's gaffe, just as the last remains were removed from the bottom of the pit, the LMDC finally released its first policy paper, "The Blueprint for the Future of Lower Manhattan." It was a local development document with a markedly national view. "In the aftermath of September 11, the entire nation has embraced New York, and we have responded by vowing to rebuild our City—not as it was, but better than it was before," the preamble read, confirming the role of political and urbanistic opportunity in the process. "Although we can never replace what was lost, we must remember those who perished, rebuild what was destroyed, and renew Lower Manhattan as a symbol of our nation's resilience."[14]

In the "Blueprint," nearly all the middle-of-the-road assumptions that had been bubbling through the public hearings and the press, those that served the interests of the LMDC and the Port, were given an official imprimatur. Its fifteen points ranged from "reserve an area of the site for one or more permanent memorials"— the beginning of the end for the families' full-sixteen-acres crusade—to the endorsement of the goal to create a "24/7" downtown, long a dream of the local real estate establishment. The street grid was in, naturally, as was a Downtown Grand Central (to ease the arrival of consumers), cultural facilities (to keep them spending at night), an opera house (a pet project of enthusiast John Whitehead), and a network of new and refurbished parks (on all counts, the residents, via Madelyn Wils, were being heard). The idea was floated here, too, for a "Freedom Park" that would coordinate the Statue of Liberty, Ellis Island, the New York Stock Exchange, Federal Hall, and a September 11 memorial under one tourist-friendly rubric. The "Blueprint" also revealed for the first time plans for a "Museum of Freedom" on the site, an idea proposed to the LMDC by Tom Bernstein, the well-connected civil-rights lawyer–cum–Chelsea Piers developer. As the "Blueprint" had it: "Create a museum dedicated to American freedom, tolerance and the values that the World Trade Center represented."[15]

To the straightforward Port Authority, the principal value that the World Trade Center represented was still, above all, value itself. While the LMDC was busy aligning the redevelopment with the sentiments of the national response to September 11, the Port had its eye on the bottom line. From the beginning, the two agencies were on a converging course—their power was balanced but their objectives were not—and their first public collision took place over the first tender issued for master planning consultants.

Miraculously, a request for proposals (RFP) was rushed out by the LMDC less than a week after Andrew Cuomo questioned the project's pace and made it an issue in the governor's race. Then, just four days after that document was issued to the handful of large architecture and planning firms deemed suitable—those with ten or more years of experience on similarly thorny mixed-use, transportation-intensive projects—a second RFP was released, this one from the Port. It was prefaced by a letter urging recipients to ignore the LMDC's initial invitation; there had been an ugly fight over jurisdiction behind the scenes. But both calls were the product of Pataki-inspired haste: proposals for the largest, most complex, and most important development project in memory were due by the close of business on May 6, two weeks hence.

Cuomo's intemperate remark jump-started the process of actually designing the site. It fueled a politically motivated rush that begot the contract that resulted in an ill-received batch of prematurely presented site plans that were handily and inevitably rejected by opinion-makers and the public, and then, in turn, led to a second round of planning launched to erase the memory of the first. Cuomo never made it to election day. Wounded mortally by his coat-holding remark, his campaign went nowhere; he abandoned the race in September, a week before the Democratic primary, leaving State Comptroller H. Carl McCall to lose to Pataki two months later. But he will be immortalized at Ground Zero: by spurring action when and how he did, Andrew Cuomo is among the foremost architects of the next World Trade Center.

The first cursed commission was won by Beyer Blinder Belle, a well-respected but decidedly uninspiring Manhattan architecture and planning office that had burnished its reputation in the years before with sensitive renovations of Grand Central Terminal and the immigration station on Ellis Island. The firm's short passage through the process would be marked by controversy, beginning on the day of its selection. Alex Garvin, a professor at Yale and a stalwart of the conservative urban planning establishment known as the "bow-tie mafia," had by then been brought into the LMDC as its vice president for planning. Many reacted to his arrival as the second coming of fabled planning czar Robert Moses; development-tested, articulate, and tough, Garvin was seen as a man—like Moses, who had masterminded the construction of most of the city's parks and highways—who could push big plans through the expediencies of a politicized process.

But Garvin was most like Moses in his vanity—he was always mugging to his best advantage for the cameras that increasingly sought him out as he expounded on correct futures for the site—and his arrogance: he was always right (the title of the popular textbook he wrote is *The American City: What Works, What Doesn't*).[16] During the voting to winnow the respondents to the planning RFP, each member of a joint committee of the LMDC and the Port was asked to rank them on a scale from zero to a hundred. When the votes were counted, Beyer Blinder Belle had won, but Garvin appeared to have freaked the system: he had given the firm a score of eighty-two, twenty points higher than his next highest pick, while his colleagues had all voted along a much tighter spread. Had he single-handedly determined the outcome by hoarding his approval? Fighting broke out again among Pataki's sibling agencies, and there was a week's worth of tea-leaf reading in the press.

That episode was cleansed by an in-house, bi-agency review that found no wrongdoing. And then the real problems started. Though he had clearly favored Beyer Blinder Belle, Garvin abandoned the firm after it began its work on an incredibly short five-week deadline (it had been fixed by a two-stage political calculation: show progress by the November 2002 gubernatorial election but do not reveal a final plan until December). Garvin "would come to our meetings, maybe spend a third of the time in the meeting," John Belle said in 2003. "He seemed to be very preoccupied with his own way of moving forward. Probably he saw us getting more and more in trouble publicly, so he distanced himself a little bit from us."[17]

Trouble arrived early in the person of Herbert Muschamp, whose definition of architecture does not expand much past the blobbier work showcased in the Max Protetch Gallery. "The selection of . . . Beyer Blinder Belle to design a master plan for ground zero and the financial district confirms once again that architecture will play no more than a marginal role in the redevelopment of Lower Manhattan," Muschamp wrote the day after the contested vote. "Mediocrity, the choice of this firm reminds us, is not a default mode. It is a carefully constructed reality."[18]

Muschamp went on in his own default mode, praising some snazzy new Manhattan buildings by snazzier architects and nicknaming the firm "Blah, Blah and Blah." He attacked the contextual approach—"which calls for new buildings that imitate adjacent old ones"—favored by Beyer Blinder Belle on those occasions when they were called upon to build from scratch. But this was not such a case—the job ahead was not about style, not even about architecture. The language in the RFP was clear: the successful firm would study the whole of Lower Manhattan, map existing and pre-attack conditions, conduct traffic and use studies, calculate costs, and then, after analyzing that larger context, come up with six alternatives for positioning buildings on the World Trade Center site itself (a number apparently chosen at random by the Port) that would be presented for further public and governmental review as a basis, down the line, for architecture that might traffic in symbols. Beyer Blinder Belle had been hired as planners, and that is what planners do. In Muschamp's circles, the boundaries between planning and architecture had become very porous. Throughout the 1990s, name-brand architects were proposing wishful changes at the city scale, and in Europe, occasionally, they were allowed to implement them. But in old New York, at least until this process, the two pursuits were very much distinct. And for good reason: except in the biggest firms—Beyer Blinder Belle, SOM—the skill sets of planners and architects rarely overlap. Planners crunch a developer's numbers, ideally with civic need in mind, to see what is possible; architects are brought in to dress those numbers. And it's hard to see the advantage of playing dress-up before the details of a story line are in place.

Denied Garvin's potentially mitigating presence, Beyer Blinder Belle found themselves at the mercy of the Port. The first thing that greeted them was a drastic change in scope. The RFP to which they had responded had specified an exhaustive planning study for all of Lower Manhattan, exactly what the goo-goos and better-informed public opinion around town had been calling for. Step one: examine the potential uses of the site within the context of what is needed across a wider area, in preparation for step two. Step two: bring in architects to design buildings to house those uses and to address the emotional demands of the redevelopment. Following this sequence could have resulted in a new program for the site beyond rebuilding what had been there and adding a memorial and sundry conventional wisdoms, a program that might have helped to foster a more appropriate setting for symbolic architecture than the commercial concerns alone could provide. Beyer Blinder Belle pushed to conduct the full urban plan and even to explore alternate futures—"plans that could have had a lower density, that could have had housing," Belle said—but the Port Authority wouldn't allow it: the firm was limited to a study of the site alone, the final product of which would necessarily be closer to architecture than the broader planning for which Beyer Blinder Belle was so well qualified. "I don't agree with them, but they had a rational argument," John Belle remembered. "They said, 'Our mandate does not permit us to build less because of the lease agreement.' Now that's a very narrow legal point of view, which, in my humble opinion, they had a responsibility to go beyond. But they chose not to." Here again, the lease was proving more durable than the buildings leased. As a *New York Times* real estate reporter wrote in the summer of 2002, assessing the sway held by Silverstein and Westfield, the Australian firm that controlled the World Trade Center mall: "The powerful Port Authority, which managed to clear the whole site in the 1960s, is now legally bound to protect the right of two private companies to recover their lost commercial potential."[19]

Beyer Blinder Belle found itself in a three-way squeeze, between the Port's defense of its tenants' unforgiving numbers, Pataki's newly fast-tracked election-year redevelopment calendar, and a simmering revolt against plans not yet drawn. The revolt was fueled by criticism like Muschamp's, but also by public opinion of the sort represented months earlier in the long line of symbol-seekers outside the Max Protetch Gallery. The emotive visions of the new folk architects and the speculative work hung in the Protetch show had helped to create a climate that made responsible planning impossible; Beyer Blinder Belle's plans would be judged, whether the firm liked it or not (and it did not), as an attempt to give meaning to the events of September 11 through symbolic monuments.

The indignities piled up. John Belle and his team were not allowed to present directly to the LMDC board—Alex Garvin would appear on those occasions to describe the work—so their primary point of contact with that agency was the planning committee headed by Roland Betts, co-developer of Chelsea Piers and surprisingly liberal-minded (and left-leaning) friend of George Bush. "They met with us a couple times, maybe three, and in a very grievous kind of way there was very little discussion or evaluation of alternatives," Belle reported. "It was incredibly superficial." The effects of the Port Authority/LMDC rivalry only made it more so. Committee members "would meet for hours and write memorandums of understanding regularly, so it was hard to get their attention focused on what we thought were the physical planning issues at hand," Belle said. "And all of this was being driven by a political agenda that certain things had to happen before the election."[20]

Garvin was not more actively asserting the right of Beyer Blinder Belle to conduct a proper planning study because he also had another horse in the race. A week before the vote he appeared to have skewed, Garvin had urged the LMDC to hire Peterson Littenberg, a solidly traditionalist New York urban design firm with which he had previously collaborated on some work for Battery Park City. Without any competitive bidding—the LMDC cited the need for haste in its defense—these insiders were given a contract for $375,000 and permission to silently contribute ideas to two of the six forthcoming plans. Brookfield Properties, owners of the World Financial Center, were allowed to bring in Alex Cooper, one of the original urban designers of Battery Park City, to provide another unattributed proposal. Not to be outflanked, Larry Silverstein lobbied for and won the right for his architects, SOM, to participate. Beyer Blinder Belle was now responsible for integrating the ideas of three other firms into an increasingly doomed presentation that would bear only its name.

On July 16, days before the second "Listening to the City," the first six official plans for the World Trade Center site were unveiled. Lest anyone forget that these exercises in accommodating the leaseholders' square footage were also symbols of national resurgence, Matt Higgins, the LMDC's communications director, always thinking, had chosen to announce them with high pomp at the flag-draped Federal Hall on Wall Street. The next morning, images of the six plans were on the front page of the *New York Times*: a grid, in each square of which was another nearly identical cluster of white skyscrapers massed around one or more green memorial parks. Within the paper were the beginnings of what would be three weeks of public opinion–whipping excoriation.[21] But the public needed little encouragement. The reaction of one New

Yorker, spotting the *Times* that day at a Brooklyn bagel shop, was representative: "They got *paid* for that?"

The universal negative reaction that would kill the plans was not only a knee-jerk response to unsatisfying architecture—symbols were needed and none were found—it marked the death of reasoned planning at Ground Zero; from this point forward, the Port-protected leases and the LMDC-promoted "public" assumptions would be the primary forces shaping the plan. It was a long-delayed death, really: all sobriety had ended in September when the towering middle fingers arrived in thousands of e-mail in-boxes, and a deliberative pace was precluded by the associated politics of revenge. "This is a process that has proved time and again that it's not the value of the ideas, it's the political backroom wheeling and dealing that's running the show," Belle said. "We got slammed because we did something very un-American: we tried to plan."

The absence of open, inquisitive planning led to six designs that were very close variations on the theme of the lease; Ada Louise Huxtable called them "six cookie-cutter losers."[22] The manner in which the plans were presented exaggerated their similarities: each was rendered from the same angles and, to appeal to the public sentiment that they otherwise ignored, given a name that began with "Memorial." All four participating firms chose to bring back at least some of the grid, along the lines the streets had occupied before Yamasaki and the Port designed them out of existence in the 1960s. Because the six plans also restored the lease-mandated square footage under the Silverstein-mandated height limit, they all shared the low, crowded, fat-towered aspect those numbers dictated.

But those similarities can be overstated; three of the plans did not preserve the footprints, and two of those—Peterson Littenberg's "Memorial Park" and "Memorial Promenade"—were distinctly in the New Urbanist mode: contorting the site into regular blocks and comforting symmetries. The stealth SOM proposal,

"Memorial Garden," which did preserve the footprints, was notable for the degree to which its signature tower had been developed beyond the blank boxes of the other five plans and toward the visions of so many amateurs: reaching for patriotic height while respecting the developer's comfort level. SOM's David Childs had been busily developing the tower for Larry Silverstein: a seventy-story office building with an empty, memorializing top, a tower that would get "more and more ethereal—until it disappears into the sky."[23]

That idea was just beginning its long, successful life in the process; the three proposals that obliterated the footprints were dead on arrival. Just two weeks before the plans were revealed at Federal Hall, Governor Pataki had made his first important statement about the redevelopment. At a gathering of the family groups at a Midtown hotel, Pataki put his considerable election-year weight behind the idea of sanctifying the footprints. "They will always be a permanent and lasting memorial to those we lost," he said. "Where the towers stood was hallowed ground."[24]

The activist mourners would hold Pataki to those words. But where the footprints actually were in space, and to what use they should be put, would be one of the major flash points of the battle going forward, not to be resolved completely until the selection of a final memorial design. And all the while a representative of the Coalition of 9/11 Families was making the rounds with a piece of evidence that made it all too clear: a photograph taken on a day when the mud churned by construction equipment at the bottom of the pit had parted to reveal the towers' closely spaced perimeter columns, still rooted where they had been cut about four inches above the living rock, still describing the two pinwheeling squares that Minoru Yamasaki had drawn in 1963, now with so much more symbolic heft than their architect had been able to give them. The designation of the footprints as holy ground had a devastating effect on the planning possibilities at Ground Zero, but the two enormous squares also made a very awkward site for the memorial they were fated to contain. Their sanctification was Yamasaki's revenge; with the families soon claiming the zones untouchable "from bedrock to infinity," his critics were forced to genuflect to his meaningless geometry.

Pataki's low public profile at the time of his footprints pronouncement was explained by a spokesman as considerate caution. The governor was concerned that any comments he made regarding the site would "take on added weight."[25] He was not wrong; with his decree—three months after the Cuomo-induced acceleration, six months after the first public hearing, and only ten months after the attack—all the major limits that would ultimately define a plan for Ground Zero were in place. You can do this at home: Draw the outline of the World Trade Center site, a square, more or less, with one side canted. Bisect it vertically and horizontally with Greenwich Street and Fulton Street. Drop the footprints into the southwest quadrant. Then arrange your offices, hotel, and shopping mall in the L-shaped space remaining outside that sacred precinct, put your busy train station at bedrock beneath it, and season lightly with "cultural institutions": the "Museum of Freedom" or equivalent, Whitehead's opera house. Garnish with platitudes and serve it up in red, white, and blue. Though the process would churn on in search of a master plan, one adorned with the longed-for symbols, the only politically acceptable solution was already apparent in the summer of 2002. The site would be rebuilt as a crowded, mixed-use, shopping-intensive corporate development surrounding a large but compromised memorial. It was all over but the shouting.

7

STAR LIGHT, STAR BRIGHT

IN JANUARY 1947, *Architectural Review* published an essay by the historian Henry-Russell Hitchcock that remains one of the most relevant critiques ever made of the practice of modern architecture. Fifteen years earlier, with Philip Johnson, Hitchcock had curated "Modern Architecture: International Exhibition" at the Museum of Modern Art in New York, the show that gave its name to the International Style and did so much to consolidate American interest in the new way of building. In *Architectural Review*, Hitchcock was assessing how modern architecture, after its ascendance during the war, might weather the postwar years. The article was a product of the critical anxieties that were then driving the debate on the New Monumentality—how will functional modern buildings evolve to address the impending demand for public symbols?—but Hitchcock was also concerned with a problem at the city scale: how will such buildings coexist with the other, less grand type, those that needed to solve practical problems first? The division was laid out in the title of his article: "The Architecture of Bureaucracy and the Architecture of Genius."

"Bureaucracy," as Hitchcock used the term, had none of the disparaging overtones we hear in it today; to him it implied competence and humility: "By bureaucratic architecture I mean all building that is the product of large-scale architectural organizations, from which personal expression is absent."[1] Writing just after the war, Hitchcock stressed that it was that category that was demanding the most urgent attention; serviceable structures of all types would have to be built rapidly to satisfy pent-up need as soldiers returned home and society carried on. But Hitchcock worried that the penchant of modern architects to favor experimentation at the expense of utility would pollute the necessarily mundane work. "During a certain stage of adaptation and apprenticeship, a large body of architects got, almost literally, ahead of themselves," Hitchcock wrote of American modern practice in the preceding years. "Instead of being content to develop the fruits of a particular architectural revolution which had already taken place"—that is, modern architecture—"they aimed at a sort of permanent revolution."[2]

As an example of the architecture of genius, Hitchcock cited Frank Lloyd Wright's design for the Guggenheim Museum in New York—more than a decade away from completion but already well known through drawings and models. Again, he was careful to define his categories: "The term refers to a particular psychological approach and way of working at architecture which may or may not produce masterpieces." He deferred criticism of Wright's building, but noted the risks involved in trusting one architect's eye—not so much of a problem in a private museum, he acknowledged, but potentially fatal in public work. For Hitchcock, that danger was unacceptable: to indulge in the architecture of genius was to take a chance, one that was not appropriate for the majority of building types—offices, housing—or for urban planning, in which art was of secondary concern to public welfare. "In other words," he wrote, "the architecture of genius is a kind of artistic gamble which may or may not come off, but rarely just gets by."[3]

Hitchcock's distinction touched the core issue that needed to be addressed in the late summer of 2002, by the now klieg-lit public process—high from its perceived victory in rejecting the first master plans—and by officialdom working in the shadows to find a new way to move forward. The redevelopment of Ground Zero had begun as a problem of bureaucratic planning, as common sense suggested. But the grievously misunderstood attempt to plan first and emote later had been thoroughly condemned in the press and effectively shouted down in the redevelopment's sole moment of universal public solidarity. Governor Pataki piped up a week after the unveiling of the master plans to say that the people must be heard; the trajectory of the process would be reconsidered, he said, perhaps even the inviolability of the commercial and retail square footage enshrined in the World Trade Center leases. That was an obvious bluff—Westfield alone had contributed $100,000 to Pataki's reelection campaign—although the governor's display of sensitivity to the "will of the people" might have helped to mollify voters as the election approached. The leases were sacrosanct, the commercial future of the site secure; but to bury the memory of the infamous six plans would require the LMDC and the Port Authority to take another, superficially different tack. Genius, which the choice of Beyer Blinder Belle had responsibly deferred, would now have to be rallied to the service of the ordinary kind of bureaucracy.

In choosing to defenestrate Beyer Blinder Belle, that was the path taken. The firm was the very face of an architecture of bureaucracy, perhaps even more than the giant SOM, which, though it had pioneered the corporate-scale, full-service office, has often promoted individual geniuses in its ranks. Beyer Blinder Belle continued on through December per its contract, but would not again appear in the process except as an epithet—although it became clear to all, much later, that genius or bureaucracy, the basic use of the land proposed in the six plans was the only one possible at Ground Zero, barring the lightning-strike departure of Silverstein, the Port Authority, and Governor Pataki.

The *New York Post*'s Steve Cuozzo had preemptively defended Beyer Blinder Belle in Hitchcockian terms just after its selection in May. "The firm, which conceived the wonderful restoration of Grand Central Terminal, is too wedded to the past, critics grumped, and insufficiently visionary to be charged with a broad-brushstrokes plan for the devastated zone," he wrote under the headline "The Wrong Stuff: Keep World's Architects Away from Ground Zero." "Who, then, would make the critics happy?" Cuozzo continued. "Only a superstar world genius. One who'll throw out rules, shrug off political shackles and give us something new and 'out of the box,' brimming with unspecified esthetic and humanistic wonders. But what they really crave are the far-fetched fantasies that clog the pages of unreadable design magazines—not exactly the thing for the Financial District, generator of $3 trillion in capital annually and one-fifth of the city's tax revenue."[4] To push the point, the *Post* ran the article with a photo of the Pan Am Building, a star-designed ugly duckling maligned by New Yorkers since its birth for the way it straddled Park Avenue and blocked the view. " 'Geniuses' scarred Park Avenue with the Pan Am building," the caption read.

In New York in 2002, it was safe to replace *genius* with *star*, or even with the noisome term *starchitect*, which was occasionally found in the design journals Cuozzo described. No one had done more to establish that formulation than Herbert Muschamp. His position at the *Times* made him the only American architecture critic with a truly national reach, and for years he had used that power almost exclusively to advocate the work of a small group of already enthroned international stars—Frank Gehry, Rem Koolhaas, Peter Eisenman, Steven Holl—and more local but equally well-sung avant-gardist favorites such as Liz Diller and Ric Scofidio (the duo that had suggested, within days of the attack, that "it would be tragic to erase the erasure").

Muschamp's usual mode when discussing projects in New York, which he applied to the redevelopment of Ground Zero, was to bemoan the absence of stars, whose "progressive architecture" was underrepresented in the city, not, as he often suggested, due to some conspiracy of bad taste, but because such architects rarely gain the trust of Manhattan's necessarily risk-averse developers. At a public symposium at the Museum of Modern Art in 1999, Muschamp—not on the panel, though it was taking on one of his signature topics, "urban spectacle"—hijacked the microphone to state his preferences more clearly than he ever had in print: "Why can't you just say that people are going to walk two or three blocks out of their way to see something that's *good*?" He explained that none of the developer-built skyscrapers around town could pass that "two or three blocks" test. "You know, they're real estate projects, not architecture, that's been built in this city for twenty-five years," he said. "We've seen great operas . . . but we haven't seen one fucking *building*."

Muschamp's emphasis on aesthetic satisfaction, his own above all else, filled a void left by the lack of a consistent platform to undergird his criticism. He often tried to promote his stars with wandering arguments for the importance of glamour or "desire" in architecture, set within a celebration of urban life in the age of globalization. But just as often Muschamp would construct other, single-use justifications, more remote and more elaborate, that gave his criticism of the lively, dirty art of building the detached air of art-historical inquiry. "Forgive a cultural journalist for trying to plug up the void of meaning with pieces of art history," he wrote in his first response to the attack at the end of September 2001. "As I gazed down on Lower Manhattan from the 44th floor of a residential highrise"—his own, on the edge of Tribeca—"the scene brought to mind Karl Brulloff's 'Last Day of Pompeii.' The small figures below, running north through Foley Square, evoked the frozen panic of fossilized Romans trapped by ash as they fled the eruption of Vesuvius. Or Breughel the Elder's 'Landscape With the Fall of Icarus'. . . . Myths, stories and pictures are useful at times of terror and isolation."[5]

After having contributed to the destruction of Beyer Blinder Belle, Muschamp's search for solace resulted in a list of solving names: Peter Eisenman, Charles Gwathmey, Zaha Hadid, Steven Holl, Rem Koolhaas, Richard Meier, and Diller and Scofidio. Those stars were among a group of sixteen architects he convened to put together a new blueprint for Ground Zero and its environs, personally presiding over the creation of work by designers he continued to champion, directing an unsolicited contribution to a redevelopment he continued to criticize. Going to the mat for genius, Muschamp entered deep into the process, not as a critic but as a player.

In an analysis of the Beyer Blinder Belle plans published the day after their unveiling at Federal Hall, Muschamp included this strange note between parentheses: "Disclosure: The *New York Times Magazine* is sponsoring an architectural study project on the future of the financial district. I have advised the editors on the composition of the design team. An overview is scheduled for publication in September."[6] That told part of the story. In fact, the project began as a chance conversation between Richard Meier and Charles Gwathmey in the building that houses both their offices on a desolate stretch of Tenth Avenue in Midtown. Muschamp naturally played matchmaker with the *Times Magazine*, and then went well beyond a mere advisory role: meeting repeatedly with his handpicked team, sitting at the head of a conference room table in the *Times* headquarters, directing the efforts as a client might to reach his preordained end: a heroic repudiation of bureaucratic planning.

Muschamp's architects had met four times when Alex Garvin was tipped off about this gathering insurrection. The LMDC's planning czar responded that he was already "picking up word" of Muschamp's efforts—he predicted "ideas that will look as though they came from the Protetch Gallery"—and added that the LMDC was "seriously considering issuing a new RFP for designers."

The LMDC's gamble with genius was announced on August 19, 2002. The Port had asserted itself, taken the first shot, and missed the target completely. Now the LMDC's Innovative Design Study, launched over the Port's objections, was to right all wrongs. Unlike the previous planning round, this one was open to all architects; anyone who thought he could contribute to "an innovative and bolder range of ideas and designs"[7] was invited to supply up to ten pages of supporting credentials by the deadline in mid-September.

No actual designs were to be submitted; at least one large New York firm was disqualified for ignoring that rule. The LMDC was looking only to assemble five or more individuals, firms, or other teams who would then spend one month studying the site under the direction of Alex Garvin. An insultingly inadequate honorarium of $40,000 was offered to participants, though some were likely to be based abroad and expected to fly in to New York for meetings at their own expense (the LMDC was then sitting on $2.5 billion in federal funds). The goal of the study was to produce and present—again, after the gubernatorial election—the bold visions lacking in the six bogeyman plans. "An architecture that is compelling, meaningful over the long term and culturally ambitious not only respects the past," the text of the tender pointed out, "but also takes great risks to create the future." Initially the Innovative Design Study was not conceived as a competition. "The results . . . will be presented to the LMDC and to the public to promote a free-flowing exchange of ideas," the document stated, continuing in bold type: "This is NOT a competition and will not result in the selection of a final plan."[8]

Planning committee chair Roland Betts was the primary force promoting the Innovative Design Study within the LMDC. At first, he was an unlikely champion. His own Chelsea Piers development demonstrated no great faith in architectural genius, and standing high on the stage at the Javits Center "Listening to the City" meeting, his poised delivery quadrupled on the projection screens, he had seemed genuinely enthusiastic about the six plans as he presented them into the teeth of public loathing. Betts himself characterized the decision to change course as common sense: the Port had tried one way, and it hadn't worked; the LMDC should try another. A top official there offered another explanation: "Roland just loves competition."

Max Protetch promoted his own theory about Betts's conversion, which hinged on the influence of Max Protetch. The scene was not a smoky back room but a steamy locker room. Betts had gamely dropped into the gallery on the day Protetch was hanging "A New World Trade Center," and the two made plans to talk architecture. As it happened, Betts and Protetch worked out every morning at the same gym in the Chelsea Piers complex, and their lockers were not far apart. According to Protetch, "One day he said, 'Well what do you think of our proposal?' "—referring to the Beyer Blinder Belle plans—"and I said, 'I think it's really pathetic. It's everything that I was afraid of. I'm terrified that those of you who are in power would do something like this.' And I really lit into him—I wasn't mean, but I certainly wasn't pulling any punches. And I was in my underpants—you know it wasn't a place to be doing diplomacy. . . . Our talks continued, and I was shocked at the reversal. And then he began saying to me, 'You're going to be really happy with what we're doing.' "[9]

As the first anniversary of the attack arrived—commemorated at the site with safe recitations of the Gettysburg Address and a grueling reading of 2,819 names—two cavalries of great minds were coming to try to help the process move beyond the recent, failed attempt at planning. The first to appear was Herbert Muschamp's group; its work was published in the *New York Times Magazine* on Sunday, September 8, with the cover line "The Masters' Plan: Downtown Manhattan Reimagined by a Team of Architects Daring New York to Think Big."

Muschamp was named as the plan's "curator," but he might have been more accurately described as its developer. Over the years, as he regularly derided the corporate firms still carrying the torch of Hitchcock's bureaucracies, Muschamp had often gone out of his way to savage the developers who hired them. He began his introduction to the article in this spirit, warning that "the official planning process was following a pattern conventionally used by real-estate developers and that, in this instance, it had to be broken." That pattern, he explained, was to "chop up [a] development into parcels, develop guidelines for each one and then hand them over to developers, who subdivide the building project among an assortment of specialists, including lawyers, interior-space planners, retail consultants, construction companies, architects and construction managers." This is exactly what Muschamp himself had done, though his finance-free, no-stakes exercise had allowed him to proceed without all those essential if unpalatable players; while the plan was presented as a coherent, triumphant whole—"a revised mythology of our place in the era of globalization,"[10] he wrote—Muschamp's stars had each merely designed a stand-alone building for a discrete parcel on or near Ground Zero.

Several of his favorites took center stage at the site itself. Richard Meier was given a choice spot for his proposed urban studies school, just north of the vacant footprints, one of many fanciful notions that Muschamp's plan put forward. Steven Holl, whose work had been singled out in the publicity for the Max Protetch show, designed a low-rise version of the spiraling "street in the sky" that had hung in that gallery eight months earlier; the now ground-hugging coil was to house a "Confluence Center of World Religions." Rafael Viñoly, a close friend of Muschamp's and perhaps the most accomplished of the bunch, designed a looping version of the de rigueur Downtown Grand Central. Peter Eisenman, the greatest American proponent of an architecture of permanent revolution, was given a site bridging West Street and stretching the entire four-block length of Ground Zero. He indulged there in his trademark irreverence, drawing a line of squat office towers with glass facades fractured and folded (even melting) to mimic the one-year-old catastrophe. Muschamp sanitized Eisenman's design, referring to it as "a critique of the Cartesian grid." But appearing on television, Eisenman said his design was meant to capture "a certain beauty coming . . . a moment before a disaster."[11]

Eisenman's comment underscored the callow aestheticizing of the attack and the site that suffused the whole exercise. Muschamp had unwittingly succeeded in reminding the development powers that contemporary architects of the genius type, when left to their own devices, played stylish, self-serving games. As Kevin Rampe, the ultra-effective second director of the LMDC, remarked, "[Muschamp] doesn't understand what's going on. He thinks this is a paper project."

The inability to transcend the congenital limitations of artsy practice obscured what could have been Muschamp's positive contribution to the Ground Zero debate: his plan was influenced by one of the most inventive concepts for the site that was then in the air. Reacting to the dawning tenacity of Silverstein's lease-backed numbers, a pair of ideas had emerged that sought to free Ground Zero from real estate fetters by compensating the Port with larger, less contested spaces elsewhere.

Aides to Mayor Bloomberg, led by Deputy Mayor Dan Doctoroff—whom Bloomberg had placed on the LMDC board—proposed a visionary deal that came to be known as the "land swap." In exchange for Ground Zero, the Port Authority would be given outright ownership of the land it leased from the city under the two New York City airports it operated, La Guardia and John F. Kennedy International: 5,610 acres in Queens traded for sixteen acres in Manhattan. The deal's appeal to the mayor, marginalized by the heft of the other players, was clear: if he could succeed in ejecting the Port, a near sovereign state-within-a-state, the World Trade Center site would once again fall fully under the legal dominion of New York City. Removing the Port would also make it possible for the city to buy out Larry Silverstein's lease and send him packing, opening up all options for Lower Manhattan. The city's own expert planning department—usurped by the in-house operations at the LMDC and the Port and given no role—might then even be allowed to participate.

It was considerably less clear how the land swap would benefit Silverstein and the Port Authority. The deal would have required both parties to give up control of the place that each so clearly loved, now more than ever, as well as the worldly thing that most motivated them: revenue. New Jersey's governor, James Mc-Greevey, exercising his co-trustee power over the Port, came out against the swap in his only big move in the process. Governor Pataki was forced to comment at times—whenever the on-again-off-again negotiations made the papers—but as usual he remained purposefully noncommittal. The land swap died a quiet death in the fall of 2003, when the Port Authority renewed its leases at La Guardia and JFK.

Muschamp's plan was loosely based on a second swap idea. Several parties had realized that more than sixteen acres could be recouped out of thin air by burying about half a mile of the block-wide swath of West Street where it ran alongside the World Trade Center site. That boulevard, technically a state highway, fell directly under Pataki's control, which was seen as an advantage, potentially smoothing the transfer of the Port's nearly twelve-million-square-foot burden to this adjacent land. As Muschamp pointed out, this strategy did not preclude building on Ground Zero itself, but would channel the commercial urgencies of the redevelopment to where they could do less harm.

Like nearly every other proposal for the site, the idea of exploiting West Street had many authors, each operating independently in a kind of convergent evolution. By the first anniversary, the concept had been proposed in some of the more skillful unsolicited designs, and it had also been studied by a subcommittee of New York New Visions, the well-intentioned but politically maladroit architecture-world pressure group. It first came to public light, however, in a July 2002 *New York Times* article by Muschamp himself, in which the critic gave credit, and the first glimpse of process-garnered fame, to a mid-career New York architect who was soon to be ubiquitous in the follies.

More than any other architect involved with the redevelopment, Fred Schwartz internalized the ample pain to be found at Ground Zero. Prior to September 11, he had been well known in New York architecture circles, not so much for his work—his major building, a new Manhattan terminal for the Staten Island Ferry, seemed to be forever coming soon—but for his genial, late-night omnipresence at parties and openings. As a student at Harvard's Graduate School of Design in the 1970s, Schwartz had made a name for himself as a master of disguise. Three years in a row he had won an annual costume contest there, first by dressing up as a duck to catch the eye of a visiting lecturer who had popularized the bird as an architectural metaphor, then by transforming himself into Boston's John Hancock Tower—famous for its habit of ejecting windows from forty stories up (Schwartz's outfit included a sound track of breaking glass)—and finally, in a bold act of body-art minimalism, shaving his head and hippie beard in a silent performance on a stage before the entire school.

Recounting those stories one day as he stood near Ground Zero—he had just kept vigil at an LMDC board meeting—Schwartz managed a glimmer of what must have been his previous delight in things impish. But his earlier, lighter incarnations were unrecognizable to those who knew him only after the attack. As it was for so many of the folk architects drawn to the problem, for Schwartz, September 11 was intensely personal, not because he suffered directly but because he had made it so. The architecture firm he heads has its office in Lower Manhattan—he saw the whole thing go down from there—but the building is full of architects, none of whom became as caught up in the disaster or in the process meant to assuage it. Schwartz's obsession took a toll, but his heart was in the right place; Max Protetch said that Schwartz's submission to his show was the only one he had to reject: a single black question mark centered on a white board. Too early for form.

As a civilian in the process, and later as a leader of Think, a team of architects that became a short-listed contender to redesign the site, Schwartz attended all the public hearings and even the most minor events organized by the victims' families, to whom he must have felt a kind of kinship. He missed only two of the monthly LMDC board meetings in 2003, and each time the regular beat reporters asked one another, as concerned as amused, "Where's Fred?" He would become a kind of tragic conscience in the redevelopment, enough that when he was nominated for a National Design Award in the fall of 2003, an honor that would have been inconceivable without the raised profile the process had given him, it was not a stretch when a press release described him as "an architect and a humanist."[12]

Though he was known around town, in the summer of 2002 Fred Schwartz was not yet a star; with a practice that did not forefront an individual style, he might even have been fairly characterized as a bureaucratic architect. Before he had run too far with Schwartz's idea for building on West Street, Herbert Muschamp had to change that. On September 19, an aggrandizing profile of Schwartz was published in the *Times' House & Home* section, a corner of the paper in which Muschamp exercised considerable behind-the-scenes editorial sway.[13]

"The Masters' Plan" placed a parade of idiosyncratic buildings on the repurposed West Street. On the site itself, Muschamp situated a carefully curated constellation of structures and one enormous anomaly: rebuilt twins. The renderings in the magazine were dominated by two towers of familiar proportions but unfamiliar form: twisted from top to bottom like candlesticks. Since the attack, this idea had been vigorously publicized by Richard Dattner, a respected local architect—as Muschamp acknowledged—but also by nearly everyone else. It was the choice of Philippe Petit, the man who had danced on a very high wire stretched between the towers one morning in 1974. "I envision the twin towers *com' era*, *dov' era*, but with a twist, a dash of inventive panache," Petit wrote, captioning a sketch of twisted towers he included in a post-disaster book about his walk. "Architects, please make them more magnificent."[14]

In Muschamp's plan, Guy Nordenson, a celebrated engineer, was charged with making them more magnificent. He also gave the empty form some much-needed justification, illustrating structural studies that showed how the twist might increase a tall building's rigidity and decrease the effects of the wind. "For me,"

Muschamp wrote of the twisted twins, "they signify resilience and the civilizing conversion of aggression into desire."[15]

When, on September 26, 2002, the LMDC announced its selections for the Innovative Design Study, many of Muschamp's stars were included—Richard Meier, Peter Eisenman, Charles Gwathmey, and Steven Holl, together again in what was soon being called the Dream Team; Fred Schwartz and Rafael Viñoly, heading the Think team and now joined by Shigeru Ban, who had contributed his profoundly humble idea for a paper-tube memorial tempietto to the Max Protetch show. Filling out the initial roster of six participants were Daniel Libeskind, who had first been approached as a juror; Norman Foster, the leading modern architect in the United Kingdom; a team of trendy young bucks under the name United Architects (led by the same Greg Lynn who had so disgraced himself with his stylized war-mongering in the Protetch gallery); and a large team assembled by SOM's resident star designer, Roger Duffy. These architects who had followed the rules (though, in the case of SOM, the LMDC had specifically asked that they participate) were soon joined by a seventh who had not: Peterson Littenberg, the LMDC's in-house urban design consultants, still operating under the same Alex Garvin–given contract that had allowed them to interfere so effectively with Beyer Blinder Belle. Except for that exception, it was all genius all around.

The LMDC crowed that it had received entries "from every continent except Antarctica," 406 in total. But strikingly few of that number were the stars the study had been designed to attract. Using the most generous measure of who might qualify, only about a dozen such architects had been moved to submit their credentials. (Frank Gehry, keeping the process at arm's length, and Rem Koolhaas, then busying himself with work in China, were notable no-shows.) The final group overlapped with Muschamp's "Masters' Plan," not because the LMDC was trying to flatter or sabotage the critic—although with busy Matt Higgins handling the press strategy, such things were always possible—but because so few other stars had responded. The list of 406 was padded with the usual suspects: Ethan Ernest, giving his name only as "Ripple Effects," and dozens of others who had already logged their unsolicited designs.

So where was the process at the end of that first long year? Political forces had co-opted a set of unimaginative, time-worn assumptions as the coin of the realm. A master-planning study had been mistaken for a failed exercise in healing form and had been pilloried into nonexistence (though its underlying land-use principles would continue to be the only ones possible). Thousands of inspired neophytes had put their dreams on paper and crashed as one against the ramparts of bureaucratic indifference. And after embarrassing themselves in similar efforts, the great minds of architecture had come under the sway of officialdom.

But first it was time for a victory lap. Just before the anniversary commemorations in New York, the city's architectural stars decamped for the opening of the biennial architecture exhibition in Venice. The Max Protetch show was installed at the domed, brick United States Pavilion—a bent and dusty piece of World Trade Center steel decorated the forecourt—and, at another hall, Herbert Muschamp's plan was put on display. Muschamp himself was there, in his glory, at the Gritti Palace, holding court on a terrace overlooking the Grand Canal, on one occasion weighing the future of Ground Zero—far from its unsightly, unseemly complications—with a group that included Daniel Libeskind, the architect who would soon emerge to provide that catalyst the process so desperately craved: genius. And there was not a bureaucrat in sight.

8

PRIME TIME

WHEN THE north tower fell on September 11, it appeared to unzip about as neatly as one could hope for a building 1,362 feet tall. As the first high floors pancaked in what engineers later called "progressive collapse," the television transmission mast dropped straight into the core of the building and disappeared, and then it all came down. For a few seconds, a spike centered around the heftier, ganged columns of the southwest corner, maybe sixty stories tall, was left standing, and then, when the rumble subsided and the needles on distant seismographs stopped twitching, all that remained of the great tower was a shaft of brown smoke, heavy enough to resist the wind.

The top ten floors, home to Windows on the World, The Greatest Bar on Earth, various kitchens and function rooms, and the charnel house of Cantor Fitzgerald, veered off in the fall and landed in West Street, spraying the much shorter towers of the World Financial Center with the supersize shrapnel workers at the site called "spears." The Winter Garden, the pride of Battery Park City—a cavernous, glass-vaulted, palm-filled atrium nestled at street level between two of those towers—was smashed and packed with dust. Minutes earlier, thousands had escaped through it to the safety of the riverbank after crossing a covered pedestrian bridge over West Street. As they fled they were treated to the sight of the remains of several jumpers who had sailed away from the towers, passed through the Winter Garden's glass roof, and come to rest between the benches and palms on the richly pat-terned, high-gloss marble floor, the site, in better times, of con-certs and dancing.

When morning broke over Manhattan on December 18, 2002—one year, three months, and one week later—the once again grand interior of the hastily resurrected Winter Garden rang with the din of an assembling media scrum. As planned, the previous month's vote for governor had come and gone with progress im-plied. George Pataki had been reelected in a walk, having silenced charges of inaction by sheltering behind the crowd-pleasing mech-anism of the LMDC's Innovative Design Study. Now the veils could be lifted; in the weeks after the election, the papers began to fill with a steady pulse of official and officially leaked enthusiasms intended to raise hopes that the study had in fact resulted in the promised genius: a set of inventive, symbol-laden, and appropri-ately monumental solutions for the physical, political, and psycho-logical mess at Ground Zero.

Now, in front of a well-guarded stage, behind a barrier of re-tractable ticket-line ribbons, a phalanx of miniature heroic futures waited, each world's-tallest totem of renewal suggesting its potency by the size of the peak it pushed up in a tented white sheet. Every vantage on those proud models not obstructed by the restored grove of sixteen palms was taken by rows of VIP folding chairs and banks of network cameras. Reporters eddied around the margins, traded scuttlebutt, and complained that there was no coffee. At the back of the room, on the now dead-end stairs that had led from the lost bridge to the World Trade Center, representatives of Team Twin Towers, the Coalition of 9/11 Families, and all the other groups lobbied noisily, hunted for camera time, and waited for the worst. At ten o'clock sharp, in what may stand forever as the high-water mark of architecture's popular presence in American cul-ture, the unveilings began, covered live on television and on local radio, where a prominent design critic was asked to provide color commentary as if it were the Macy's Thanksgiving Day Parade.

John Whitehead, hanging on as chairman, was the first to speak. He asked the big question: "What does September eleventh represent?" He went on to claim that the plans about to be shown would provide answers through the medium of architecture. Lou Tomson, the LMDC's Pataki-backed director, evoked the ferment of the year before and remarked that the designs were "forged in a democratic process." "It is no accident that every plan repairs the skyline," he said. "No accident that each represents the foot-prints." Planning committee chair Roland Betts, underscoring his relationship to George Bush, reported that as the Innovative De-sign Study got under way, his old friend had told him simply to "do something that makes people proud." Then, describing the programmatic constraints under which the seven teams had worked all fall—essentially the terms of the World Trade Center leases, plus sites for a memorial, cultural buildings, and a train station—Betts noted that each plan included "ample commercial space, ample retail space, ample hotel space." Still, somehow, he thought those burdens had been overcome by art. "This day," he said, "belongs to the visionaries."

The first visionary to appear was Daniel Libeskind. Each of the seven teams was given a twenty-minute slot to explain its site plan, and Libeskind's place at the top of that patience-testing or-der was a calculated play. Alex Garvin had worked closely with the architects, vetting their developing designs every two weeks after a kickoff meeting they had all attended in early October, so the LMDC knew exactly what to expect. And it was shopping for fresh faces as much as fresh forms. As the morning progressed, it became clear that the agency had front-loaded the proceedings with per-sonalities the cameras couldn't help but adore.

Topping out in a gray brush cut at not far over five feet, invari-ably in black from his cowboy boots to his thick, shieldlike de-signer frames, Daniel Libeskind was a star architect well primed for mainstream celebrity. He looked the part and he came with a compelling backstory. Libeskind was born in Lodz, Poland, in May

1946, a year and a week after VE Day. Much of his extended family had been killed in the Holocaust. His parents had fled separately to Russia, finding themselves imprisoned in camps in Siberia and the Volga, and then, between 1943 and 1946, free but stuck in the "Wild East" of Kirgizia, where they met, married, and welcomed the birth of Daniel's older sister. After ten years back in Poland— years in which Daniel Libeskind flowered as a musical prodigy on an unlikely instrument: the accordion—in 1957 the family moved to Israel. In August 1959, when their son was thirteen, the Libeskinds relocated to New York City and an apartment in the Bronx.

Later, Daniel Libeskind would continue to wander. After attending Bronx Science, one of New York City's elite, specialized high schools, he studied architecture at The Cooper Union, in Greenwich Village, departing soon after graduation to become an itinerant scholar and visionary-at-large, winning dozens of awards and showing his work—ruptured, counterintuitive spaces in tortured geometries, all of it on paper—at more than sixty exhibitions in the following years. Libeskind would eventually teach at fourteen schools in seven countries, including an eight-year stint as head of the architecture program at the prestigious Cranbrook Academy, outside of Detroit. In 1985 he stepped down to found his own alternative architecture school, in Milan—he called it Architecture Intermundium—before settling for a decade in Berlin to oversee the construction there of his first and only important realized building, the zigzagging Jewish Museum, into which he poured his heart and soul and every last ounce of his (and his wife, Nina's) political nerve.

This immigrant-cum-nomad's course left Libeskind with "starchitect" credentials, a compelling coming-to-America story, and a peculiarly persistent hybrid accent, the most charming feature of which is a tendency to add a *k* to his terminal *g*'s, as in "buildingk." Speaking at a mesmerizing, rushing clip, high-pitched and sibilant, Libeskind can leave listeners scratching their heads, struggling to parse his sentences as he toggles from nostalgia to pathos to hope. But through it all, one emotion comes loud and clear: a kind of joy. Daniel Libeskind is almost always smiling, and when he smiles his face is nothing but teeth and squinting eyes behind those enormous black glasses—the kind that popular myth tells us deep-thinking architects are supposed to wear. He has a habit of rocking back on his heels, his chin lifted slightly, arms spread, as if he is receiving glories from the divine. That is how he faced the Winter Garden on the morning of his process debut.

"I arrived by ship to New York as a teenager, an immigrant, and like millions of others before me, my first sight was the Statue of Liberty and the amazing skyline of Manhattan," Libeskind said, speeding through a prepared text. "I have never forgotten this sight or what it stands for. This is what this project is all about."

As he spoke, masterfully despite his handicaps, with the echoing volume of the high atrium momentarily hushed, the plan he called "Memory Foundations" unspooled on video screens behind him. He proposed to turn the site into a kind of shattered crystal city ornamented with captured cosmic rays and puzzle-locked Tetris chits. The white sheet came off the model to reveal a piercing needle spire—a flashback to the improbable splinter of the gored north tower, the last steel to fall. The spire was stacked with hanging gardens—"the Gardens of the World . . . a constant affirmation of life"—and welded in its lower reaches to a standard, mid-size glass-skinned office building with a sharply sloping top. Below, an off-kilter museum would wrap around and hang over the footprints, left exposed at bedrock seventy feet down, at the bottom of the World Trade Center's pit. That day Libeskind called his museum a "museum of the event," though he was also at the time referring to it as "the Museum at the Edge of Hope." Arranged around the site's now-official sacred quadrant—as in some of the Beyer Blinder Belle plans—were three au courant versions of the fat, low office towers that Silverstein's lease, and his leeriness of excessive height, had made an intractable requirement for all.

"When I first began this project, New Yorkers were divided as to whether to keep the site of the World Trade Center empty or to fill the site completely and build upon it," Libeskind continued in his hasty, ebullient way. "I meditated many days on this seemingly impossible dichotomy. To acknowledge the terrible deaths which occurred on this site, while looking to the future with hope, seemed like two moments which could not be joined. I sought to find a solution which would bring these seemingly contradictory viewpoints into an unexpected unity. So, I went to look at the site, to stand within it, to see people walking around it, to feel its power and to listen to its voices. And this is what I heard, felt and saw."

Unlike nearly everyone else who had made the descent into the pit—workers mining it for remains, families for memories, artists for meaning—Libeskind did not fixate on its bedrock floor. Instead, he was moved by the sloppy, haphazardly patched, often leaking expanses of the pit's seventy-foot-high, three-foot-thick concrete retaining walls—the enormous dams, studded with hundreds of rusty steel fittings, that formed the four sides of the bathtub and kept the nearby waters of the Hudson River at bay. "The great slurry walls are the most dramatic elements which survived the attack," Libeskind told the crowd at the Winter Garden. "The foundations withstood the unimaginable trauma of the destruction, and stand as eloquent as the Constitution itself, asserting the durability of democracy and the value of individual life." The specific memorial to September 11 was outside the purview of the Innovative Design Study—an open competition for its design was already being planned, and the architectural teams had been asked only to provide an appropriate setting—but it was clear from Libeskind's drawings and delivery that he felt those decrepit walls, with his veneer of Americana, were that memorial in waiting.

Other elements of Libeskind's plan were similarly freighted with symbolism. Across from his glass lantern of a museum, in front of the large train station that had not yet been given specific form, he imagined a triangular public space, opening to the east, which he called the "Wedge of Light." It would serve as a pedes-

trian forecourt to the train station in the European mode—
renderings showed the plaza filled with chic shops and shoppers—
but also as a mystical link to the moment that had brought about
this whole architectural dance. With the aid of rough white-on-
black sketches, Libeskind explained that the lines of the two facades flanking the "Wedge" pointed at the precise locations of the
sun in the sky at the onset and the end of the attack. The result
was a kind of urban Stonehenge: "Each year on September
eleventh, between the hours of eight forty-six a.m., when the first
airplane hit, and ten twenty-eight a.m., when the second tower
collapsed, the sun will shine without shadow, in perpetual tribute
to altruism and courage."

Continuing the theme of democracy he applied to the slurry
walls, Libeskind had designed his garden-filled spike of a tower to
stand at 1,776 feet tall. As it was connected along one side to a
seventy-story office building, the glass-and-steel spire looked
vaguely like a spear held aloft by its lower, leasable neighbor—
that old pride-mending and Silverstein-soothing compromise
again. To Libeskind, it was a torch; the shape of his Declaration of
Independence tower was an evocation of the Statue of Liberty.
The one rendering of the tower from afar showed it pasted into
the Manhattan skyline behind a standard postcard shot of Lady
Liberty herself, the conjoined buildings, later to be given the
name Freedom Tower, aping in abstract form the statue and its
upraised flame.

Daniel Libeskind, the foreign-born, Jewish expatriate, a dual
citizen of Israel and the United States, a man who had lived so long
in Berlin that the American press frequently called him a German,
would be the only architect that day to offer politicians a politicized architecture. As Washington ramped up to the war in Iraq, at
the very moment White House rhetoric was so effectively eliding
Saddam Hussein with the events of September 11, Libeskind
served up a graphic talking point: a tower said to mean freedom, at
the site where freedom was said to have been attacked, on the eve

of an invasion said to be freedom's defense. Of all the architects to pass through the process, only Libeskind was shrewd enough to wrap his vision of Ground Zero in the flag.

Libeskind's assignment of patriotic and heroic meaning to otherwise mute forms was the hallmark of his plan. "A skyscraper rises above its predecessors, reasserting the preeminence of freedom and beauty, restoring the spiritual peak of the city, creating an icon that speaks of our vitality in the face of danger and our optimism in the aftermath of tragedy," he said in a single breath as he concluded his presentation. "Life victorious!"

All of this was perfectly tuned to the day—to the viewers at home and to the public patrons in the room. Libeskind's presentation was met with spontaneous applause, affirming with his first turn in the spotlight that he was capable of providing what the process so desperately needed at that moment: a human face uttering inspiring words, a reprieve from its battle-scarred businessmen and bureaucrats, an apolitical presence who could simplify and sanitize the image of this numbers-driven development. There was a distinct buzz in the air, but no time to consider it: Alex Garvin rose immediately to introduce the next architect, seeming to delight in calling him Lord Foster.

A short, trim man in his late sixties, Norman Foster is the father of the "high tech" school that has thrived in the United Kingdom and been exported throughout the world—though not as yet to New York City—in skyscrapers and lesser buildings that revel in exposed structure and advanced, environmentally correct technologies. Foster quickly pointed out that, like so many top architects, he had been in Manhattan on the morning of September 11. "How do you measure emptiness, loss, memories?" he asked, leveraging that credential. "How do you give a physical presence to such intangibles?" His answer, which he had been considering since the day of the attack, took the form of two faceted, triangular towers rising well above the height of the vanished twins they so eerily resembled. At several points, the towers were joined structurally to increase their strength and to allow multiple exit routes in the event of a second strike. Foster described them memorably as "two towers that kiss and touch and become one"—a sound bite that stuck in the press, where they became known as the "kissing towers." He also reached for deeper meanings, writing in an accompanying statement that his towers' many triangles were "cross-cultural symbols of harmony, wisdom, purity, unity and strength."

Alone among the designs shown that day, Foster's plan resisted the conventional wisdom of restoring the grid and retained the World Trade Center's superblock and elevated plinth, even increasing the area by extending it over West Street as a park-topped bridge. Though such moves were often decried as anti-urban and even anti-human, the plan harkened back to the kind of monumental humanism practiced by Minoru Yamasaki and others at mid-century: grand gestures that sought to stir the heart and the mind, even as they inconvenienced the body. "Architecture is about needs," Foster said early in his presentation, "the needs of people." And the people whose needs he met most completely were those such as Jon Hakala and the "silent majority" promoted by Team Twin Towers, people whose equanimity hinged on the return of a defiant statement to the skyline. The next morning, Foster's towers were on the cover of the *New York Post*.

Foster, like Daniel Libeskind, also had a keen sense of the redevelopment's emotional riptides. He tempered his heroic modernism, presenting his plan "through the eyes of a child." Nearly every drawing showed a little girl in an orange dress, reminding many that day of the little Jewish girl in a red dress who flits through the scene of a ghetto purge in Steven Spielberg's otherwise black-and-white film, *Schindler's List*. Speaking confidently, in the kind of high-bred London tones against which the American press has no defenses, Foster described his Girl in Orange as she took a parent's hand and toured the vacant, steel-lined footprint memorials he had proposed—"Why is it empty?" he said she might ask—before boarding a glass elevator to ascend to one of the open-air observation decks on a high floor of his kissing towers. The environmentally correct engineering of those towers, their appeal to the build-'em-as-they-were crowd, Foster's canny proposal to create private mourning zones for the victims' families, the twenty-acre park he sketched in for the locals, and the comfortable feasibility of the whole added up to a rhetorical grand slam. There was more eager applause and a palpable buzz. Maybe, just maybe, the redevelopment of Ground Zero could transcend its political and economic imperatives; maybe this gamble with genius would pay.

Lord Foster was a hard act to follow. Perhaps that was why Richard Meier kicked off his team's presentation with an attempt at ingratiating shtick. "We're the New York team," the tall, shambling, white-haired architect said to the world with a thud as his colleagues—Peter Eisenman, Steven Holl, and Charles Gwathmey—stood by in varying degrees of obvious discomfort. "Some say we're the Dream Team. But that's not true. We're very real. And we're presenting a project that we'd like to think is also very real."

His qualification was the clue; the Dream Team's plan was embarrassingly undeveloped: five identical, faceless towers arranged in the requisite *L* around the sacred zone, all tied by fat skyways into an imposing waffle that reared over a plaza offering little more than windswept déjà vu. The buildings were immediately compared to a steroidal game of tick-tack-toe. The tone-deafness of the plan was underscored by its name, "Memorial Square," which had also been given to one of the six dismissed Beyer Blinder Belle proposals from the summer before. Peter Eisenman had brought a drawing of the gridded towers into his team's first meeting, and the design had not advanced far beyond that over the course of the collaboration. Eisenman, a closet numerologist whose devotion to the number eleven had moved him years before to schedule his second wedding on November 11 at eleven o'clock, had also determined the five towers' height: 1,111 feet. In this way, form would somehow be made to bear meaning. And as with Libeskind's symbolic dimensioning, pedigreed architects were playing catch-up with the numerical superstitions of the unsolicited amateurs.

The Dream Team got a pass from most architecture critics—Herbert Muschamp actually published a preemptive defense of the scheme—but an architecture-school studio critic would have had to give Meier et al. an incomplete. The poverty of the design, a blank onto which any idea could be projected, gave credence to reports that this ego-rich collaboration had not gone smoothly. Speaking candidly, Charles Gwathmey, the most grounded and least star-struck of the four, described the difficulties: "I wouldn't wish this project on my worst enemy."

Though the concept was so clearly botched, blame for its failure fell on Richard Meier's uninspired presentation that morning in the Winter Garden. The truth, of course, was more painful: the greats of New York architecture had been given a chance to solve the greatest architectural problem the city had ever faced, and they had come up very visibly short of greatness.

Think, the second of the day's bizarre star clusters, brought together David Rockwell, the master of themed, good-times architecture (in an advisory role); Shigeru Ban, a genuine prophet of an ethical, bare-bones alternative; Fred Schwartz, whose career in the trenches had been interrupted when Herbert Muschamp adopted his idea of a West Street land swap; and Rafael Viñoly, whose tortured presentation, on the heels of Richard Meier's, somehow failed to sink his team's bid for glory. The coalition covered its bets with three alternative master plans: "World Cultural Center," twin, openwork constructions in white steel; "Sky Park," a plan for three towers looking down on a green plateau; and "Great Hall," which imagined a site-spanning thirty-story-high glass room that, despite Viñoly's liberal use of the word "quiet" in describing it, looked like a louder, loftier version of the press-choked Winter Garden itself.

That morning, all three Think schemes appeared to be nonstarters. Viñoly is a fast-talking émigré from Argentina, and as he rolled on in his heavily accented English, many in the audience saw the opportunity to take a break from the event, then approaching the end of its second hour. The plans also polled poorly with the public in the days after, when every newspaper and Web site intuitively pitted the noncompetitive teams against one another. Together, the Think schemes made every urban planning mistake in the books—they relied on long, forbidding walkways; they privatized public space; they hid plazas and parks from the streets around them—and invented some more for good measure. So it was a surprise to many that the World Cultural Center was tapped to go head-to-head with Libeskind's "Memory Foundations" when an ad hoc, competitive second round was announced six weeks later.

What the World Cultural Center had going for it—as nighttime renderings of the two towers made clear—was its allusion to the "Tribute in Light," an instant memorial that projected two ghostly stand-ins for the towers into the sky over Lower Manhattan. During its monthlong, dusk-to-dawn commemoration at the half anniversary of the attack, the "Tribute in Light" had become by far the most beloved artistic response to September 11, despite the fact that the twin blue beams were the wrong size, had risen from the wrong site (across the street in Battery Park City), and had a clear art-historical precedent in the form of Albert Speer's "Cathedral of Light," shot into the Nuremberg night in 1936. But the World Cultural Center also proposed something less conspicuous and considerably bolder than a melodramatic light show: it was the only plan that came out of the Innovative Design Study with a challenge to the redevelopment's codified land-use assumptions.

In that plan, the full lease-mandated square footage could be accommodated in a dense quarter of towers proposed (for other architects to complete over time) on the north, east, and south sides of the site, but the area directly above the footprints—where the two towers of the World Cultural Center would rise—was not given over to mourning. Had this scheme prevailed and been realized, the centerpiece of Ground Zero would not have been a memorial (or memorials) but two pieces of speculative infrastructure that would have become "sites," as the team described it in a statement, for the construction of "the first truly Global Center, a place where people can gather to celebrate cultural diversity in peaceful and productive coexistence." Though that language recalled Minoru Yamaski's vision of peace and "the cooperation of men," the engines here would be strictly noncommercial: a "9/11 Interpretive Museum," a performing arts center, an international conference center, an amphitheater, and assorted "public facilities for exploration and discovery in the Arts and Sciences"—all hanging from the exposed steel "latticework" of the towers in blobs and pods to be supplied by other architects as needed. It was by far the most radical proposition to make it out of the galleries, off the Web sites, and into consideration in the conference rooms of the LMDC. Good thing everyone was focused instead on its resemblance to the Twin Towers; despite all the radical imagery filling the Winter Garden, no one was looking for radical ideas.

The last three teams to present on that long December morning, as television viewers were no doubt beginning to find other diversions, were the mercy cases and the long shots: United Architects, a group of computer-wielding digerati; Peterson Littenberg; and the ever-present Skidmore, Owings and Merrill.

In addition to Los Angeles–based Greg Lynn and New Yorkers Kevin Kennon, Jesse Reiser, and Nanako Umemoto, United Architects included jet-set architecture-scene mavericks from London (Foreign Office Architects) and Amsterdam (Ben van Berkel and Caroline Bos of UN Studio, slumming here with less accomplished contemporaries). Using presentation materials developed with the design and branding firm Imaginary Forces (the wizards behind the title sequences in the Harry Potter films), Greg Lynn—tall, shaggy, and no longer celebrating urban warfare as he had a year earlier at the Max Protetch Gallery—presented his team as nextgeneration utopians. He did so despite the fact that United Architects' design featured classic elements from New York futures past: a street-spanning megastructure, a "City in the Sky." Lynn came armed with a short, advertising-slick film—set to percussion and a klezmer-mad violin—in which ethnically diverse young models were shown rounding corners or emerging from subway stairs to gaze up at the team's design with wonder and reverence. Desire had come again to Ground Zero.

The design the cosmopolites in the film were responding to—in vignettes that were a happy inversion of all those looking-up-at-Doomsday street scenes from September 11—was a wall of five canted, triangle-trussed gray-glass towers that melded into one excruciatingly sinister blob. It is safe to say that no speculative product from the bleeding edge of architectural experimentation has ever had such an enormous audience. But beyond the hip bits and bytes of their spellbinding presentation, United Architects' design, though full of insurgent pluck, was not quite ready for prime time.

The plan was arranged so that the view up from the subterranean footprint memorial sites was not of the sky but of the crotch of the leaning, looming office buildings—a vantage that Greg Lynn had the nerve to compare to the domed interior of Istanbul's Hagia Sophia mosque. Lynn noted that it would be the largest building in the world and, at the refreshingly nonsymbolic height of 1,620 feet, the tallest. But it would also be one of the most grandiose and complete barriers ever erected in a living city. When architects start talking about "porosity," as Lynn did, slipping a hand into one of his model's erogenous slots, you know they're planning to build a honking big wall.

The insiders presented last. The plan prepared by Peterson Littenberg, the firm that had skirted two official selection processes through its consulting contract with the LMDC, was a world away from United Architects' blob and the farthest that day from the stylistic and urbanistic mean. Where others had tried to bring life across the barrier of West Street to Battery Park City, that still-sterile annex to Manhattan, these urban designers in the reactionary mode sought to impose an identical impotence on Ground Zero: awkward towers jammed into a cheap facsimile of Rockefeller Center, cozy pocket parks, the familiar easy streets of ersatz urbanism. They even had an obelisk. The plan was readily comprehensible—in the way that classically inspired architecture can be—but in all other respects it was a dud. Peterson Littenberg would have created a wonderful beginner's pedestrian district for any car-wracked American city that needed one, but New Yorkers expect much more from a street: vitality, for instance, even surprise. Apart from the self-defeating Dream Team, it was the weakest of the "innovative designs," and, because of what it revealed of official taste, the most disconcerting. It was a pitch-perfect paean to the status quo, a developers' delight. And it came with a whiff of exclusivity. Barbara Littenberg, speaking to a very skeptical Winter Garden, remarked that the walled park planned for the center of the site was hallowed by tradition: walls had always been built in English gardens to keep out rabbits. Who were the rabbits here?

At the very end came Skidmore, Owings and Merrill. Originally the firm had not planned to participate—the partners were aware that their ongoing work with Larry Silverstein was a conflict—but the LMDC had insisted and, at the last moment, with their work for the developer momentarily suspended in an exchange of letters, Roger Duffy had fielded a team. A half dozen artists were brought on board—SOM had most other expertise in-house—but like so many of the instant partnerships, this collaboration proved unwieldy; an official at the LMDC said the team fought like "cats in a sack." In front of the cameras and the thinning crowd, Duffy presented a phased array of nine nimble, crooked glass towers that would cover the entire site, replacing the public ground acre for acre with tree-lined plazas in the sky. Particular attention had been given to a very beautiful (and, given the firm's engineering chops, very buildable) train station—the grandest of the Downtown Grand Centrals shown. But Duffy barely mentioned it; he took only six of the twenty minutes allotted to present his very intricate plan. He had watched the process unfold for more than a year from within the walls of SOM. He knew he shouldn't waste his time with hothouse flowers. And with that quick exit, after four hours, having treated the world to a revealing look at the state of architectural invention, the rollout of the Innovative Design Study was done.

As the media spectacle played out in the Winter Garden's center ring, office workers, many likely survivors of the generative event, looked on. They stood at the mezzanine rails—above the press, politicians, and palm trees—or sat on the wide stair at the back of the hall. Four or five of the Innovative Design hopefuls had hired public relations firms to increase their traction with the media. So, under the witnesses' mordant gaze, those inevitable lubricants of contemporary enterprise, smiling flacks, were doing their thing. Some of them were telling all who would listen, "Our team should win."

Win? As things stood, there could be no winner in the redevelopment game, not one worth rooting for anyway; a compromised process could result only in compromise. And even if it had been a competition—as it would be soon but was not quite yet—there could have been no winner that day. This was bread and circus for the chattering class, smoke and mirrors for the viewers back home, a feint by the development powers to protect their left flank from charges of Philistinism, a dodge to buy time as they got their publicly financed house in order for a final push at that fearsome fait accompli: rebuilding on the World Trade Center site every last square foot that the leases required and society could be made to tolerate.

LMDC chairman John Whitehead reappeared to close down the event. He thanked the architects for their many plans, which, he said, his agency now had the task of editing and recombining into something that could be used. With the designers parading before the cameras—the public, via the press, serving as a de facto jury—it was easy to forget the original, limited goals of the Innovative Design Study: "This is NOT a competition and will not result in the selection of a final plan." But at that moment it looked as if the architects had fattened themselves for the cannibals' feast. By the end of the following month, the LMDC intended to digest the architects' ideas, by means unspecified, into a single master plan. And the Port Authority had promised it would soon reveal another transparent-process wild card: its own proprietary land-use vision being drawn up in characteristic secrecy.

Roland Betts had not been dissembling when he said that the day belonged "to the visionaries." It was a generous sentiment, and it was true; after the *New York Times* editorial board deemed the designs "a gift" ("The government's obligation . . . is to protect the scale and ambition of these plans against what are almost certain to be challenges from commercial and political interests"); after the online polls were closed at the *New York Post* and CNN (Foster's "kissing towers" won both); after the plans were splashed on front pages around the world; after the submissions were put into vitrines at the Winter Garden for public review, the news cycle was immediately swallowed up by the annual slide into styling an American Christmas just like the ones we used to know. Whether by chance or tactic, that snowbound intermission took two weeks out of what was only a six-week window for the LMDC to assess its harvest of ideas, gather and weigh public comment (from the exhibition, online, and at public meetings), stitch together a master scheme, and somehow stretch that exquisite corpse around the unknown angles of the Port Authority's Plan X.

What does haste make? Here, a wealth of rumors that the fix was in. And in a sense, it was; the redevelopment process, though subject to deflection and amendment by every party involved, would continue to be ruled most surely by the formidable combination of George Pataki's ambitions and the codicils of Larry Silverstein's lease. Which is not to say that the Innovative Design Study changed nothing; it tilted the scales ever so slightly in favor of architectural quality—insofar as quality is synonymous with the products of architecture's star system, deployed in the time-honored New York way: decorating the developer's box, a signature skin job. After the big splash in the Winter Garden, it was no longer possible for any of the powers to backtrack from the public's assumption that at least one marquee name would be attached to the project. It was that realization, in part, that caused the LMDC—pushed again by competition-loving Roland Betts—to float the idea that a single winner would be chosen.

By late January 2003 the decision had been made: the cherry-picking of ideas was ruled out and the nonbinding design study segued into what it was perceived to be all along: a contest in search of a winner. The LMDC may have hoped that none of the now openly competing teams would remember the language of the original Request for Qualifications: "This is not a design competition. It is a design study." But at least one team, after having lost under the new terms, briefly considered filing suit.

The sudden appearance of the long-sought competition between architectural stars—though operating without a jury or a clearly defined program and not a whit transparent—led some observers to dance little victory jigs in print. But it offered only small comfort to all those still hoping for *difference* at Ground Zero. Those who control the program and the publicity and the calendar and the money and the land and the sky above it can hardly be said to have bent much if they contracted out for aesthetics. When the design teams dispersed from the Winter Garden and the satellite trucks rolled away down West Street, the odds-on future of the site remained a trains-below, cubicles-above, memorial-in-the-footprints, shopping-everywhere dollop of old-normal Manhattan. And as in so many other local real estate ventures, a star architect would now be brought in to prettify the developer's numbers. No one should have been surprised; that is the bone that is always thrown, and this time we saw the windup broadcast live on TV.

9

WHEN ARCHITECTS ATTACK

"IT HAS been known for some time that Libeskind and his wife are in fact Raelians," an anonymous architect posted to an online forum, referring to the cult whose followers believe that life on Earth was seeded by UFOs and whose leaders were just then in the news for their home-cooked attempts at human cloning. "The Libeskinds have incorporated many Raelian beliefs and systems in much of their work, most notably in . . . their recent WTC proposal, as a kind of landing platform for future generations. The recent cloning news attributed to the sect has great implications for the Libeskinds . . . and their hopes for world domination."[1]

Coming only ten days after the press fiesta in the Winter Garden, the libel was among the first and perhaps the most creative to be leveled at the architect and Nina Libeskind, his wife, business partner, chief political strategist, and—with her reduced height, cropped gray hair, European-Jewish antecedents, and on-message intensity—nearly his clone. As they rose to a prominent and then a central position in the redevelopment, the Libeskinds drew fire from their colleagues and returned it redoubled.

Throughout the intrigues surrounding the fate of the World Trade Center site, pettiness had been present, and the personal was never out of bounds; it was Andrew Cuomo's "coat-holding" attack on George Pataki that had helped set in motion the events that made the Libeskinds' participation possible. But in 2003, with the national and international media now fully engaged and the redevelopment achieving its full potential for the baroque, the art of the takedown reached new highs and lows. And as with every other related conflict, this discharge of enmities would rattle through the process to find itself reflected in form.

With the nonbinding Innovative Design Study now a winner-take-all competition, with architects marketing their personas alongside their designs, the stage was set for a Herculean street fight. Tarring the Libeskinds as alien-worshipping cloners was not likely to destroy their apparent early advantage, but it indicated the extremes to which their enemies would go. And in New York, they had many enemies waiting. They would soon make more.

One of the seminal set pieces in the Libeskind biography—an old story retold and republished a thousand times as the mainstream press descended on their new love object—involves Daniel and Nina in the spring of 1989, just after they won the competition for the Jewish Museum in Berlin. The Libeskinds had been living in Milan but were at that very moment in the process of relocating to Los Angeles, where Daniel had accepted a coveted appointment as a senior scholar at the Getty Center. With their household already packed into a freighter working its way through the Panama Canal en route to California, the Libeskinds arrived in Berlin to accept the competition award. "Our children were wearing shorts," Daniel Libeskind remembered. The family planned to proceed on to the Getty, where the scholarly architect would live "a life without cares," he said, "with assistants and computers and access to this incredible institution—just to think." But as they crossed Berlin's wide Helmholtzstrasse after collecting the award, Libeskind recalled, "Nina turned to me and said, 'You realize what this means?' and I suddenly knew that if we were serious, we couldn't leave. Because of the politics, how is anybody going to build without the architect being there every day, talking to everybody?"[2] The Libeskinds called the Getty Center and the shipping company, checked into a hotel, and stayed—through the completion of the museum building in 1999 and the delayed opening of the exhibitions within it on September 11, 2001.

This part of the museum's genesis myth—the two Jews, one a descendant of Holocaust victims, shelving their aversion to things German in order to push their building against all resistance—was well known in architecture circles; it served as shorthand for the considerable savvy and tenacity the Libeskinds had shown over ten years of successful political battles in Berlin. So it was with special alarm that New York architects received the news, around the time of the Winter Garden presentations, that the Libeskinds were planning another move: from Berlin to Manhattan.

As he reminded the city at every opportunity, Bronx-bred Daniel Libeskind was a native New Yorker. But he had not lived there for decades, since shortly after graduating from The Cooper Union and beginning the international peregrinations that brought him his fame. Libeskind's time at Cooper was well spent—he'd earned the trust of the dean and gotten the nickname "Danny"—but it had also generated much of the rancor that awaited his return. One of his professors there was Peter Eisenman. An angry stalwart of the city's in-fighting avant-garde, he would be among the most vocal of Libeskind's opponents, in public and elsewhere. And Eisenman had the ear of important process players, ranging from Herbert Muschamp at the *New York Times* to David Childs of SOM.

Ground Zero was not the first place where Eisenman and Libeskind tangled. In 1998, both men had entered the competition for a national Holocaust memorial in Berlin. Not long before the submissions were due, Nina Libeskind reported, her husband received a strange phone call from Eisenman, during which he asked if Libeskind was planning to adapt the design of his memorial garden at the Jewish Museum—a field of forty-nine featureless, closely set concrete columns—for his competition entry. Libeskind said that he was not and hung up. When Eisenman's entry—a much larger field of featureless, closely set concrete columns—later won that competition, things got nasty. The Libeskinds made far-fetched sub rosa accusations of plagiarism, fueling the curiosity of reporters, several of whom cornered and embarrassed Eisenman at a public forum. There was hissing. Though the flap soon subsided, the confrontation resulted in several articles in the German press examining the relationship between the two designs.

At the same time, there was an unholy row over the commission for a Jewish Center in San Francisco. Peter Eisenman got the job, left it, and then the Libeskinds swept in. On top of their simmering student/teacher rivalry, the episodes exacerbated the tensions between two men already divided by temperament. Like Daniel Libeskind, Eisenman is an extraordinarily introspective and cerebral architect; but unlike that free-flowing empath, Eisenman's more rigorous cerebration has at times led him to creative immobility. It took him forty years to complete his masterpiece, a formalist study of the work of the fascist architect Giuseppe Terragni that was finally published in 2003 (as a student, young Libeskind had prepared drawings for that book), and he once worked for years with Jacques Derrida on a project for a park in Paris. That collaboration generated an intricate correspondence but only a paltry architectural product: a grid of nine squares, one slightly turned.

It is easy to see why Eisenman would recoil from Daniel Libeskind's comfortable trade in emotions, which, as brought to Ground Zero in full flower, many felt was at least overdetermined, if not also tastelessly oversold. To those architects, like Eisenman and his embittered Dream Team partners, who had staked a claim to the site on their proximity, the specter of Daniel and Nina Libeskind winging in from Berlin to redeem New York was not appealing. As a junior architect in Charles Gwathmey's office said at the time of Libeskind's arrival: "We're going to crush his nuts."

The anti-Libeskind rhetoric so much in the air was given explicit form by Peter Eisenman and Steven Holl, overheard at a magazine launch party. Their conversation was posted on the Web (with annotations) by Gawker.com, a popular gossip-mongering site:

SH: She [Nina Libeskind, partner/wife/PR engine/sister to a special envoy to Kofi Annan]'s so political. When we were selected, she called me up and congratulated me. What's that for??

PE: I saw the dirty pool she was playing. I'm not going to get in the gutter with that. It's not worth it.

. . . a minute later . . .

PE: You've got to promise me, if he [Daniel Libeskind] is up for the spot [Dean of Columbia Architecture School, where Holl teaches], you'll step in. That would be a fucking travesty.

SH: There's no way.

PE: You have to step in.

SH: There are a lot of people who'll step in. It's ok. It'll never happen.

That exchange was also quoted in the *Daily News* and the *New York Observer*. After the spike in press coverage, there was agreement in architecture circles that the redevelopment was "good for the profession." Certainly the process had raised architecture's profile in the public imagination; "From now on," Daniel Libeskind told the *New York Times*, "architecture will be as interesting for people to talk about as the taste of wine."[3] But much of what the public got a taste of, between generous helpings of sentiment and jargon, was the sort of everyday bile served up by Peter Eisenman and Steven Holl—now for the first time newsy enough to make reporters reach for their pens.

As they came to terms with their professional eclipse, the local boys of the Dream Team found another target for their venom. Though he'd had little contact with the redevelopment process that had been increasing the visibility of his peers, Frank Gehry was still the biggest name in American architecture. He had mostly declined to comment on the future of the site, but he had been thinking about it. In January 2002, Gehry was scheduled to begin teaching a studio class at Yale. "I didn't know what to do," he said, "and I thought, 'Maybe Ground Zero'? But I didn't want to touch it." Then he saw Rudy Giuliani give his valedictory speech, the one in which the departing hero-mayor argued for devoting the entire site to a memorial. "Giuliani got on TV and said that there should be a soaring public memorial that everyone can come to," Gehry said. "Well, I had no idea what he was talking about, but I said, 'That's a one-room building' "—an assignment Gehry favors when teaching because, he said, "students have to go right to architecture, they can't fuck around." Off the cuff, at the first meeting at Yale, Gehry told his students that the only space he could imagine as a precedent was the Hagia Sofia. The school's dean, Bob Stern, said right there he would send the class to Istanbul, and off they went with Gehry to see what lessons a domed mosque from the sixth century might hold for a memorial at Ground Zero.

Having declined to send a pretty picture to Max Protetch or to join a team for the Port Authority's first attempt at planning in early 2002, and having declined to contribute to Herbert Muschamp's "Masters' Plan" or to enter the LMDC's Innovative Design Study that summer, Gehry returned to his deliberate non-participation—until he gave a telephone interview to the *New York Times Magazine*, published on January 5, 2003. Gehry shared there his idea for building a single, inspiring space as a memorial, a little reluctantly, adding, "I don't want to come off as the white-haired wonder from California telling New Yorkers what to do." But the interview opened with an exchange in which Gehry seemed to attack those architects who had played along with the LMDC:

Q: So, how have you managed to stay out of the debate over the twin towers site? You're the only architect who's a household name in America, so naturally people wondered why your name was missing when the Lower Manhattan

Development Corporation presented seven new proposals
for the site last month.

A: I was invited to be on one of the teams, but I found it
demeaning that the agency paid only $40,000 for all that
work. I can understand why the kids did it, but why would
people my age do it? Norman Foster or Richard Meier or
any of those people? When you're paid only $40,000 you're
treated as if that is your worth.[4]

Gehry knew immediately he was in big trouble. "She asked me
why I didn't enter the competition and I told her the whole story:
Giuliani, Yale, the Hagia Sophia," he remembered a few months
later, referring to the interviewer, Deborah Solomon. "And I told
her that the competition focused too much on the commercial aspects. I told her I didn't know the politics—the LMDC or the
'ABD' or the 'World Authority.' At the end she asked me a question that worried me—about the money. I got off the phone and
got worried. I wanted to call her back, but I didn't have her phone
number. I dialed four one one, and there were three numbers—
three Deborah Solomons in New York. I called all three and I got
her. I told her I was worried about the last question. Then that article was published in the magazine. So, as far as I'm concerned,
I'm staying out of Ground Zero."

Though poorly put, Gehry's view of the $40,000 was more than
justified; each team had likely spent over $500,000 out of pocket
on their elaborate submissions—Charles Gwathmey later said his
team had spent that on models alone—at a time when the LMDC
was being very generous in its contracts with other consultants. But
the architecture world went into a tizzy over Gehry's comment—
providing services on spec is a perennial point of controversy
within the profession—and the national media, newly conditioned
to notice architects, fanned the flames. On January 9, Aaron Brown,
the anchor of CNN's late-night news program, read Gehry's remark

about the stipend and then made these observations: "Well, excuse me, Mr. Gehry. How much do you think the firefighters who perished in the building that day made? And I can't imagine any firefighter said, 'I'm not running into that mess for what I make every year.' And how about the people down at the morgue here in New York, who now say it will be years before they can identify all the remains? You think they're paid big bucks? We can go on, but the point was best made by someone who did submit a plan. Earlier this week he got big applause at a meeting of architects saying this, 'It doesn't matter a damn, Frank Gehry, that we were paid only forty thousand dollars.' "[5]

The architect in question was none other than Peter Eisenman, speaking at a packed forum for the Innovative Design Study teams organized by one of the architecture trade magazines. (The other big applause that night came when a former executive of the Battery Park City Authority said that it was "ethically, morally and, possibly, illegally wrong for the Port Authority and a developer to be calling the shots" at Ground Zero.[6]) Before that meeting, Eisenman had logged more directly his displeasure with Gehry's economic critique. Charles Gwathmey had already sent a letter representing three-fourths of the Dream Team. "Frank Gehry: Peter, Richard and I think you are a total prick," the opening line read.

It is a curious document, especially considering that only five months prior Gehry had been invited to join his old friends in the Innovative Design Study. "I got a call one night from Charlie Gwathmey," Gehry said. "He was out drinking"—actually he was calling from Richard Meier's office where the newly formed Dream Team was enjoying a bottle of champagne—"and he said, 'This is a very historical call.' I said 'Shoot.' He started ringing off the names of the apostles—'We want you to be on our team.' I said, 'Charlie, I can't do that. I'm not in New York. I'm not there. I can't do it.' He said, 'It's really important.' I said, 'If it's so important, call me in the morning and we'll talk about it.' He never called."

Despite the interview flap and that spat with his fellow stars, Gehry's distance from the process was having the perhaps intended effect of increasing his already considerable cachet. Just a month later, when five of the Innovative Design Study teams had fallen away and the LMDC had winnowed the field to two, Gehry was approached by both finalists—Rafael Viñoly, for the Think team, and the Libeskinds—to see if he would come in from the sidelines as a ringer to help decide the pitched battle to come. Still playing the long game, he turned them down, sparing himself a role in that next, far uglier clash.

On February 4, 2003, those making and covering the news at Ground Zero convened at the nearby offices of the LMDC to mark another process milestone: the announcement of the Innovative Design Study finalists. There were about seventy people in the large conference room, mostly reporters, and seventeen cameras. But before they could go live with the presentation, the networks had to wait for George Bush to finish speaking at the day's other big event, a memorial in Houston for the astronauts who had died in the crash of the space shuttle *Columbia*. There was a forty-five-minute delay, during which one reporter jokingly asked an LMDC staffer, "Why are we here?" Smiling, he replied, "We designed something. I don't know what."

Nobody knew what, but the writing was on the wall—*genius*—and Larry Silverstein, an unwilling patron of the arts, was getting nervous. Five days earlier, the developer had written a nine-page letter to LMDC chairman John Whitehead—cc'd everywhere and instantly leaked to the press—in which he asserted his right (clearly stated in his lease with the Port Authority) to choose an architect for the reconstruction of his vanished office space. He had chosen SOM: "As you know, we have engaged Skidmore, Owings and Merrill to work with us on a site plan. We understand that LMDC shortly will select one or more architects to work with it in developing a plan over the coming weeks; and the Port Authority, of course, has its own extraordinarily qualified architects and planners. We have been and remain fully amenable to having SOM work with any architects selected by the Port Authority and LMDC over the coming weeks."

Silverstein's language was business-letter-ese for *don't test me*, and the selection of the finalists was hastened and their announcement choreographed to do just that. The decisive meeting of the LMDC's site planning committee had taken place the night before, and now the press was to be treated to one of those rare displays of political camaraderie that always signaled Pataki-applied pressure behind the scenes. If Silverstein chose to brandish the terms of his lease—threatening to undo all the face-saving work undertaken since the rejection of the six misbegotten plans the summer before—then the public officials would pull out their trump card: the public.

Each speaker that day went to great pains to describe the scale of the public input received during a brief return to "listening mode" that had begun after the release of the seven teams' designs in December. John Whitehead said that twelve thousand comments had been received and would be considered. Roland Betts claimed to have read six thousand himself. Lou Tomson noted that the "overwhelming majority" of that feedback was "favorable." Diana Taylor, the governor's liaison to the LMDC and the mayor's girlfriend, said that both of the plans under consideration were "beautiful, compelling, meaningful"—in short, they gave the public what it had been demanding: symbolic monuments.

Joe Seymour, director of the Port Authority, was also there, burying for the moment his own agency's opposition to the Innovative Design Study and its results in order to join in putting down Larry Silverstein. He referred to the whole murky mess as "the most open public process in the history of New York City," though, later, answering a reporter's question about the next steps in refining any selected plan, he broke the spell and spoke the truth: "The best parts of the concept will survive, and it will still be recognizable."

The architects who would have to run that gauntlet were brought out, to applause led by LMDC staff, and images of their plans were unveiled yet again: the blob-hung twin towers of Think's World Cultural Center, the broken angles of Daniel Libeskind's symbol-soaked "Memory Foundations." Each team was then given a chance to speak. Representing Think, Fred Schwartz, shell-shocked and with a catch in his voice, evoked the dead: families torn apart, children without parents; it was a sentiment that many in the room were then, almost a year and a half after the attack, ready to move beyond. Daniel Libeskind, with Nina at his side, had a better read on the political moment; he kept to the day's populist theme. "Cities are made out of citizens," he said, promising to heed the people's voice should he have the honor to go forward. "I don't have to tell you that everyone in the world has been looking at this site since the disaster happened."

Two days later Herbert Muschamp took sides. His first assessment of the Innovative Design Study plans had run in the *Times* the morning after the Winter Garden event. He took up the designs then "in almost no particular order of preference." Libeskind's came first. "If you are looking for marvelous, here's where you will find it," Muschamp wrote. "Daniel Libeskind's project attains a perfect balance between aggression and desire." He continued, riffing on Libeskind's immigrant backstory: "On a mythical level, at least, most of us have experienced the wonder and fright of arrival in the big city, the simultaneous sense of freedom and intimidation, the exhilaration of moving into the unknown . . . Mr. Libeskind has captured these emotions."

In that same article, Muschamp also found kind words for the Dream Team ("continuity with the epic ethos of the modern era"), for Norman Foster ("terrifying thoroughness . . . elegant logic"), and for United Architects ("The designers might want to rechristen themselves The International House of Voluptuous Beauty").

But of the three Think proposals, he offered very little, ignoring two of them and giving only a polite and uncharacteristically dry description of the World Cultural Center.[7] So it was with something close to shock that students of the process greeted Muschamp's new line on the finalists that day in early February: the Think plan was now "an image of peacetime aspirations," suggesting "a place beyond armed combat," with spaces "as eloquent as a cathedral's" that had the power to transform "our collective memories of the twin towers into a soaring affirmation of American values."

Daniel Libeskind, on the other hand, had managed to lose his "perfect balance between aggression and desire." His design had become, per Muschamp, "a startlingly aggressive tour de force, a war memorial to a looming conflict that has scarcely begun." Compared with the Think plan, it was "stunted"; in the context of the buildup to the war in Iraq, it was "demagogic," even "Orwellian." "Had the competition been intended to capture the fractured state of shock felt soon after 9/11, this plan would probably deserve first place," Muschamp wrote. "But why, after all, should a large piece of Manhattan be permanently dedicated to an artistic representation of enemy assault? It is an astonishingly tasteless idea. It has produced a predictably kitsch result."[8]

Clearly, something had happened to alter Herbert Muschamp's views in the seven weeks between his two appraisals. The Libeskinds' supporters thought they knew what that was: personal politics. They were soon reminding reporters about Muschamp's friendship with Rafael Viñoly, and that Muschamp had pushed him to the foreground and practically invented his partner, Fred Schwartz, in the plan the critic had developed six months earlier for the *New York Times*.[9]

There is an old saw about the Libeskinds, originated many years before but on everyone's lips in the winter of 2003: *Every architect needs a Nina*. Daniel Libeskind's wife is a thoroughbred political creature. Her father, David Lewis, founded Canada's left-wing New Democratic Party, and she had an iron grasp on the lessons to be learned in a political family. As she had in Berlin, at Ground Zero Nina Libeskind led the strategic effort to get her husband's design approved and built. But in New York she was also conducting a more momentous campaign: transforming Daniel Libeskind from the eccentric artist he had always been to the enchanting public figure he now had to become. "He's started to get into stuff that's more complicated than form or ideas or theory," a former employee observed in early 2003. "He's started to *architect* the people. Nina's making him do it."

Still, there were battles to be fought on the ground. The day after Muschamp's thorough panning of "Memory Foundations," Nina Libeskind's war in the shadows began in earnest with a round of outraged calls to journalists. Asked about her husband's reaction, she replied, "Danny said, 'Here I am, I just won the Hiroshima Peace Prize, and this man is calling me a warmonger?' It's preposterous." Actually, he had won the Hiroshima Art Prize. The same day, as if in sympathy, the national terror threat alert level was raised from yellow to orange.

As Nina Libeskind worked the press in New York, many of them were also receiving a letter mass e-mailed by an assistant out of her office in Berlin. "Herbert Muschamp wrote a vicious and close to libelous [article] in the *New York Times* yesterday," it began. "We have been advised by 'people in the know' . . . to start a write-in campaign." The e-mail then offered four sample letters:

1. I have been a longtime reader of the *New York Times* and have always enjoyed reading about architecture. Yesterday's article by Muschamp is over the top.
2. I am not an architect but I follow architecture. . . . I read with dismay (or increasing anger) Herbert Muschamp's article. . . . Mr. Muschamp seems no longer to be a critic but rather a campaigner!
3. Muschamp's article . . . was incoherent and almost crazy. . . . I will not be reading him for a long time.

4. This time Muschamp went too far. Why is he still writing for the *New York Times*! . . .

In a second round of calls, Nina Libeskind retracted the hapless
e-mail, calling it the unsanctioned effort of an overzealous staffer;
she and Daniel were embarrassed by it. That was easy to believe;
the stillborn anti-Muschamp backlash lacked the cunning of a sophisticated attack.

At that time, it was widely assumed that the Libeskinds were
running an organized war room and that Nina was the commander
in chief. On-the-record confirmation would not come until nearly a
year later. For the site-planning aspects of their design, the Libeskinds had collaborated with Gary Hack, a respected urban planner
and the dean of the Graduate School of Fine Arts at the University
of Pennsylvania. In October 2003 Hack gave a freewheeling lecture at the State University of New York at Buffalo in which he
detailed the ways that design, politics, and propaganda had interlocked in the promotion of "Memory Foundations." Unfortunately for him, William Neuman, the enterprising beat reporter
for the *New York Post*—always a step or two ahead of the pack, as
many of his rivals acknowledged—got wind of that talk, and, after two months of lawyerly persuasion, succeeded in acquiring a
videotape of the lecture over the resistance of the speaker and the
school.

Neuman wrote two articles on successive days in early December 2003—another dicey moment in the process. The first article,
"Libeskind Pushed Ground Smear-O," blew the lid off of Nina's
actions the February before. "Hack praised Libeskind's wife Nina,
whose father was a Canadian political leader, saying she 'is absolutely critical to the team . . . because she comes from a family
of politicians,' " Neuman wrote, describing the lecture. " 'So she
took this on as a campaign while we took this on as a design and
it's no accident the two things were as intimately related as they
were . . . because she's so attuned to . . . how you can package the

images into messages. She's actually had a huge role in helping shape the design.' "[10]

One way in which Nina Libeskind contributed, Hack revealed and the *Post* reported, was to devise a way to counter the public image of their plan's central feature: the seventy-foot-deep depression around the tower footprints that was intended to serve as a site for a memorial. Understandably, that pit was immediately labeled "the Pit" by opponents of the plan, which included Wall Street business leaders (concerned about the image of the neighborhood), local residents (concerned that it was repeating in negative the raised barrier of the World Trade Center's superblock), and the editorial page of the *Post* (concerned that imported genius had run amok and would turn the site into a "Disneyland of Death").[11] As Gary Hack later explained in that ill-advised lecture, the solution, as old as politics itself, was to redefine the opposition:

> The conditions for producing a scheme like the one we did were created by the media. They were created by a set of events. We understood that, and in fact developed a design and described our design in ways that played to the way the project had already been framed in a media context. Many of the other competitors did not—either they didn't understand it or they didn't want to do it. So in fact the media positioned them. . . . Both Think and we had public relations firms working on this project. And they managed to get positioned in the press as "soaring towers." "Towers of the future." The things that were written were using those words. . . . We got positioned at that point, despite our best efforts on this thing. Many people were enthusiastic about our scheme, but the newspapers— in particular the *New York Post*—were referring to it as "the Pit." And we figured we would never get chosen as long as we were "the Pit." Especially competing with these "symbols of the future." These "spires." And so we

began to refer to the other scheme—and got others to refer to it—as "the skeletons." [Laughter] In other words,
we had to reframe what they were doing, just as they were
reframing through the press what we were doing. And so
it became a competition about what was appropriate in
this place—a set of ideas where the press was an active in-
termediary in the process of making this choice. . . . I
wouldn't say that I'm absolutely clear on where you stop
with this and where you start. But I am absolutely clear
that in a case like this . . . you can't afford not to be doing
this, because others are doing it. It's like a politician saying, "I'm not going to try to produce slogans. I'm only going to produce good government."

Daniel Libeskind first aired the "skeletons" attack publicly on
February 20, in an online chat hosted by Gothamgazette.com.
"There is a dramatic and urgent need to repair the skyline," he
wrote from Berlin. "I do not believe that two skeletons in the sky
asserts the vitality of New York or the courage of America."[12]
Three days later, Marvin Trachtenberg, an architectural historian,
repeated that slur with gusto in a scathing attack on the Think
team published in the *New York Times:* "In Think's predictable
scheme . . . gigantic twin spectral tombstones rise over the New
York skyline, flayed skeletons of the World Trade Center, with
various cultural and memorial spaces dangling within, including
one that—really—rather resembles an airplane shooting through
both buildings."[13] That same day, the *Los Angeles Times* ran a long
profile of the Libeskinds in which Daniel referred to the Think
team's name as "Orwellian" and its proposal as "Stalinist." Nina
Libeskind saved her anger there for the man who had touched off
the ruckus; if she saw Herbert Muschamp, she said, she'd "kill him
on the spot."[14]

As things got hot, Rafael Viñoly responded in kind. In conver-
sations with reporters, he began to refer to the exposed concrete

perimeter of the Libeskind pit as the "Wailing Wall." The Libeskinds naturally bridled at that characterization. But, in other con-
texts, Daniel Libeskind was not averse to carting out a closely
related metaphor. In early March 2003, a Jewish weekly reported
that Libeskind had recently told a German newspaper that the
Temple Mount in Jerusalem—the western flank of which is but-
tressed by the Wailing Wall—was an apt precedent for Ground
Zero. "It is one of the most positive places in the world," he said,
"and yet a site of utter destruction."[15]

On a second front, another threat to Think was gathering. As
the barbs were being traded and the redevelopment of the World
Trade Center site spun irretrievably into the gutter, Daniel Libeskind received a mysterious e-mail. It was sent from an untraceable
Hotmail account with only a ridiculous, cloak-and-dagger *nom de
procès* affixed: John Smith Smith. The letter began with a pasted-in
excerpt from a short profile of Rafael Viñoly that had run a few
weeks earlier in the *New York Times:*

> [Viñoly's] take on what should happen at ground zero is
> informed by what he says happened to him decades ago in
> Argentina, first when a 1966 coup resulted in raids, and
> murders, at his university, and later when the military, no
> friend to intellectuals, raided his home and suspected him
> of Communist ties because of his Larousse dictionary. To
> them, Larousse was code for La Russie. To him, it was
> time to leave, and with help from Rabbi Marshall Meyer of
> Amnesty International, he did.[16]

"John Smith Smith," less of a native English speaker than the
name would suggest, then offered a refutation of that passage:

> Mr. Viñoly, as you can check, built his curricula working
> with the military regime in Argentina, during the so call
> "Dirty War," he was very much involved with the regime.

His main building was a State TV station (Channel Seven) and some other important building for the regime.

When he left the country, he did so, at request of [a developer] who was trying to design and built, a big lot in the Upper West side, after completed by D. Trump.

He was never in clash with the military on the contrary and of course is a complet lie that Rabbi Marshall Meyer, help him to fled the country.

He left for bussines.

You can check this with Mr. Meyer's wife that up today is living in New York City, or in the files of Amnesty International that has a list of all political exiles.

It is unbelivable that Mr. Viñoly is trying to get simpathy in a dirty way, re-inventing a story so sensitive for Argentinians, Americans and Jews, he might have said that he was also in Aushwitz, for completing the script.

Is a sad thing that Viñoly is using 30,000 dead for getting an edge in the Towers contest.

A friend.

Hope it can help.

Conveniently, the scathing Smith Smith letter was a veritable connect-the-dots for journalists, with whom it was soon shared. And it appeared to be accurate: Rafael Viñoly was not listed on any Amnesty International registry of the oppressed, and Naomi Meyer, the rabbi's widow, had no recollection of her husband having aided Viñoly in his departure from Argentina. As a young man, Viñoly had designed major buildings for the military regime, including a television station and a soccer stadium for the 1978 World Cup, and he had profited, as he himself wrote, from the association. Rafael Viñoly had come to New York for business, with $40,000 in his pocket.

No one contested the details. In fact, the stories relayed by the Libeskinds' tipster had been around for years, getting little traction as Viñoly built up his local and international reputation with projects everywhere from the Bronx to Japan. In a profession whose revered "dean," Philip Johnson, was an admitted Nazi sympathizer—even following the blitz into Poland as a correspondent for a Jew-baiting American newspaper—the threshold for tolerating dalliances with fascism was high. But now at Ground Zero, in this way at least, everything was different: the gravity of the response required architects with the appearance of clean hands, and there was a busy press eagerly looking for dirt.

On the morning of February 26, the day a master plan was chosen, the *Wall Street Journal* ran a damning article that detailed Rafael Viñoly's work for the Argentine junta. "Ground Zero Finalist's Past Draws Questions," the headline read, adding in a subtitle: "Argentine Architect's Work For Junta Emerges as Issue as Trade-Center Plan Gains." In this story, Viñoly backtracked from the refugee implications in the *Times* profile of the month before— "after hearing from concerned Argentines, he realized the article 'could be misconstrued' "[17]—but by then the damage was done. "I lost a lot of friends in that dirty war," Nina Libeskind later said.

The last week of February 2003 began nice enough. On Monday, February 24, Fred Schwartz, Rafael Viñoly, and Daniel Libeskind appeared on *The Oprah Winfrey Show*. The theme of the day was "Why I Love My Job." Eating a cookie baked by the previous guest ("Imagine this warm with some milk. You could hurt yourself"), Oprah segued into a segment taped with the architects at Ground

Zero: "All eyes will be on the ultimate job of the century, which is to rebuild the devastation of the World Trade Center that will not only memorialize the lives lost on September eleventh, but will create inspiration where attackers meant to create nothingness."

Daniel Libeskind spoke first, giving a condensed version of his spiel. "It is quite unbelievable that we are sitting—looking at sixteen acres, not just emptiness, it's sixteen acres of potential," he said with his usual joy and haste. "I came to the city as an immigrant on a boat, when I was thirteen years old, from Poland. My parents were survivors of the Holocaust. But, you know, part of my culture, part of my background is that you have to turn these evil things into something for—into hope." Winfrey narrated a bit, let Viñoly ("the most emotional experience") and Schwartz ("a really kind of mind-blowing experience") have a brief say, then she cut back to give Libeskind the last word: "I love architecture, because as an architect you have to be an optimist. You always have to believe that there is a better future."

Herbert Muschamp notwithstanding, Oprah's pro-Libeskind bias was shared by legions of architecture critics at newspapers across the country (including the ever-influential Ada Louise Huxtable) and by the editorial board of the *New York Times*, which endorsed his scheme. Despite what Daniel Libeskind would later claim, however, "Memory Foundations" was not the choice of the people. Public opinion at that point still leaned toward rebuilding the Twin Towers or, as the popularity of Norman Foster's "kissing" skyscrapers had shown, a close equivalent. Just after the announcement of the finalists, an online poll conducted by NY1, the local all-news cable station, had found that only 13 percent favored the Libeskind plan, while 15 percent supported the Think team, and an unambiguous 70 percent agreed with the statement "I don't like either of these plans."

No wonder the architects were scrambling. But the Libeskinds probably needed to scramble somewhat less, and the Think team a great deal more. Think's World Cultural Center, with its emphasis on not-for-profit venues, was asking New York to consider a novel alternative to developer rapine. "Memory Foundations" was merely putting that wolf in sheep's clothing: beneath the veneer of Libeskind's signature forms, it was every bit as amenable to commerce as the plans proposed by Beyer Blinder Belle. The week before the final decision, under the word "SHAM" in enormous page-one wood, the *New York Post* reported that the Libeskind plan was favored by development officials, and was expected to win, because it could be so easily adapted to the redevelopment's status quo. "Officials see Libeskind's plan as flexible, something they can shape to their needs," William Neuman wrote, before quoting a source close to the discussions. " 'The feeling is that Libeskind is going to be easier to do.' "[18] It didn't hurt, too, that since nearly the moment of its unveiling, the Libeskind plan was the favorite of the governor of the State of New York. As the week of the selection approached, George Pataki's preference was widely reported. But there was still the necessary kabuki of official procedure to endure.

On Tuesday, February 25, the selection committee, chaired by Roland Betts, met at the offices of the LMDC. The warring teams presented—isolated in separate rooms—and for four hours the committee reviewed both plans, assessing changes that had been made in consultation with the Port Authority. Daniel Libeskind, responding to concerns about the stability of the slurry walls, had raised the floor of his sunken zone about halfway up, to thirty feet below street level, where it could act as a brace. This move made room under the memorial site for a tour bus parking lot, something that would later cause the victims' families much pain. It also, crucially, allowed the Port Authority to continue using the site as a train station, since the deeper pit at bedrock would have compromised access to the mouth of the Trans-Hudson tubes. The new Libeskind plan also simplified the facades and shape of the office towers on the site and, by adding an additional fat tower where a shorter, slimmer hotel had stood, brought the square footage, previously at only 7.5 million, back up to Larry Silverstein's full ten.

The Libeskind plan was also, at $330 million, by far the cheaper of the two proposals to develop. The Think plan was first priced at $800 million, then steeply discounted to parity with the competition, but the question of who would pay for its noncommercial centerpiece was never resolved. And the Think towers could not be so easily reengineered in response to the Port Authority's needs. The major issue discovered during the Port's review also involved the train station. Because of the enormous load they had to carry down to bedrock, it was determined that the footings for the two open towers would compromise the placement of the PATH station's tracks and platforms. In solving this problem, the Think team confronted the limitations of their initial idea. To lessen the weight of the towers, they had to make them shorter and narrower, and they specified that they would be built with lighter, stronger, more beautiful, but more expensive stainless steel. The new renderings of the World Cultural Center showed its two reduced towers supported by significantly less structure, some of it now taking the form of a double helix. If anything they looked more skeletal.

Still, bucking conventional wisdom and the well-known feelings of the man in Albany from whom all process power flowed, when Roland Betts convened the LMDC committee that Tuesday in February, its eight members—including representatives of the mayor, the governor, and the Port—decided in favor of the Think plan. "Many people looked at the Viñoly towers as something that would be a magnet, as an inspiration, for the city and the country and so on, that would propel tourism and commercial development," Betts told the *Times*. "That's how I saw it. What I didn't realize was that other people saw it as the skeletons of the original towers and a constant reminder of the attack and of death."[19]

After being informed of their victory, the Think team gathered with its supporters at a loud and lively bistro in Tribeca. They went to bed late that night thinking it was all over. "It was the first time I could sleep after nine eleven," Fred Schwartz remembered.

"There was nothing else I could do. And I had won." He would later claim that his team had not been told beforehand of a second round of deliberations that was to take place the following day. At nine o'clock the next morning, Schwartz said, he and Viñoly were asked to return to the LMDC at noon for a presentation to Mayor Bloomberg and Governor Pataki. Nina Libeskind had been more than aware of that truly decisive meeting. When asked a few weeks earlier, she had ticked it off among the big events on the decision-making calendar: Tuesday, Betts's committee meets; Wednesday, present to the governor; Thursday, a winner is announced.

On the morning of Wednesday, February 26, the *New York Times* reported the news that the selection committee, acting as it had been empowered to do, had chosen Think: "The unexpected decision appeared to set the stage for a showdown today among city and state officials." As it happened, that showdown, when it came, was between Roland Betts and George Pataki, with Michael Bloomberg present but noncombative. In that same article, the *Times* reporter wrote that "several of the committee members believe that the mayor and the governor should pay heed to their preference," going on to quote one of them: "We don't expect anyone to overrule us."[20] That official spoke on condition of anonymity, but, just as there was also only one "anyone" with the power to overrule the committee, there was only one "committee member" in a position to stand up to the governor: Roland Betts. "Roland is the only person that neither the city nor the state . . . wants to mess with," an unnamed source had recently told the *Times*. "Roland is really a power right now."[21]

Since he had risen to prominence at the LMDC after championing the Innovative Design Study, Betts had been a salutary presence. He was fair, he listened with obvious concern, and he seemed to be taking on his political responsibilities as a New Yorker first. It was not unusual to find him lurking in the back of a public hearing, among the process addicts and eccentrics, just to see what was going on. Betts was also more independent than most of his fellow

Pataki-appointed directors, a quality attributable to his character as well as to his connections: his close friendship with George Bush. In addition to being college friends and fraternity brothers, they had been business partners. Betts had included Bush in the group that purchased the Texas Rangers in 1989, a deal that brought that son of fortune his first earned wealth—$15 million on an initial investment of $600,000—and rescued him from a string of failed oil companies where he had been sinking dry wells and muddying his name. Bush's visibility as an owner of that baseball team, and the money he netted in its sale, prepared the ground for his political ascent in Texas.

As Betts's own public profile was rising during the redevelopment, his relationship with Bush was a source of fascination. Betts, who lives on Manhattan's famously left-leaning Upper West Side, is married to a black woman (they met while teaching in Harlem) and he generously supports liberal causes and Democratic candidates. He does not seem to share any of the values of those with whom George Bush was spending his time in Washington, or of those across the country to whom Bush's divisive politics were designed to appeal. But Betts's ties with Bush ran deeper than ideology. A month after the selection of a master plan for Ground Zero, as the war in Iraq began, he traveled to Camp David to support his old friend. "He is just totally immersed," Betts told the *New York Times* a week later, defending Bush from charges that he was a figurehead.[22]

It was that higher source of power that Roland Betts took with him into his final meeting with Governor Pataki and Mayor Bloomberg that Wednesday. The two teams presented once again—Think collecting itself, Daniel Libeskind cruising—and then Betts and the two politicians retired to talk through their differences. Pataki was angry at Betts because of his poorly concealed quote in the morning paper and also, perhaps, because he could not now exercise his gubernatorial fiat in private. All through the ostensibly democratic process, Pataki had called the shots at one remove; this time he would have to rule with no political cover.

Betts made his case for the Think plan. At length he described the towers' innovative engineering to the impatient governor. Then he underscored his views with a scarcely veiled threat: "Well, remember, there are three people in this room—the mayor, the governor, and the White House." That didn't sit well with the most powerful man in the Empire State. "I may just be a hick from Peekskill," Pataki said, "but those towers look like death to me." It went downhill from there; the governor reportedly told Betts, "There's no goddamn way I'm going to build those skeletons!"

Late that afternoon, just before the news broke on the wires, John Whitehead had the honor of calling Daniel Libeskind to tell him he had won the commission of the century. As they had been throughout their campaign for Ground Zero, the Libeskinds were bivouacked at Midtown's posh Four Seasons Hotel. Strangely, they seem to have been the only people in town unaware that, for weeks if not months, they had been favored to win that peculiar design study that had become a competition. In a proposal for his book on the redevelopment—leaked to the *New York Post* and widely circulated among reporters—Libeskind looked back on the moment he and Nina were surprised with the news of their victory:

> When the phone rang that February afternoon, I . . . didn't even notice it. I know I was reading *God, Death and Time*, a book by Emmanuel Levinas, the great philosopher and Talmudist. I had chosen the book in part because, since such heavy stuff requires a lot of concentration, I knew it would provide a happy distraction from the hullabaloo surrounding the announcement of the competition's winner. As Levinas is one of the most important thinkers on ethics, ontology and Judaism after the Holocaust, his work also provides a reminder of the relative importance of the personal successes and failures we spend our lives chasing after and worrying over, and that there are so many larger questions to ask ourselves.

. . . Nina gestured toward the receiver. My first reaction was to pretend I didn't notice her, so that I could
finish a passage. I closed Levinas over my index finger—
intending, I suppose, to get back to him once the fateful
news had been delivered. After telling me it was John
Whitehead and making sure I took the phone, Nina
headed out of the room—she was feeling nauseous. She
had worked harder than anyone on this, and we had spent
almost our entire savings on the submission. Her visceral
reaction seemed to foreshadow the worst, only preparing
me further to hear the bad news.

"Mr. Libeskind, you won," Whitehead said, and it was time for
a triumphant return to the Winter Garden. The next day, in a singular display of bureaucratic unity and implied bonhomie, everyone was shoulder to shoulder in the great glass atrium for another
blowout press event. All the players were there: Madelyn Wils and
most of the LMDC board, sundry officials from the Port Authority, Roland Betts (looking glum), Mayor Bloomberg (indifferent),
and Governor Pataki (elated). Even the guy from the Department
of Housing and Urban Development had come up from Washington to remind everyone from whence the LMDC's dollars flowed.
Shigeru Ban, who had been distancing himself from his work with
the Think team, stood off in a corner.

He wasn't the most unlikely new supporter of the Libeskind
plan. Larry Silverstein made his entrance alongside the draped
model of "Memory Foundations" as it was being rolled in from the
wings. He found Daniel Libeskind, high as a kite, and congratulated him. Silverstein had lost this battle long ago—a genius architect was now ensconced—but he was not conceding the war.
He brought his own architect to Libeskind's coronation; David
Childs sat in the front row, as if eager to get onstage.

As the decision makers gathered in the Winter Garden, members of the Coalition of 9/11 Families were down the hall con-

ducting a quiet protest for a much smaller klatch of reporters. One woman, whose twenty-four-year-old son had died in the south tower, was repulsed by the media-driven chaos of the recent brawling. "This is America's memorial," she said. "Unfortunately it happened in New York." It was a hard stance to fault. People do behave differently elsewhere; had the attack targeted Denver or Seattle or even Chicago, it seems unlikely that it would have devolved quite so quickly or so far into vanity—though Los Angeles could probably have given the city a run for its money in that department. To counter the festive mood, to keep press eyes on the prize, a spokesman was handing out copies of one of the most disturbing documents the process had produced: a plan of the site, prepared by the Fire Department, on which every found body part was mapped as a red dot. The Coalition's intention was to show the density of remains corresponding to each of the tower footprints, which had been promised to them as a memorial but were not yet secured. But the dots spilled copiously from the footprints—the greatest concentrations were between the two—swirling out to cover the whole neighborhood, with outliers on distant blocks that had never seemed a part of the disaster.

The mood was different at the main event. "This is a great day for New York, and I think it is a symbolic day for America," Governor Pataki said. "The Libeskind plan was born out of tragedy but forged in democracy." Then, inevitably, he paraphrased Winston Churchill: "This isn't the end or the beginning of the end, but the end of the beginning." (That sentiment was shared by Fred Schwartz. Sort of. At the opening for an architecture show at the Whitney Museum that night, the Think front man appeared, looking more burdened than usual. A well-wisher approached with condolences. "Don't be sorry, do something!" Schwartz said. "It's not over.") Daniel Libeskind followed the politicians to the stage. He gave an ecstatic version of his stump speech, adding a significant new line that foreshadowed the dramas of the year to come: "Architecture is the art of compromise."

The next morning, the last of a long week, the front page of the *New York Times* recorded the event with an above-the-fold photograph of the architect in his glory, standing in the Winter Garden in front of his already out-of-date model, hands clasped in front of him, chin up, all in black except for the flag pin on his left lapel, smiling an impossibly complete smile, eyeless behind his designer frames: the apotheosis of Daniel Libeskind. The same photograph was shown that night on *Real Time with Bill Maher*, a new cable television vehicle for the comedian pundit who had been run off the air after September 11.

"All right, let me go to the World Trade Center, because this is obviously a big story this week," Bill Maher said. "They had been trying to come up with a design for what's going to take place and grow in the footprints of that horrible tragedy. And they finally have it. Can we see what it looks like? There it is. That's the vision of what the World Trade Center site, Ground Zero, is going to look like. And show the one with the designer. Yes, that's—look at—that's the guy who designed it. He just broke up with Elton John."

Just shy of eighteen months after the attack, and only two months later than originally scheduled by the LMDC, the World Trade Center site had a working master plan. It wasn't pretty, but the stars and the pols had aligned. And the result seemed storybook perfect: the site of America's most murderous event was consigned to the one architect among all the glitterati who had spent the preceding boom years maundering about hope and death and recovery. There was closure of a sort. On February 27 the terror alert level was adjusted again, ticking back down to yellow.

It might have gone up to red. For a day or two the process was at rest—stunned—but the gossip engine soon kicked back in with a vengeance. It was fueled by the Libeskinds' now legion detractors, old and very new, the latter led by supporters of the Think team who were just beginning to nurse their very legitimate grievance over Governor Pataki's eleventh-hour application of force. There were new rumors. Had Daniel Libeskind really emigrated to New York Harbor on a ship, the perfectly named SS *Constitution*? Some said he had flown over from Israel by plane (manifests for the ship were located and checked). Had he been secretly working with SOM all along? Was his accent even real? Everything short of the Raelian clone libel was coughed up to try to discredit the Libeskinds' win. And there was something darker, intimations of a real scandal, passed from mouth to ear in the back of conference rooms, shared by guarded sources in bars. Like "What is the Matrix?" it was a test to identify initiates in a secret brotherhood, and it always took the form of a question: *Who bought Ground Zero?*

For those inclined to believe that taste and merit alone had not shaped the governor's choice, the answer to that question was Ronald Lauder. After the selection of Daniel Libeskind, many people close to the redevelopment, even some at the LMDC, seemed willing to entertain the possibility that this wealthy and politically engaged Republican—son of Estée Lauder—had used his influence to steer George Pataki's preference. Whether there was truth in it or not, that assertion took on a life of its own, becoming as much a part of the Ground Zero landscape as the milling tourists and the pit itself.

The Lauder rumor went public five days after Daniel Libeskind's moment of glory at the Winter Garden. The agent was a man named Steve Anderson, a New Yorker who had built a vast and wonderful Web site on the history of the city's bridges and roads and who, like so many, had transferred his love of the city to concern over the state of affairs at Ground Zero. On the evening of March 4, 2003, Anderson sent a note to a popular Internet forum maintained by the *New York Post*—"Corruption at the WTC site! . . . Certainly, an investigation is called for."—in which he named Lauder, Pataki, and Libeskind.[23] The accusation was soon picked up elsewhere online, as such things are, and what had been traveling only in elite whispers broke into more open alarm.

The roundabout path that the Pataki/Lauder/Libeskind formula had taken to reach that first airing illuminates the shadier, livelier byways of the process that always ran parallel to its officially dictated course. For every board meeting, policy speech, or camera-ready unveiling there were a thousand such lurking transactions: a chance exchange between two people touched by the tragedy, each driven in his own way to affect the built response to it.

Some time after September 11, a Brooklyn resident named Mark O'Rourke sat down to write a poem about the attack. His father was a chief in the New York City Fire Department who had lost countless friends. His brother, a New York City cop, had worked in the recovery operation at the Fresh Kills Landfill. O'Rourke himself was a former army captain who had served in Kuwait and Saudi Arabia in the mid-1990s. In addition to the friends he had lost on September 11, one of his soldiers had been killed in the 1998 al Qaeda truck bombing of the United States embassy in Nairobi.

For the subject of his poem, "I Will Wait," O'Rourke chose that lone New York City monument to American values, the Statue of Liberty, describing the attack in eleven stanzas from the statue's point of view. It began:

> Before your noble ascent, I waited to glimpse
> your towers above the majestic blue.
> It was '72 when I welcomed you.

On February 6, 2003, O'Rourke sent an e-mail to Herbert Muschamp with the poem attached. He was moved to contact Muschamp, who that very day had established himself as the most vociferous supporter of the Think scheme, because he felt that the design reflected "the sentiment and resonance" of his poem. Muschamp responded eight minutes later—"It is the most wonderful letter I have ever received"—and the two continued their correspondence. Soon the veteran-poet wrote again, asking Muschamp if he would forward the poem to the Think team: "I truly believe that . . . the poem . . . speak[s] to the mystical and harmonizing qualities of the Think project design: 'Celestial blue beams paid quiet tribute to precious lives lost.' " Again, Muschamp replied within minutes, offering to share the poem with Roland Betts.

Later that month, as Daniel Libeskind's triumph was being announced in the crawl at the bottom of every cable news screen, O'Rourke wrote Muschamp a third time. He was bereft: "I hope the leaders who chose this design really accorded the time and attention that this process and these two final designs warranted." The next day, after attending the gala for Libeskind at the Winter Garden, Muschamp sent a reply in which he credited Libeskind's selection to Ronald Lauder's influence with Pataki. O'Rourke sent that e-mail to four friends, one of whom, Steve Anderson, soon posted the news online. "Laudergate" was born.

For those who wanted to find a connection between George Pataki and the Libeskinds, Ron Lauder was the shortest distance linking them: he knew both parties and he gave a lot of money to at least one of them. Pushing the story, partisans made the rounds—*Just follow the money . . . Don't any of you guys want to win a Pulitzer?*—and at one point or another, nearly every reporter on the beat took some time to look into it. There wasn't much to see. The presumably covert nature of the transfer, if there had been one, obviated the possibility of any direct evidence. And the scale of the money known to have openly changed hands made it hard to follow in any Deep Throat sense. The cosmetics heir—also a former ambassador to Austria, a major philanthropist for Jewish causes, and an important collector of modern art—had donated $150,000 to the Republican National Committee in early October

2002, as the election for governor approached and the Innovative Design Study got under way. But Lauder had made comparable contributions in each of the preceding five years (offset by his brother, Leonard, who sometimes matched him dollar for dollar with gifts to Democrats). Only one donation recorded in the public campaign finance records raised any eyebrows. On September 26, 2002—the day Daniel Libeskind was announced as a participant in the Innovative Design Study—Ron Lauder and his wife gave $58,000 to the Friends of Pataki.

That was the closest thing to a smoking checkbook. And it wasn't much. But there were enough personal connections to keep the pay-for-play rumor alive. The governor's wife, Libby Pataki, worked as a consultant for Ron Lauder. And Ron Lauder had worked for Pataki. In the late 1990s, the governor had appointed him to lead a task force to determine which assets of New York State might be privatized. One result of that committee's work was the push to privatize the World Trade Center.

The Libeskinds also had ties to Lauder, however tenuous. The woman Nina called her best friend, Daniella Luxembourg, was married to an architect who had designed a house for Ron Lauder and his wife in Tel Aviv, and she was close to Lauder herself. Luxembourg, a well-established art dealer at a boutique auction house, had worked for many years with Lauder in the acquisition of his substantial collection. There were also older ties. Daniel Libeskind and Ron Lauder both went to high school at Bronx Science, four years apart, and Libeskind's sister, Annette, had been class secretary the year Lauder was the equivalent of class president. She confirmed that the families had known each other since the 1960s. Yet as late as the winter of 2004 Libeskind continued telling reporters that the two had rarely met. Nevertheless, there was widespread unsubstantiated speculation that Lauder had at least funded the Libeskinds during the crucial, expensive months of the Innovative Design Study, when they were working nearly *gratis* for the LMDC while conducting their campaign to secure the commission—at one point paying fees to two public relations firms—from their command post at the pricey Four Seasons Hotel. Prior to the selection of the Libeskinds' master plan, a close source said Daniel and Nina had quietly retained a lobbyist in Washington for $15,000 a week; rumormongers reflexively invoked Ron Lauder's support, though the Libeskinds strongly denied it.

These stories would probably not have gotten the traction they did were it not for George Pataki's near-instant devotion to the plan. Pataki, the self-described "hick from Peekskill," is no architecture aficionado, and even initiates found it difficult to decipher "Memory Foundations" when it was first presented. The dense stand of angular buildings and one decorative memorial feature—the "Matrix of Heroes," lines inscribed in the pavement to record the arrival of responding fire companies—combined to give images of the design an agitated quality that obscured Daniel Libeskind's flag-waving deployment of American motifs. Had he not spoken of it so effectively, the plan would have been dead on arrival.

Something had to account for the governor warming so quickly to such an avant-garde idea, but his attraction can be explained without recourse to conspiracy. Early on, Pataki had gotten some help in seeing the straightforward patriotic symbols hiding just beneath Libeskind's zigzags. A few days after the Innovative Design Study debut in December, the governor's people called the LMDC and said he was coming down to view the plans. He had been shown a PowerPoint presentation before the unveilings, but he wanted to see the exhibition of all the work mounted in the Winter Garden. It was a museum-quality installation, with interviews of the architects on plasma screens, wall-size renderings, and many expensive models. To accommodate their three proposals, the Think team had built an extravaganza with a concealed robotic arm. At the touch of a button, the mechanism would pop a model of each scheme up through a Ground Zero–shaped hole.

Pataki arrived that day with a sizable entourage of his closest associates, including Ed Hayes, a celebrity attorney (Andy Warhol, Robert De Niro, Puff Daddy) and bona fide architecture buff who had also been the future governor's law school roommate. Andrew Winters, then the number two in the LMDC's planning department, walked Pataki through the show. For forty-five minutes the group looked at the plans, giving equal time to each. When he paused at Norman Foster's towers, Pataki said they looked like the World Trade Center, adding, "but I never liked the World Trade Center."

To everyone's surprise, the governor wanted to go around again. This time, he stopped cold in front of the drawings and models depicting the Libeskind plan. Ed Hayes was at his side, singing it, pointing out its politically potent features: the wall that meant democracy, the 1,776-foot tower, the generous amount of space set aside for a memorial within the pit. The governor stood there, nodding; he had seen past the architecture. At that point, George Pataki's earlier pronouncement on the footprints— "They will always be a permanent and lasting memorial to those we lost"—was still his only specific comment on the future shape of the site. More than any of the other designs, "Memory Foundations" put the footprints, and the families, first. It was also the only one that made the site a shrine to patriotism. And Daniel Libeskind had already shown he could perform. Within weeks of that tour, Ed Hayes was advising the Libeskinds. The governor had made up his mind. He would give his support to the scrappy power couple, fresh off the plane from Berlin. And once it was given, it protected them well, right up until the day it was taken away.

10

SHOW AND TELL

WITH THE commission in hand, at the height of his influence in the process, Daniel Libeskind made the rounds. Even with the governor's backing, he needed to shore up support. And despite the pervasive labeling of "Memory Foundations"—"The Wedge of Light," "1776"—the intricate plan required its author's interpretation. So in the spring of 2003, Libeskind began a goodwill tour of the city's boardrooms, ballrooms, and dining rooms—speaking, inspiring, and pressing the flesh: a retail politician at full tilt.

That's how he found himself on the morning of May 8, eating a light breakfast at one of Manhattan's storied Jewish delicatessens, sandwiched between former Mayor Ed Koch, representing the governor, and Fyvush Finkel, an actor and one of the few living heroes of the Yiddish stage. When they had finished their bread and tea, the three men—joined by Nina Libeskind and representatives of the Folksbiene Yiddish Theatre—were led outside to the corner of Second Avenue and Tenth Street, where a klezmer band, a small pack of reporters, and all the trappings of a minor civic moment were waiting. That day, Daniel Libeskind was going to get his star added to the Yiddish Theatre Walk of Fame.

Libeskind had grown up speaking Yiddish in Poland, in Israel, and even after moving to New York. As a young man, he spent his summers in the Catskills at a Yiddish-friendly camp for children of Holocaust survivors, where he had worked as an arts-and-crafts counselor and had met his wife-to-be. But he was never an actor,

and his inclusion in the Walk of Fame was an exception that bene-
fited all parties: it allowed the theater company to leverage publicity off of the architect's newfound fame—he was also an
attraction at its fund-raiser a few months later—and it gave Libeskind another opportunity to sell the project as he worked to wed
himself to his newfound hometown.

"I think that what is happening at Ground Zero, what is happening with rebuilding that place, with the memory that it represents, the heroes that perished on that day, New Yorkers who went
to work that day, who were just being human beings, *menschen*,
what does that mean for us for the future?" Libeskind asked,
standing at a microphone, protected from a light rain by the deli's
awning as he accepted the honor.

> New York is an optimistic city, a city second to none. It's
> the capital not only of finance, it's the capital of emotions,
> of creativity, of intellect! I think those two things to-
> gether really form a body, and I think that's what the Yid-
> dish theater is, and I can tell you it's not just an
> intellectual desire to continue Yiddish, for Yiddish to
> flourish, but it's an emotional and human desire, because
> that's the air that I breathe and it's certainly part of the
> culture and it's part of the memory and I think when we
> speak Yiddish we speak to the voices—those unheard
> voices—who are with us here today and are part of our
> mission to take the legacy to a new generation of Yiddish
> speakers, and to offer Yiddish to all people, because I think
> people love it. It's a language of joy, and it's a language
> that, just like New York, speaks of the victory of life over
> all the events. So, thank you very much.

That gift for merging the interests of his audience with the de-
sired reading of his plan—"Life victorious!"—served Libeskind

well during this period of accelerated salesmanship to any and every group that might afford him, and the project, political traction. At the Plaza Hotel, he charmed the four hundred–plus business leaders gathered under the auspices of the Association for a Better New York—Manhattan's de facto Chamber of Commerce—introducing his plan, retelling his arrival story, and riffing passionately about freedom, freedom, freedom. He tamed a hostile crowd at a Community Board 1 meeting in Tribeca. One man there, concerned about the shadows to be cast by Libeskind's 1,776-foot spire, had asked why the architect couldn't pick another, lower symbolic height: 1,492 feet, say, or 1,066? Nina Libeskind, standing at her husband's side, snapping her gum like a pro, touched his arm, and he managed a delayed laugh. In front of the community board, in a neighborhood heavy with intellectual parents, the erudite architect cited Walt Whitman and talked about parks. Speaking to an association of downtown businessmen in a hotel near Ground Zero on the morning after the "shock and awe" bombing of Baghdad had begun, Libeskind used his persuasive ways to different ends. "To be here at this moment," he said, was another reminder that "there is no greater act of optimism" than building. Not long before he had rung the bell to begin the trading day at the American Stock Exchange.

At each stop Libeskind found a way to personalize his attachment to the city, the site, and the job ahead. When a downtown resident made a plea that the architect not forget her isolated neighborhood to the south of the site, he responded that he never could: his father had worked for many years in a printing plant on a nearby street, so naturally he was more than aware of the particular psycho-geography of that district. At another event, confronted by one of the legions of vocal Twin Towers fans, Libeskind claimed to share the love of those buildings, telling a story about his brother-in-law, a long-serving Port Authority engineer who had worked testing materials during the construction of the World

Trade Center. Facing a crowd of hardened, up-by-their-bootstraps businessmen, he had warmed them up with a few kind words for the Bronx.

The day after his sidewalk star was unveiled on Second Avenue, Daniel Libeskind (class of '65) went back to his old high school, Bronx Science. He was being honored as "Principal for a Day"; his duties included meeting with faculty and a group of architecture students, and he delivered his full stump speech, with slides, at an all-school assembly. At the beginning of the tour, the real principal pulled out Libeskind's file and read aloud an autobiographical essay she had found there. "I was surprised to see the amount of freedom in the United States," the young Libeskind had written of his recent immigration. "It had by far exceeded my expectations, but I still realized that if this freedom is to continue, the public must take a more active interest in governance."

Later, Libeskind gave some unusually frank answers to a set of questions posed by a girl reporting for the student newspaper. Asked about the experience of "working on a project that has so much significance for so many people," Libeskind replied:

> Well it's a very special process. It's really a project without precedence because it has so many stakeholders and people with different interests, and so many cynics and skeptics who think nothing good will ever come out from that—sort of that conflict that's there. It's not really easy, but certainly if I didn't believe that something integral will emerge from it I wouldn't be involved in this. So, yeah, it's a process of negotiations too. Most people think that negotiations only take place in politics, but architecture is the art of compromise. Because you can't just say, "I like this. I want to build this," or somebody says, "Build me this," or an investor says, "Give me this." The Port Authority tells me, "Give me this kind of infrastructure here!" The LMDC says, "No, give me this kind of infra-

structure!" You have to reconcile these interests. And of course an architect is responsible for the civic result.

Did he think the project might come out differently from how he planned it?

> Put it this way: that's what toughens a project, the limits, it's what makes a project better. Because it is so clarified what the issues are, the limitations make it more creative. All great architects are limited.

At the end the student asked Libeskind if his background—"coming out of the Holocaust"—made him "more sensitive to issues of memory and remembering," giving him a special advantage at Ground Zero. The man a critic had recently called "a human Yahrzeit candle" caught that one on the bounce: "I don't think of the future as just something based on the past, as something not really having kind of an open horizon." Libeskind also toured the school's Holocaust museum, a surprisingly rich collection of images and artifacts housed in a small room off the library. His old biology teacher, a survivor herself, walked him through with some student caretakers while she talked of her experience at Auschwitz.

At such moments, Daniel Libeskind seemed like the only possible choice of architect for the World Trade Center site. As he stood in the little museum, a patient, practiced listener to such things, it was as if the whole bureaucratic structure of the redevelopment were paying its kindred respects, cleansing itself, atoning for whatever nastiness it had generated in its commemoration of mass death. And though they soon tired of Libeskind's rhetoric, the political powers knew they needed it. His ability to mask the ugliness of the process was so important to the LMDC, to the redevelopment as a whole, that the architect's role as a humanitarian ambassador was spelled out in a rider to his first contract. "Mr.

Libeskind has proved to be an effective spokesman on behalf of this project, and we believe it is essential that he be available and accessible to as many constituent groups as possible," the agreement read, going on to list those with whom he was required to speak at official request: "Government leaders, public agencies, civic and professional groups, advocacy groups . . . community boards, public 'town hall' meetings, professional forums . . . newspapers, TV, radio, magazines and internet." In short, his job, per this unusual amendment to LMDC contract no. A40327, was to "increase public understanding of the work and to build broad-based support."

And so the world's leading architect of recovery found himself on Second Avenue, the official human face of Ground Zero—as ever smiling, his arms crossed and his chin in one hand, dressed in black but for the red-white-and-blue enamel of his lapel pin—dwarfed by the enormous Ed Koch, as Fyvush Finkel, a comedian as well as an actor, entertained the small street corner crowd with an off-color joke:

> So this woman goes into a bar and she's obviously in search of some male accompaniment and she happens to meet three guys at the bar but they all have a problem—they're all stutterers. So she goes up to the guys and she says, "What's your name?" And the first guy says, "Ph-ph-ph-phil." And she goes up to the next guy and she says, "What's your name?" And he says, "D-d-d-daniel." She goes to the third guy and says, "What's your name?" He says, "R-r-r-robert." She says, "Listen, guys, I got something for you. I'm going to cure you. A guy that can answer one of my questions without stuttering can have his way with me." And she was a gorgeous, gorgeous woman. So she asked the first guy, "Where are you from?" He says, "Ph-ph-philadelphia." She asks the second guy. He says,

"T-t-t-texas." She says, "You guys are in bad shape. What about you?" she asks the third guy. He says, "Miami." You're in! Well, they have a great time. And immediately thereafter he says, "B-b-b-beach."

It's almost allegory. The Daniel Libeskind roadshow was so important because his architecture alone could not make itself understood. Like most modern civic buildings, divorced from the certainties of the classical canon, they proudly wore their novel attempts at communication—here a coat of slashing lines and shards. But despite their symbolic pretensions and heavy-handed labels, the forms themselves said nothing. New Yorkers and the greater audience beyond the city had been searching for an architecture that would speak of what had taken place at the site, what it all meant, and, again and again, architects had promised that such a language could be found. To a remarkable degree, the process was driven by that search. You could see it in the popularity of the Max Protetch show, in the endless eurekas of the amateur architects, in the civic raspberry that greeted the six Beyer Blinder Belle plans, blindsided for their failure to give the public shelter for its grief. You could see it in the resulting calls for innovation that delivered Daniel Libeskind to the scene. But when by twists and turns the city at last got its star-brand monumental symbols, when its political leaders had gotten into bed with genius, the chosen design turned out to be more of the same: without interpretation in plain English, without captions, without the hint of its title, "Memory Foundations" was silent. Or, at best, stuttering.

More than any other prominent architect, Daniel Libeskind had, in the preceding years, staked his name on creating architecture that could speak to people directly, as writing can. "Architecture is a communicative art," he wrote in a newspaper article, beginning a belabored explanation of the meaning of the typically difficult war museum he had just completed in Manchester,

England. "All too often, however, architecture is seen as mute," he continued. "Buildings are understood as disposable consumer items whose sole fate is to disappear with their use."[1]

Though Libeskind often spoke of creating a living monumental architecture—one that could tell bracing, tragic, hopeful stories—he had yet to achieve it convincingly in a building. His Felix Nussbaum Museum, in Osnabrück, Germany, the first he completed, was a mess of narrow, ramping halls and awkward, prow-ended galleries meant to evoke the work of the painter, who was killed in the Holocaust. To Libeskind it was "The Museum Without Exit," a composition that "retreats to form a background of hope" for the existing art museum to which it was attached. Because the angles of the building followed certain mystical alignments on the site—with a neighboring villa that had housed a Nazi headquarters, with an excavated Roman bridge—Libeskind felt it would mean more than the sum of its concrete, glass, and cinder blocks. The Nussbaum Museum "transmits the mysterious irreversibility of time and destiny,"[2] he wrote in 1997, defining the building a year before its completion might invite other views.

His Jewish Museum in Berlin came much closer to communication. Though its form was generated by the same voodoo of crisscrossing lines that Libeskind had used in Osnabrück—and that he would later import to Ground Zero—many visitors came away from the building, even before the exhibitions were installed, claiming that it elicited emotion. "I wasn't skeptical, but until you do it, it's not done," Frank Gehry said after he first saw the museum in the summer of 1998. A "kid from the office" had initially taken him through it in the wrong direction, leaving Gehry to mistake the six centerpiece voids for "shafts in a New York tenement." But once he was oriented in the museum he was impressed by the way it expressed "anger." That anger, Gehry said, was visible in the lightning-bolt path of the long building across its site, in the erratic diagonals of its more than one thousand slit windows, and in the presence of the empty shafts that interrupt the museum's crooked galleries. "Libeskind expressed an emotion with a building," Gehry said, "and that is the most difficult thing to do."

High praise, but Gehry was judging the Jewish Museum according to his own aspirations in his own work. Sober beyond what the acid-trip convolutions of his architecture might suggest, Gehry had set a realistic goal for himself: to communicate a sense, a feeling—but not meaning—through the inert stuff of building. Libeskind, by contrast, was attempting to apply to the design of real buildings the same haunted intellectualism found in an impenetrably dense series of line drawings of nightmare geometries—he called them "Micromegas"—that had propelled him to notoriety years before he had begun to build. And through those means he aimed to cajole stubborn materials to expound universal truths. Libeskind's goal was not that the Jewish Museum should generate emotion but that it should be a repository of epic meanings.

As Libeskind explained in the statement that accompanied his submission to the museum competition, the building's form was derived from four ideas. First, responding to a feeling that "the physical trace of Berlin was not the only trace, but rather that there was an invisible matrix or anamnesis of connections" between Germans and Jews, Libeskind constructed "an irrational matrix in the form of intertwining triangles which would yield some reference to the emblematics of a compressed and distorted star: the yellow star that was frequently worn on this very site." Plotted on the map of Berlin, this "matrix" connected the homes of Jewish artists, poets, and composers to the addresses of their German counterparts, creating, Libeskind wrote, "a cultural constellation of Universal History." Through a series of graphic manipulations, this pattern became the basis for the geometry of the museum's windows.

The second inspiration was Arnold Schoenberg's unfinished opera *Moses and Aaron*. Libeskind wrote that he was drawn to it because it ends in spoken words, not singing, so "one can understand very well the missing word which is uttered by Moses, the call for

the Word." In the museum building, this idea became associated
with the play of absence represented by the periodic interruption
of the galleries by empty shafts. The third idea related to Libeskind's research in the Gedenkbuch, an alphabetical list of the
names of Holocaust victims with the times and places of their
deaths. He cataloged the variations on the name "Berliner," a common German Jewish name. Reproductions of those lists were applied to various study models over the years, usually on the inside
walls of the shafts, where they telegraphed that those six moments of emptiness in the museum were meant to correspond to
the Holocaust's missing six million. The final idea, reflected in the
number of sections in the museum's zigzag plan, came from Walter
Benjamin's *One-Way Street*, a collection of vignette fantasias on life
in Berlin before World War II. Sixty vignettes, sixty kinks in the
plan; certainly an attentive visitor would see the connection.

For Libeskind's design of a Jewish center and museum in San
Francisco, he subjected the Hebrew letters *chet* and *yud*, which form
the word *chai*—life—to a series of devious geometric contortions.
Though unrecognizable in the spaces they formed, the shape of
the letters was meant to charge the construction from within, like
a battery or a relic. "That whole geometry is generated in order to
experience in space the experience of the letter," Libeskind said in
1998. "It's about the substance of the letters—What are the letters of life?—because life is in those letters also."[3]

At the Jewish Museum in Berlin, Libeskind had a similarly un-
shakable faith that the hidden meanings carried into the building
by his four form-giving precepts would create spaces through
which those meanings could be read. Interviewed a few months before the museum's completion, he offered the reactions of its
builders as proof. "It doesn't matter" that they didn't know about
his various generative moves, Libeskind said. "The workers have
told me: They have no idea what they are building. Nobody told
them anything. They don't even know about the Jewish Museum.
But they look and they tell me things, and it's clear that the build-

ing has its own life. And it communicates." One of the workers was so moved by the undertaking that he surreptitiously stenciled his own contribution in red ink on a concrete wall at the bottom of one of the symbolic shafts. It was a common saying: "When the Jews start leaving, a city's in trouble." Of course it was decided the graffiti should stay; it was the permanent caption the cryptic building needed.

Daniel Libeskind later acknowledged that his esoterica had served another, more mundane function. The museum building's unusual forms, and the rich rhetoric that enlivened them, had helped to win over Berlin's politicians and citizens, easing the project's passage through the city's cultural minefields. "If this building had been a box it would never have been built," he said. "Because nobody would have the money to build a box. But because the building communicated to them through these issues of the void or whatever, it sparked their own involvement. And I think that's important for any project: unless one gets the involvement of the public, what is the use of doing it?"

Libeskind's master plan for the World Trade Center site relied on all the same ploys. The ostensibly meaningful shapes returned. Generating lines—the "Matrix of Heroes" and the angles of the sun that defined the "Wedge of Light"—were drawn again to help mold those shapes. The numbers—in Berlin the six shafts and the sixty segments, in New York 1776—were redeployed. The void, a catchall for scattershot meanings, was repeated in the "Pit". And, of course, as on the Lindenstrasse, an ensorceling veil of language was cast over Ground Zero to bridge the great gap between form and message.

Language was so central to Libeskind's efforts at the World Trade Center site that he literally refused to discuss the project's architectural basics. Why was his Downtown Grand Central rendered as a glass basket hemmed willy-nilly by canted columns? Why was the proposed "Museum at the Edge of Hope" clad with red or pink polygons, no two the same? Why was a tower evoking the birth of the United States laced with steel at erratic angles, seeming to serve some master other than gravity? How would any of these things, alone or in aggregate, communicate the plan's elaborate narratives? When pressed on these matters in an interview, the architect retreated to his stock phrases about memory and democracy and freedom. As it turned out, that scarcely mattered; most of Libeskind's architectural ideas failed to live long enough to receive serious criticism. Soon after its selection, the plan was subjected to a much more rigorous review—by New York City.

Despite all his time on the stump, despite Nina Libeskind's backdoor politicking, "Memory Foundations" could not withstand the assaults it would have to endure to stay whole—from Larry Silverstein, working to shape the buildings to his needs; from the Port Authority, going its own way with the construction of the rail station; from the ever-growing pool of detractors; from the press. Though that last group gave his actual architecture a pass—reading it back to the public most often in variations of the architect's words—as Libeskind toured the city, selling, reporters began to abet the dismantling of his design by testing the rhetoric against reality, by parsing the personality of the man who had used his personality as a credential.

Sixty-four days after Daniel Libeskind's apotheosis, his unraveling commenced. It began with the "Wedge of Light." While presenting his plan at the Winter Garden, Libeskind had claimed that "between the hours of eight forty-six a.m., when the first airplane hit, and ten twenty-eight a.m., when the second tower collapsed, the sun will shine without shadow" in the plaza to be formed by two angled buildings on Fulton Street—"a perpetual tribute to altruism and courage." At the many public events thereafter, Libeskind repeated variations on the formula; indeed, those very words were written large on a panel in an ongoing exhibition in the Winter Garden.

Again, because of the speed of events, no reporters had

stopped to dissect Libeskind's claims. But Eli Attia, a local architect and critic of "Memory Foundations" as well as the process as
a whole (who was also, naturally, pushing a plan of his own), had
taken the time to build a computer model that instantly put the lie
to the theatrics. Attia found that the Wedge would never be
bathed in light: at 8:46 each September 11, 40 percent of it would
be in shadow; at 10:28 it would be 99 percent dark. At those moments and in between, there would be only stray patches of direct
sun. While the results of Attia's study were reported in the *New
York Times* under the headline "Shadows to Fall, Literally, Over
9/11 'Wedge of Light,'" the news was hardly shocking: there were
ten blocks of skyscrapers between the site and the nearest open
sky to the east. It must have pleased Attia that a main source of
the inconvenient shadows would be the black glass tower of the
Millenium Hotel, right at the rim of Ground Zero, a building he
had designed.[4]

The exposure of the "Wedge of Light" fiction was the architectural equivalent of a campaign trail bimbo eruption, and the
Libeskinds reacted like red-faced candidates caught with their
pants down. They spun vigorously, digging themselves in deeper
as they tried out a series of ever more fatuous excuses. At first,
Daniel Libeskind claimed that the intention had been to reflect
light back into the plaza from the adjacent buildings' glass facades.
"I'm a little perplexed by the simplemindedness" of Attia's calculations, he said in the *Times*. "If you think of the sun being a ball of
fire, only at Stonehenge could you get . . . straight lines of light."
However, as Libeskind surely knows, the sun's rays reach us as parallel lines; all architectural light studies are premised on this fact.
And even had reflection been intended—and this was the first
mention of the word—a facade in line with the sun at a given moment presents no surface against which its light can reflect, whether
it is considered a ball of fire, a point of fire, or a great seething
chariot of fire filling the sky. Shortly after the story broke, Nina
chimed in that Eli Attia had failed to consider daylight savings

time. This only meant that darkness would fall one hour earlier in a space intended to celebrate heroism with light. Daniel Libeskind's words had become fatally detached from his forms.

There was an audible civic scoff, and the "Wedge of Light"— the organizing idea for about half the site plan—was soon being called the "Wedge of Shade," the "Wedge of Night," the "Wedge of Lies." At a press conference, a reporter shouted a question about it to Governor Pataki. "I'll have to talk with my astronomer first," he answered with a smile. The Libeskinds' patron had a personal interest in quelling the teapot tempest. Beyond the necessity of keeping his legacy on track, the governor had recently repeated Libeskind's "shine without shadow" line verbatim in a major speech on the future of Lower Manhattan. Because of the very public way he had chosen "Memory Foundations," Pataki was bound to the plan, and to the slippery words around it. As criticism swelled, the LMDC countered with lulling statements. But some there were not surprised by the discoveries. The bureaucrats may not have thought to vet that example of architectural eyewash that had escaped the galleries and lecture halls and was ready to imprint itself on the city; if they had doubts, they would not have let Libeskind's words merge with the governor's. But the LMDC's planning department knew all along that the "Wedge of Light" could not function as described. It formed a nice enough public plaza, a site for commerce; it served as a forecourt to the train station and opened sensibly to allow commuters to flow east along two cross streets. Certainly that was enough. As one LMDC planner later said of Libeskind's light, "We thought it was metaphor."

Daniel Libeskind's way with metaphor would soon get him into more hot water. In what would become a steady drubbing, eroding the architect's credibility when he needed it most, Wedgegate gave way to Versegate. The *New York Post*, the city's foremost vehicle for Libeskind bashing, had early on attacked the architect as an artsy-fartsy carpetbagger. Steve Cuozzo, the paper's acerbic real estate columnist, had inveighed weekly against the commercial viability of "Memory Foundations" (he was also the first writer to point out its resemblance, beneath the skin, to several of the dreaded Beyer Blinder Belle plans). Page Six—the *Post*'s must-read gossip sheet—had previously called the architect out for everything from his funny glasses to his repeated accounts of being hailed as a savior daily on the streets of Manhattan. One month after the flap over the "Wedge of Light," Page Six "unearthed" a copy of *Fishing From the Pavement*, a collection of Libeskind's poetry, published in 1997.[5] It provided the *Post* with a bottomless reservoir of new calumnies.

The item on Page Six—"Ground Zero 'poet' exposed"—quoted two stanzas from Libeskind's "Miniature Cages: for Angels"—one perhaps critical of American media culture, the other, referencing Marcel Proust, completely eluding comprehension. The *Post*'s finds also included references to "the bishop's phallic culm," a lesbian's "sex Torah," and a man's "third leg dreaming of crawling inside any woman's rib cage." These were picked up by other news outlets and republished all over the world. Soon after, Deroy Murdock, a *Post* columnist and prominent advocate for reconstructing the Twin Towers, decried various lines within the poems that seemed to slander Christianity, Judaism, and Islam ("Moslems resent that neither Allah nor the scent of a future B.C. can be resurrected by gently pulling the nose's hard ridge with a somber gesture of the hand—the same one they use to launch little paper airplanes in the market"). Then he argued for tossing "the nutty architect" off the job. "Given Libeskind's jarring literature, tasteless self-promotion and the absence of affection for his work, the LMDC should hand him a severance check and let WTC leaseholder Larry Silverstein rebuild," Murdock wrote. "Until then, Americans should live by these words of wisdom from the mind of Daniel Libeskind: 'If you could delay the cat from joining a zero laterally with itself, you might be the last to die.' "[7]

In a way, *Fishing From the Pavement* is a brave book; in it, the architect had turned his intellect inside out and dumped its ferment raw on the page. More than anything, his poems, written some two decades before they were published, clearly revealed to his new constituency the nature of the old Danny: the enigma-loving eccentric who had thrived in the closed world of academic architecture, the "cherubic picador, peaceful survivor of Armageddon's circle" (as he wrote in one poem) who had not troubled himself with clarity, or construction, before his wife had begun urging him to "architect the people." Read as a whole, the poems have a rigor that would be impossible without some underlying purpose. But like the play on "time and destiny" in the Nussbaum Museum in Osnabrück, like the multiplexed meanings of the Jewish Museum in Berlin, like the thin scrim of pathos and patriotism over his plan for Ground Zero, Libeskind's poems showed his blind trust in the tenacity of intention. As with his architecture, if there were meaning in those verses, without his full-time interpretation it was lost.

Live by the press, die by the press. As the Libeskinds' collaborator Gary Hack pointed out so clearly, much of the team's early success had resulted from its efforts to control the way "Memory Foundations" was defined by the media. But now the architect himself was being questioned. With Daniel Libeskind's persona colored by his poetry, with his very words in doubt after the revelations about the Wedge, no amount of spin—no quick "skeletons" attack—could position him again as the immigrant hero, come to the site of the nation's peril to pave it over with pain-erasing symbols. It didn't help that just as the *Post* published his poems, Libeskind was tied up with the glitzy debut of a German luxury sedan. Months earlier, during the media wars surrounding his selection, he had agreed to take part in a promotion for the new Audi 8—"Eight Individuals Who Never Follow"—and he had been photographed for an advertising insert. It appeared in a half dozen widely read glossies in June. Libeskind's page, nestled among those of seven other brainy celebrities, showed him standing in a large cardboard box, with only his cowboy-booted feet and his elaborately bespectacled head sticking out, the look on his face somewhere between beatific and smug.

As the PR tide was turning, the Libeskinds made themselves available to some of the more sympathetic reporters around town, but there was little they could do to counter the new memes. And Nina knew it. The attacks in the papers were very much bothering her in the summer of 2003. Worse, they were beginning to rattle her husband. The architect of Ground Zero, a man who had successfully represented himself as inspirational, almost saintly, was not happy to be redefined by the press as a kooky fabulist. But the most immediate problem was a shift in Libeskind's demeanor. His easy effusion of joy—so important that its use had been defined by contract—was now coming less reliably. At public events, Libeskind often appeared more serious, even distraught; sometimes he even forgot to smile. That was big trouble, and it was not lost on his overseers. "Notwithstanding what the plan is, it's that passion that keeps him at the table," Kevin Rampe, the LMDC president, said. "It's what got him to the table, and it's what keeps him there."

Daniel Libeskind's catalytic early passion would be missed, but the Libeskind roadshow had served its purpose: the process players had gotten from it what they needed most, a reprieve from public squawking. As Libeskind had been providing cover with his sermons, the LMDC and the Port Authority had largely smoothed over their differences with Larry Silverstein: the developer had agreed to build—with his own architects—along Libeskind's lines. But the three parties had rallied not around the specific features of "Memory Foundations" but the default program of the site and the inevitable distributions of use first laid down by Beyer Blinder Belle.

With Silverstein fully ensconced and Libeskind wounded, the way was clear for the master plan to be stripped of its bells and whistles. The working vision of Ground Zero would return again to the old givens: the ten million square feet of office space promised in Silverstein's lease; the sea of retail promised in Westfield's; the crisscrossing lines of the partially restored street grid; the prominent placement of a big train station, a theater, and a museum; the preservation of the footprints as a memorial. All of these things had become sacrosanct long before Libeskind arrived to ornament them; part of his genius in getting the job had been to let the process assumptions rest. "Architecture is the art of compromise," he had said as he explained his plan to the city. But after it had made its many compromises, the only surviving symbolic feature of that plan would be its most simplistic, its least architectural, and its most useful to wartime politicians—a single number, or dimension, or idea: 1776.

11

THE ART OF THE POSSIBLE

IN ALL the deliberations over the Innovative Design Study, in the shifting resolutions that followed, one development affected the process more than the charms of all the world's charming architects combined: the Republican National Committee's decision to stage its 2004 presidential convention in Manhattan. The Democrats had also considered nominating their candidate in New York—the advantages of gathering near the site of America's darkest and finest hour were not lost on them—but the party's search committee worried they would not get sufficient support in a city and a state run by Republicans. So the Democrats went to friendly Boston, a place untouched by resonant tragedy, and the potential public relations coup was left to, or rather won by, the GOP.

Weeks after the Republicans' decision, the LMDC shifted gears, opting to choose only one of the Innovative Design plans rather than embarking on the time-consuming task of distilling the highlights and mapping a synthesis, as had been originally intended, onto an alternate scheme prepared by the Port Authority. That alone could have taken a year, a year the process no longer had to burn. The specter of the convention, scheduled to coincide with the third anniversary of the attack, scrambled the dynamics of the redevelopment. As the mayoral and gubernatorial elections had done earlier, it sped up the clock. It also linked the construction of an appropriate symbolic architecture at Ground Zero even more closely to the national agenda. And it explained just why Governor Pataki came roaring back into the game.

Pataki's new interest was first revealed in his last-minute maneuver to give the "commission of the century" to Daniel Libeskind, overruling Roland Betts and his committee. With the fife-and-drum Americana of Libeskind's "Memory Foundations" in place, one of the governor's problems was solved: the site could be made to sing the same hymns to freedom that had been emanating from the White House since September 11. But the governor now had the problem of realizing substantial progress on the ground before the arrival of the Republicans, and that, combined with the erosion of the governor's faith through the year, would prove to be Daniel Libeskind's undoing. When George Bush stood to accept his party's nomination fifty blocks uptown in Madison Square Garden (or even, as was earlier mooted, at Ground Zero itself), the site had to be fit for polemical use. It could not be burdened with conflict or scandal. It could not be seen as a development morass, deadlocked in the usual New York squabbles. The place where George Bush had reinvented himself as a wartime president, with a bullhorn in his hand and a firefighter at his side, had to be ready for convention week close-ups on the evening news.

So while Libeskind provided a diversion with his inspirational grand tour during the spring of 2003, the governor quietly brokered a rapprochement between the LMDC and the Port Authority in which they settled some of their conflicting claims on the site. This unity allowed Pataki to lay out his first long-range time line for the redevelopment. Speaking in the ballroom of a towering new Ritz-Carlton hotel that had opened just south of Ground Zero, Pataki drove home a theme of rapid renewal.

"Centuries from now, history will record September eleventh, two thousand one, as a turning point for humanity—a date when those who believe in fear were overcome by those who believe in freedom," the governor said at the beginning of his speech, reading from a teleprompter. "But for those of us here today and our fellow New Yorkers, September eleventh, two thousand and one, will never be an abstract date in history. For us, it was the day we lost loved ones, friends, and neighbors. For us, it was the day a battle began in our own backyard. For us, it is personal. And that is why rebuilding Lower Manhattan cannot be an elusive promise reserved for another generation or a distant tomorrow. It is our honor, our obligation to rebuild. Our place in time demands that we be bold and daring and swift."

Behind him stood a ceiling-high image of Libeskind's signature tower: the 1,776-foot-tall spire married to a seventy-story glass office building, the child of Nina Libeskind's shrewd, media-friendly political calculations, the not-very-distant relative of all the monumental middle fingers proposed for the site since the earliest days. Pataki first referred to it as a building that would "defiantly reclaim our skyline with a new beacon symbolizing all that makes our nation great." Perhaps because that was such a mouthful, in subsequent references the governor chose to introduce his sound-bite coinage: "Freedom Tower."

According to the new fast-track time line for the redevelopment, the temporary PATH station at the site was set to open in November 2003, with construction of a permanent Downtown Grand Central to begin in 2005. By the end of 2006, the governor announced, the station would be complete, the construction of a memorial would be under way above it, "and Libeskind's spectacular entranceway to the site, the 'Wedge of Light'—where the sun will shine without shadow the morning of every September eleventh—will have been created." That same year—by September 11, naturally—the steel frame of Freedom Tower would be topped out and "all who come here," the governor said, "will witness the tower's imprint on the horizon and they will know our determination to overcome evil." Moreover, when the building opened in 2008 the offices of the Governor of the State of New York—moved out of the World Trade Center by Pataki himself—would return. Though he said he had authorized the relocation

with the appropriate agencies that very morning, the announcement was pure hyperbole: George Pataki's term as governor was set
to expire in 2006, and, anyway, by then he would likely have graduated to the higher office a patriotic rebuilding should earn him.

Conspicuously absent from the governor's time line was the
date of the ground-breaking for his Freedom Tower. That issue
was soon clarified. On May 1—the same day George Bush made his
tail-hook landing to unilaterally call an end to the war in Iraq—
Larry Silverstein met with the editorial board of the *Daily News*.
There, the sometimes impolitic developer let slip that "[Pataki]
wants to lay the cornerstone of the foundation of the Freedom
Tower at the Republican National Convention."[1] According to one
source, the governor's office "went nuts"; Silverstein's spokesman
called the paper to "clarify"; a Democratic congressman from
Queens fired off a letter to the Republican Party chairman,
protesting the use of Ground Zero as "a backdrop for the intensely
partisan activities that usually accompany a convention."[2]

The thread was picked up by the *New York Times* six weeks later.
But the headline of that article—"Goal Is to Lay Cornerstone at
Ground Zero During GOP Convention"—was way out ahead of
the facts reported in the article itself, which mostly concerned the
warp-speed environmental impact review necessary to meet that
date. The LMDC jumped to put the *Times* straight, forcing an immediate change on the Web site and a correction in the paper the
next day. Matt Higgins, the LMDC's resident press heavy, was living up to his nickname, "Baby Satan." He followed his pursuit of
the *Times* with a rare personal e-mail sent to his entire contact list.
His favored mode of persuasion was one to one, by cell phone or
quick retorts on his BlackBerry; this unusual response signaled a
state of panic at the LMDC. Higgins's e-mail noted that the
"false" headline "does not reflect our intentions." The construction of Freedom Tower, he wrote, would start in "August 2004, but
sooner if at all possible." It was a distinction without a difference;
much sooner was not at all possible, and the convention was sched-

uled to begin in late August. Whether the ground-breaking ceremony took place a few months before the convention, during the
convention, or any time between the convention and the vote in
November, achieving that milestone would still be a Pataki-
brokered boon for Bush.

It is not unusual for two, or three, or five years to pass between
the conception of a large office tower and its construction. Now
the governor (through the LMDC) was demanding that a skyscraper, by some measures the world's tallest, at that point only a
picture, be engineered—with novel safety systems and in concert
with an as-yet-indeterminate infrastructure—and developed from
sketch fantasy to final construction drawings in a little over a year.
Certainly it was doable—the Empire State Building, famously, had
been built in a year—but such a rush job would require the con-
certed efforts of an architecture firm that had deep experience in
building towers, not merely in describing their symbolic attrib-
utes. With the pressure on, the redevelopment had become much
more hospitable to Larry Silverstein's architects, Skidmore, Owings and Merrill. With their running start on the project, they
were the only ones who could begin to raise Daniel Libeskind's flag
at Ground Zero in time.

While the governor's haste was driven by the date of the convention and the need to put his mark on the skyline before he left
office, it was also prompted, during the hottest weeks of the war in
Iraq, by his desire to link the World Trade Center site to that undertaking so dear to the White House. That was the least responsible of all the motivations, and the least necessary: Ground Zero,
empty, already served the purpose required of Ground Zero rebuilt. As American soldiers began coming home dead from Iraq, a
new type of tribute appeared at the Port Authority's official memorial repository, a tiered wooden stand overlooking a little plaza
at the main gate to the pit on Liberty Street. Behind an aging pur-
ple wreath sent by the city fathers of Snyder, Texas, between the
unicorn insignia of a Scottish fire brigade and a turbid bottle of

sake, some parents had left an annotated photograph of their son—"Captain Benjamin Sammis, USMC, 1974–2003"—taken in the cockpit of a Cobra helicopter like the one in which he was killed. "Died in action in Operation Iraqi Freedom," the caption read, "fighting the war against terrorism."

The conflation of the war in Iraq with September 11 trickled down from the White House; the Bush administration believed in it with a fatal passion, and polls soon showed that a majority of ditto-prone Americans did too. At a pro-war rally at Ground Zero attended by twenty-five thousand construction workers, George Pataki did his part to push the party line. "Some of you may have seen yesterday in Baghdad a picture of a statue of that evil dictator being toppled and dragged through the streets by Iraqis," the governor said to the fired-up crowd on West Street. "Let's melt it down. Let's bring it to New York and let's put it in one of the girders that's going to rise over here as a symbol of the rebuilding of New York and the rebuilding of America."[3]

It was not the first time Pataki had promoted this sort of martial metallurgy. A single beam from the south tower, weighing about twenty-four tons, had already been shipped to Amite, Louisiana (population 4,110), where it was to be melted down for the hull of a new navy warship. Steel that had for nearly thirty years held offices and office workers safely in the New York sky was now destined to form the cutwater at the bow of the USS *New York*, a 684-foot, $850 million transport capable of landing up to seven hundred marines in an amphibious strike. "We're very proud that the twisted steel from the WTC towers will soon be used to forge an even stronger national defense," Governor Pataki said a few days before the symbolic beam was fished from the Fresh Kills Landfill. "The USS *New York* will soon be defending freedom and combating terrorism around the globe." Surely Minoru Yamasaki was spinning in his grave. What had become of his inspiring Twin Towers, his monument to world peace and the cooperation of men?

As a determinant of the architecture of Ground Zero, only one force gave politics any real competition: Larry Silverstein's lease with the Port Authority, all powerful but seldom seen (languishing beyond the reach of the Freedom of Information Act), a 580-page trump card in double-spaced twelve-point Times Roman. Between its encomiums to proper insurance and the loosely worded contingencies for disaster cited earlier, the lease was full of curious tangents. Section 2.2 considered the labeling of the World Trade Center's estimable art collection (". . . and if such label is affixed to any item of Artwork, the Lessee must thereafter keep such label affixed thereto"); section 64.1, "Miscellaneous," promised access in perpetuity to the memorials of the 1993 World Trade Center bombing (". . . located on the B2 subgrade level along the south wall and the enclosed area surrounding column 324").

The lease also included a piece of boilerplate that must first have appeared to be just another accessory for managing the living buildings. In an opening section defining terms, the Port Authority's lawyers had detailed the nature of architecture and engineering (A/E) firms that would be acceptable to perform work on the property: " 'A/E Criteria' shall mean A/E's that (i) (A) are currently licensed to practice in the State of New York, (B) have no less than five (5) years of experience in the planning and design of office space and have completed at least ten (10) projects in the City of New York, (C) have a staff appropriate to the size of the project . . . have demonstrated satisfactory performance on work conducted at the World Trade Center or other real property owned by the Port Authority and . . . maintain an office in the New York Metropolitan Area."

Though he had opened an office in Manhattan, three blocks south of Ground Zero on Rector Street, and though he had taken and passed his state licensing exam several months after his selection, Daniel Libeskind met few of the Port's requirements. Most important, he had never built anything taller than the four-story Jewish Museum in Berlin. How could he deliver Freedom Tower?

In private, Larry Silverstein argued that point strenuously; in public, the job was handled by the *New York Post*, which editorialized nearly every week against entrusting the job to the "bizarre" and inexperienced Libeskind. (The *Times* countered with several editorials defending Libeskind as an artist and the people's choice.) The case for bringing in Silverstein's architects had been reinforced when the governor set his politically motivated deadline. But even without that justification, the developer could have once again shielded himself behind the language of his lease: the "A/E Criteria" were describing SOM.

Many large firms later evolved to copy the model pioneered by Skidmore, Owings and Merrill, but when the office took shape in the 1930s it was unique. Confronted in its infancy with a series of large planning projects—at the "Century of Progress" exhibition in Chicago in 1933 and the 1939 World's Fair in New York—the partnership established by Louis Skidmore and Nathaniel Owings soon mushroomed into a novel type of full-service company. From its early days, SOM incorporated architecture, engineering, urban planning, and at times even construction services under one roof. "[We were] certainly not designers in the classic sense," Owings wrote of the early days in his memoirs. "We were entrepreneurs, promoters, expediters, financiers, diplomats; we were men of too many trades and masters of none."[4]

This expansive tendency was consolidated by the work SOM took on for the armed forces during World War II: first, in 1940, the design of a network of seventy-two interceptor stations intended to defend against a domestic air war that never came; and later several jobs for the Manhattan Project, including the creation of its stealth science city, Oak Ridge, Tennessee. "It isn't every day that someone drops into the office and orders a town," Owings wrote, remembering the day in 1942 when he and Skidmore were asked in whispers to deliver a complete suite of homes, schools, hospitals, shops, religious buildings, recreation centers, laboratories, and factories in less than three years for the population of seventy-five thousand drafted to the wilds of Tennessee to design the first atomic bomb. To realize this small city in time for its single product to be engineered and put to use, the firm became what Owings called "a kind of stock company." Among SOM's 650 employees on the site were a department store merchandising manager, to develop the necessary retail, and the former chief engineer of New York City's then all-powerful Triboro Bridge and Tunnel Authority, to head the firm's traffic and highway department. At one point, Owings hired an entire construction company from Grand Rapids, Michigan, "lock, stock and barrel, personnel and equipment," to "fill out" SOM's construction division.

During the war, the contracts let for design and construction by the Army Corps of Engineers were geared to favor such large, integrated firms. To ease bureaucratic bottlenecks at the newly built Pentagon, jobs were bundled into groups and given to a single party for execution. Most of these contracts went to giant construction conglomerates employing armies of engineers but only a smattering of architects to put some sugar on their designs. SOM, because of its innovative omnibus structure, was one of the few architecture firms able to compete, and prosper, during the war; more art-bound architects, purveyors of style, were shut out of the effort altogether or, as in the case of those traveling with the navy's Seabees in the Pacific, left to decorate palm-festooned officers' clubs while their engineer colleagues took on the somewhat more critical work of building the landing strips and ports that would make a bridge for American power reaching all the way to Japan.

Immediately after the war—brought to a close with the bombs born in Oak Ridge—SOM was hired to build a military base in Okinawa and five air fields in Morocco. Later, SOM designed a new academy complex for the Air Force, in Colorado, a commission the firm won with architectural vision, showmanship, and political grease in equal parts. The skills acquired interfacing with exacting military clients transferred easily to the civilian sphere when commercial construction boomed in the 1950s and 1960s. Bureaucracies, whether public or corporate, trusted these architects; politicians and executives could look across a conference room table and see their own scale and structure mirrored in SOM.

That institutional quality—and the appeal of the firm's safe, tasteful modernism—was the key to SOM's great heyday after the war. Beginning in 1952, when its glass tower for the Lever Brothers soap empire broke the brick walls of Manhattan's Park Avenue, SOM more or less single-handedly invented the look of American business at mid-century—in the suburbs, where the company pioneered the corporate office park, and in every major city across the country. In New York alone they completed prominent, trendsetting buildings for PepsiCo, Union Carbide, and the Manufacturer's Hanover and Chase Manhattan banks. The Chase project, with its shining, metal-trimmed tower and its art-punctuated plaza intruding into the old stone maze of the Financial District, was an early influence—in its form and its renovating aspirations—on the World Trade Center that would rise a decade later three blocks away. The firm remained a powerhouse; one year after the Twin Towers were completed, an SOM design, the Sears Tower in Chicago, replaced them as the tallest in the world.

In addition to their offices in New York, Chicago, and San Francisco, in 1967 SOM opened its doors in Washington, D.C. Nathaniel Owings was already a player there, working under Presidents Kennedy, Johnson, and Nixon in a long campaign to establish a master plan for the neglected stretch of Pennsylvania Avenue between the White House and the Capitol. The success of that campaign, which resulted in the appropriately regal avenue we see today, hinged as much on social tactics and the good graces of Lady Bird Johnson as it did on any particular designerly touch. "I as an individual cannot point to any major building for which I am solely responsible," Owings wrote, explaining his role in SOM. "But I can point to individual brilliant architects . . . who are

products of this entity. I can [however] claim a major role in planning projects like Pennsylvania Avenue in Washington, D.C. This
kind of thing architects just didn't used to do, and still don't."⁵

One of the "individual brilliant architects" emerging at SOM
during the 1970s was David Childs. As the head of an allied civic
group, he had worked closely with Owings to push the bill authorizing the Pennsylvania Avenue plan through Congress, and right
after, in 1971, he was hired away by the firm. He went on to lead
the Washington office as Owings's handpicked successor. In the decade that followed, Childs completed dozens of private and public
projects in the capital—including a master plan for the symbol-
laden greensward of the Washington Mall—acquiring the political
skills that would aid him as he rose to become the top corporate architect in the United States.

In 1984, David Childs and several other partners relocated to
New York City to take over the SOM office there. That move laid
the groundwork, after some years of atrophy, for a resurgence of
the firm, in the city and around the world. By any measure—
receipts, powerful clients, square footage built—at the turn of
the century SOM had become the leading architecture firm in
New York. Its overseas work included plans for everything from
Israel's major airport to a police academy in Kuwait. Closer to
home, Childs and his partners were designing new gateways to
the city, at Penn Station and John F. Kennedy International Airport; they were working on expansion plans for the New York
Stock Exchange; they were building a tower for Bear Stearns, on
Madison Avenue, and two towers for Time Warner, on Columbus
Circle; and, for the Port Authority, they were studying the development of an office building to be raised over the Port's mam-
moth bus station near Times Square. Crucially, through the
efforts of Marilyn Jordan Taylor, another partner transplanted
from Washington, SOM had also made inroads with New York
City's many civic organizations, as both a benefactor and an intellectual resource. After September 11, Taylor became a central

force in the establishment of New York New Visions, the architecture-world lobbying group, though she had to distance herself when SOM's work for Larry Silverstein began in earnest.

By September 11, SOM had designed more than ten thousand projects in fifty countries and stood alone as the standard for corporate competence in New York and around the world. Daniel Libeskind, the best choice the process had produced for a governor who required symbols, had built three buildings in two countries; his reputation in the city was as an amiable dreamer who occasionally dropped in from afar to lecture and chat up the press. But, as so many marginal participants in the redevelopment worked so hard to prove, there was more to be done at Ground Zero than merely build, and as David Childs closed in on the design of Freedom Tower, the jury was still out on his ability to soar into the artier realm. Nat Owings once wrote that "the practice of architecture is essentially the getting and executing of jobs."[6] Was Childs the firm's chief rainmaker, as his mentor had been? Or was he one of the breakthrough designers that SOM had at times so effectively nurtured?

At age sixty-two, at the top of his game and on the verge of taking over the most important architecture project in the world, David Childs occupied a lonely middle ground in the profession. He had one foot in the world of government and business—providing what Henry-Russell Hitchcock called "the architecture of bureaucracy"—and the other in the academy, incubator for "the architecture of genius." While in Washington, Childs had become close to Senator Daniel Patrick Moynihan of New York, perhaps the most architecture-obsessed politician ever to serve in Congress. Until Moynihan's death in 2003, he and Childs would breakfast regularly, establishing a relationship that eased SOM into the design of one of the senator's pet projects: the transformation of Manhattan's old Farley Post Office building into a suitably grand replacement for the original Penn Station, torn down across the street amid much protest in 1963. He had learned his politics well, but Childs also moved easily through the schools and conferences and galleries that served as a safe haven for the profession's stars, and he counted Peter Eisenman—at the heart of the "starchitect" enterprise—among his close friends. "[Childs] is tormented about being his own signature self and being in a big corporate firm," Eisenman told the *New York Post* in 2003. "He has aspirations to be a great architect, but they are limited by a lack of capacity to say what he wants to do. He's a Hamlet-like figure. On the one hand he says, 'I've got to get out.' On the other hand he says, 'What about all the years I've put in?' [SOM] is very powerful and very strong. He'd lose that backing."[7]

David Childs's suspension between architecture's two worlds was illustrated in a famous portrait of architectural all-stars taken on the occasion of Philip Johnson's ninetieth birthday in 1996. The dean of American architecture was photographed that day with a large group that included Eisenman, Frank Gehry, Rem Koolhaas, and Zaha Hadid—architects whose genius credentials were unchallenged as well as untainted by excessive contact with corporations. The man from SOM stood in the back, apart from the group and a head taller than the rest. The photo inevitably prompted the reaction, *What's he doing there?*

His ever-more overt role at Ground Zero elicited a similar response. Through the ricochets of the process, the site had acquired the aura of a domain of pure genius. But Childs was there to serve the interests of Larry Silverstein, who began lobbying for SOM during the final stage of the Innovative Design Study in a private letter to the LMDC; then, emboldened by Pataki's new convention-motivated tempo, the developer went on to openly demand that SOM lead the design process while, of course, "reflecting the spirit" of Libeskind's plan. Silverstein's case was backed by the fact that he was the only one at the table who could pay for Freedom Tower. The hopeful lawsuit against his insurers—claiming double payment for what he maintained were two attacks—was still a full year away from resolution; still, even if he lost, as seemed increasingly likely, he would nonetheless have about $2 billion to play with—not enough to develop the whole site, but more than enough to build one politically charged skyscraper.

The breakneck timeframe and Silverstein's windfall made the participation of his architects inevitable. But Daniel Libeskind was contractually entitled to his role as master planner and, more important, assumed by the public to be the sole architect of Ground Zero. He and David Childs were obliged to find common ground, yet Childs was the scion of an architectural machine while Libeskind was a mystic, a loner, an artist, a poet. And each came with his own client. David Childs was the servant party in a traditional architect/developer relationship. Daniel Libeskind was hired by the LMDC, but he would tirelessly play the populist card—he once described his clients as "every New Yorker and every American and every good person around the world for whom these events were fundamentally important." But in the end he was without a doubt Governor Pataki's man. Though at one point he claimed to have been elected by "fifty million people voting on the Internet," just as many people had seen Libeskind selected in plain view by a single vote.

The protection given Libeskind by the governor's public endorsement survived the "Wedge of Light" debacle; a month later, in June 2003, the governor again backed his architect against a greater challenge: Larry Silverstein and David Childs wanted to move Freedom Tower.

As Libeskind had drawn it, Ground Zero's skyline feature was to be built at the northwest corner of the site, acting as the crescendo of the quarter-circle of gradually ascending office buildings that the architect compared to the twirling skirts of the Statue of Liberty. Silverstein, advised by SOM, proposed to move the tower to the northeast corner, where it would be served directly by the planned train station across the street, and where, a block from Broadway, it would be far less isolated; Libeskind's location, chosen for formal and rhetorical reasons, would require Silverstein's tenants to walk two long blocks through a construction site every day for the decade or more that it would take to build the rest of the project. Moreover, the site favored by SOM was on solid ground, on the inland side of the ancient shoreline of Manhattan that ran right through the center of Ground Zero. At Libeskind's preferred location, built on land reclaimed from the Hudson River, Freedom Tower would have to integrate its foundations with the precarious concrete retaining walls of the original World Trade Center pit—symbols of a resilient democracy, perhaps, but also an expensive engineering headache.

Pumped up by the press, Libeskind's flimsy architectural notion had taken hold. Despite all the excellent reasons for relocating Freedom Tower, George Pataki was still a prisoner of the images presented with such fanfare at the Winter Garden, pictures that newspapers and television had planted in the public imagination as the first signs of progress at Ground Zero. Any responsible adjustment of "Memory Foundations" to adapt to real conditions would be decried as a return to profane bickering and an erosion of what the governor himself often referred to as "the Libeskind vision." Freedom Tower stayed put.

Daniel Libeskind won that round, but the showdown continued. By early June—just as his poems were discovered and his cardboard box Audi advertisement hit the stands—Libeskind was embroiled in testy negotiations over the extent of his role in the redevelopment. Responding to the now imminent threat of losing control to SOM, Libeskind began to claim not only the uncontested role of master planner, but also the task the public assumed he had been given: to design, rather than just position and rough in, the specific buildings on the site. He sent the Port Authority a proposal outlining a sixty/forty split of responsibility with whatever architecture firm it chose for the train station, and he brazenly offered Larry Silverstein a similar division of labor on Freedom Tower. In the *New York Post*, William Neuman reported that Nina Libeskind had gotten angry at a subsequent meeting with the Port and declared that "her husband deserved the job because he was 'chosen by the people.'" If a greater role was not granted, Neuman wrote, the Libeskinds "threatened to air their differences in public."[8] This was more than the paper's editors could resist; in an editorial on June 17, headlined "Control Freak," they rehashed the fracas, described the master plan as "a 16-acre mausoleum with a minaret in the middle," and ridiculed the Libeskinds' threat to tell all about the story of their abuse. "Ooops. Too late, Dan," the *Post* teased. "Pataki needs to go public himself, and tell Libeskind to grow up—if not to disappear altogether."[9]

Pataki did not exactly bark on command, but a month later, after still more very public friction, the governor did induce the principal disputants, Daniel Libeskind and David Childs, to get together in the same room. The meeting was called for the late afternoon of July 15 at the offices of the LMDC, and the beat reporters and TV news crews came together for a stakeout on the sidewalk outside.

Inside, the gloves were off. "When we walked in, the issue was made quite clear," Nina Libeskind said soon after. "David Childs had another design for another tower." For nearly eight hours, the architects sparred as the shape of Ground Zero's major monument hung in the balance. To Daniel and Nina Libeskind, the stakes were no less than the appropriate expression of the significance of September 11. "The Freedom Tower is not just a capricious bird in the sky," Nina later said. "It has a meaning." David Childs had no less an understanding of the events and their gravity—with its offices only four blocks away, SOM had been caught up in the tragedy—but his brief was to keep an eye on the bottom line; it was his responsibility to design a building that would work, that Larry Silverstein could afford to build and use. Each man represented one half of his profession's broken whole. Short of suturing the genius/bureaucracy or star/corporate rift that had divided architecture for fifty years and more, it was unlikely they would find common ground.

Libeskind and Childs had both come with an entourage; including the various LMDC officials, there were more than a dozen people in the room. At some point it was decided that the two designers should adjourn to other quarters and face off one-on-one. In that even smokier back room, Childs sketched out the design he had been working on for well over a year: an office building rising to seventy stories with an unoccupied superstructure rising higher to mark the skyline as the tallest in the world. The only real difference with his rival's concept was that he had placed the symbolic feature on top of the functional one, rather than having the two stand side by side. "I will not sanction an SOM tower," Libeskind told Childs. Their private session lasted twenty minutes, ending abruptly when Libeskind threatened to walk away with the name Governor Pataki had applied to his design. "You can call it anything else, but not Freedom Tower," he said. "That's our name." After nearly two years of civic ferment aimed at generating healing forms, the name of a building and the measure of its height—two words and one number—were the most valuable architectural ideas at Ground Zero.

Five hours into the meeting, after LMDC president Kevin Rampe reportedly "knocked heads," an agreement was reached. The next three hours were spent haggling over a one-paragraph press release describing the face- and schedule-saving accord. Transmitted instantly by the LMDC, it appeared in e-mail inboxes at 12:45 a.m.:

We are pleased to announce an historic collaboration between Skidmore, Owings & Merrill and Studio Daniel Libeskind to design the world's tallest building, the Freedom Tower. SOM, one of the world's leading skyscraper design firms, will serve as the Design Architect and Project Manager, leading a Project Team that will design the Tower. Studio Daniel Libeskind, which has been designated by the Port Authority as the Master Plan Architect for the World Trade Center site, will serve as a collaborating architect during the concept and schematic design phases of the Freedom Tower and a full member of the Project Team. This collaboration will facilitate the development of the Freedom Tower in a manner consistent with the Libeskind vision. We are confident that SOM and SDL will produce a world-class icon in the Lower Manhattan skyline and a powerful symbol of our nation's resilience in the aftermath of tragedy.

The two firms will begin collaborating immediately.

Though there was little ambiguity in the text—Freedom Tower was now an SOM job, Daniel Libeskind a member of the "Project Team"—Nina Libeskind was undeterred. "We don't care a whole lot about labels," she said. "SOM made a commitment to build our tower, not theirs." In reality, SOM had been given a clean win; though he would have to design a building "consistent with the Libeskind vision," David Childs was recognized as the architect of Freedom Tower by all parties, from the governor on down. As Nina Libeskind demonstrated, the agreement allowed everyone to claim victory. For her husband, it affirmed a slightly deeper involvement in shaping the tower than his title of "master plan architect" had previously guaranteed him. For Larry Silverstein, it marked the beginning of officially sanctioned work by the architects he trusted, and the end of his marginalization by the LMDC and the Port Authority; a short preamble to the late-night press release referred to him as "the developer and builder of the Freedom Tower," the first time such language had appeared in an official statement. For Kevin Rampe, brokering the agreement was a job well done on behalf of his patron, the governor, and it demonstrated the LMDC's effectiveness at a time when its future was in doubt. For George Pataki himself, an end to the standoff meant that visible progress at Ground Zero might still be possible in time for the Republican National Convention, by then just thirteen months away.

The day after the detente the two architects and their keepers appeared for a sunny photo op. They gathered at the edge of the pit, smiling and waving as they pantomimed peaceable cooperation. Childs, now able to openly enjoy the power he had long savored in private, was in a kidding mood. As he stood next to Libeskind, who reached barely to his shoulders, the new master of Ground Zero's skyline joked, generously, "This is how the tower's going to look"—a low element and a high one, serving different purposes, side by side.

That was Childs's last concession to Libeskind's design. The agreement ushered in a five-month period of turmoil that came to be called the "forced marriage." Both parties freely disparaged each other, though the Libeskinds tended to do so more often in the presence of reporters. After many more negotiations, the two teams eventually shared office space—Libeskind dispatched a group of his designers to SOM's Wall Street headquarters—but they quite literally never got on the same page: they did not share drawings or models. What Libeskind later referred to as the "so-called collaboration" progressed on distantly parallel tracks, with each architect offering many more ultimatums than insights on a common design.

For David Childs and his colleagues at SOM, so well acquainted with the intricacies of skyscraper construction, the case for their Freedom Tower began with a critique of the engineering hurdles presented by Libeskind's. Tall buildings move—the Twin Towers were designed to safely sway through more than ten feet at their highest floors—and Libeskind's side-by-side solution meant that there would be two towers, a short fat one and a tall skinny one, connected but oscillating at different rates. As a result, Childs and his engineers said, where the two structures were attached, they would grind. In the carefree world of academic architecture, it is a matter of faith that all engineering problems are soluble. This one was, but to solve it would add cost and complicate the construction. There was also the question of what use would be made of the lower floors of the 1,776-foot-tall spire. Libeskind had originally proposed his "Gardens of the World" for the upper stories (they were by then long forgotten), but a specific program was never given for the seventy lower levels, where the spire was to be joined to the adjacent building by dainty bridges. What use could be made of the small, awkward spaces set off from the main block of office floors? Larry Silverstein certainly had no idea. And developers don't build things they can't rent.

The architects carried on through the summer of 2003 and into the fall, through long periods of inaction punctuated by blowups that sometimes triggered emergency mediation by the LMDC. Not surprisingly, since the forced marriage was such a frigid one, the biggest change made to the SOM design came not from Libeskind or his small team of embedded designers, but from Guy Nordenson, the star engineer David Childs brought in to help finesse his structure. Nordenson, who had participated in the "Masters' Plan" developed by Herbert Muschamp the year before, suggested giving the building a twist—about a quarter turn as it rose from the ground to its lacy, symbolic top-hamper. This innovation—the same contribution he had made to Muschamp's endeavor—was one that Childs could use; the change would insulate him from charges of intransigence, but it would not compromise the shape of the tower's floors in a way that would make them unmarketable. The twist also provided a rhetorical advantage over Libeskind's design: Childs's tower was now arguably a better mimic of the Statue of Liberty's striding pose.

At the end of October, George Pataki returned to the Ritz-Carlton Hotel to give another major speech on the redevelopment, an update on the time line he had announced in the same room six months earlier. The fact that the centerpiece of the redevelopment was stalled in acrimony was not lost on anyone in the audience, a joint gathering of two business associations that represented a considerable convergence of Manhattan savoir faire. Near the end of his speech, the governor turned his attention to the impasse. "Nothing will stop us from building Freedom Tower," he said, mentioning the billions of dollars expected at the resolution of Larry Silverstein's legal troubles. "Now, all we await is a design. And for that assignment we are fortunate to have two of the greatest architects of our time, Daniel Libeskind and David Childs. Each of them brings to this project a long record of innovative work and a deep reserve of strong opinions."

The line was greeted with grins around the room, even at the table where Larry Silverstein, Daniel Libeskind, David Childs, Nina Libeskind, and T. J. Gottesdiener, the no-nonsense managing partner of SOM, were arranged in a row. The forced marriage had been accurately described in the papers as a stumbling disaster, and the governor was trying to deflect that story line with humor. He continued, comparing the two architects to other "great artistic collaborations," illustrating his point with slides: "Michelangelo and Pope Julius II made the Sistine Chapel. Philip Johnson and Mies van der Rohe made the Seagram Building. Just think what Libeskind and Childs will make." The general bemusement rolled into open laughter. Then Pataki, smiling, dropped the bomb. "Today, I am pleased to announce that we will know the answer to that question by December fifteenth, the deadline I have set to release the design of the Freedom Tower," the governor said, turning to face the architects. "I know everyone in this room wishes you the best of luck."

Childs and Libeskind had only six more weeks. They spent the time as they had the months before, at loggerheads—now over a primal architectural issue. David Childs favored a symmetrical structure, which would ease everything from the engineering to the construction to the leasing of the finished spaces, while giving Freedom Tower the foursquare iconic presence shared by the many towers SOM had built since the 1950s. Daniel Libeskind designed exclusively with off-kilter forms; even after he had been made to agree to a single-tower scheme—his freestanding spire reduced first to a bulge along one side of the office building, and then to an appendage on top—he insisted on asymmetry. It was, again, a question of what the tower would mean; without at least a hint of his irregular shapes, how would Freedom Tower say all the things about September 11 that Libeskind promised it could?

At the time of the governor's speech, SOM's concept was already close to its final form. Even before the addition of Guy Nordenson's twist, the open crown of the building had evolved, independent of Libeskind, into a daring suspension structure. Two massive concrete columns, extensions of the tower's elevator cores, would rise beyond the highest inhabitable floor to support a steel truss from which cables would hang down in a crossing diamond pattern that Childs said was inspired by the Brooklyn Bridge. It was on this delicate construction—one by its nature reliant on balance—that SOM eventually agreed to place Libeskind's token off-center element: a tapering triangular spike that looked like a miniature version of his original Freedom Tower.

So the building would now have three tops: the sloping roof above the highest occupied floor, the line of the truss that suspended the sheath of cables, and Libeskind's consolation prize spike. The battle then moved from symmetry to another architectural basic: proportion. The relative heights of the roof, truss, and finial were fiercely debated—the 1,776-foot tower sometimes climbing to two thousand feet and higher—with each party proposing changes in the height of one section or another to try to find the proportion that was closest to their original design. Libeskind was by then banned from SOM's offices unless his adversary was present, and he soon ended all dialogue with the firm. Testing what remained of his pull with Pataki, Libeskind began to log his protests indirectly through the governor's aides. But time was not on his side. The drawings and models and computer renderings necessary to stir public passions for the new tower could not be produced overnight; to reveal the new design by the governor's deadline, all fiddling would ideally have to stop at least two weeks prior to that date. None of this was good news for the architect who had moved from Berlin with the mission of saving New York from its pain. With the timing to the Republican convention and his own words on the line, Pataki now had a motivation far more powerful than his ties to Libeskind's nearly year-old images of "Memory Foundations." But Libeskind continued to phone in his changes to the design, threatening the governor's agenda. At the end of November, some in Pataki's circle were beginning to ponder the obvious question: *Do we still need Libeskind?*

Kevin Rampe and Matt Higgins of the LMDC were by then deeply involved in crisis arbitration, urging Libeskind to relax his objections to the SOM tower and pushing Childs to tweak his design to a point where the "master plan architect" of Ground Zero would at least not publicly condemn it. They needed Daniel Libeskind to stand before the cameras one more time and speak his essential words. But all hell was breaking loose in the weeks leading up to December 15. Late on the night of Thursday, December 4, in an episode that the *Post* referred to as "the Watergate break-in" (and some reporters were soon calling "the panty raid"), architects from Libeskind's office entered the Freedom Tower war room and photographed some of the closely guarded models and drawings prepared by their reluctant collaborators. The next day, Libeskind used those images—the only current ones he had of SOM's tower—to press his case against David Childs in a meeting with two top Pataki aides. The following Monday, December 8, there was a crucial meeting between Libeskind and Janno Lieber, Larry Silverstein's right hand on the project. It devolved into a tense standoff when the architect arrived with his powerful lawyer, Pataki's old friend Ed Hayes. Silverstein's man refused to debate the design through lawyers and called in Kevin Rampe for backup. Hayes countered by phoning the governor's chief of staff. The parties' differences were still being phrased in grand terms—*Was SOM adhering to Daniel Libeskind's master plan?*—but the real sticking point was that pointy stick on top of the building: Where exactly would it go? How high would it be? And who would pay for it?

Then another blow came, in the *New York Post*. On December 9, the first of two articles appeared describing the lecture by the Libeskinds' collaborator, the planner Gary Hack, in which he had revealed the media tactics the team had employed during the Innovative Design Study the winter before. Recounting the genesis of the "skeletons" epithet used to smear the Think team's towers, Hack appeared to revel in the fact that George Pataki had used the word to bully Roland Betts into accepting his chosen plan. The Libeskinds had spun the governor, and Gary Hack was bragging about it.[10] He was fired from the job, but nonetheless the indiscretion might have been the final straw for Pataki. He switched his loyalties from the risky architect whom the process had made necessary to the professional certainties of his natural ally, SOM.

The new lines of power were clear for all to see when the design of Freedom Tower was finally revealed, on December 19, 2003. Ever on the lookout for appropriate symbolism, Matt Higgins had chosen to return to that convenient temple to American values on Wall Street, Federal Hall—a move also intended to purge from the domed and columned space the still-vivid memory of the Beyer Blinder Belle plans unveiled there more than a year earlier. The forced marriage antagonism continued right up to the last minute— Pataki had to get on the phone himself to convince Libeskind to accept the language of the press release—but at a meeting on December 12, David Childs and all the governor's men hashed out a final compromise: the office floors would rise to 1,150 feet, the open-air suspension structure would go up to 1,500 feet, and Libeskind's meaning-drenched aerial, set off to one side, would climb another 276 feet, so the tower could top out at a legible triumphalist height.

Once that agreement was reached, SOM flexed its muscles, putting together a complete presentation that included media-ready renderings and a nine-foot-tall plastic model, now standing behind a curtain on the flag-draped stage in Federal Hall. All of the players were assembled—the governor, the mayor, the developer, the architects, some of the residents' and families' advocates, and great gangs of officials from the Port Authority and the LMDC. There was also a significant new face in the crowd: Dan Tishman, head of Tishman Construction, the company that had built the World Trade Center, recently tapped by Larry Silverstein to build its replacement.

"This is not just a building," Governor Pataki said, just before the tower model was shown. "This is a symbol of New York. This is a symbol of America. This is a symbol of freedom." He then lined up with Libeskind, Childs, Silverstein, and Mayor Bloomberg as they all pulled a string to open the curtain. And there it was: a mongrel tower with a twist, a false top, and a piercing spire—a speculative commercial office building transformed through the alchemy of the process into an emblem of the process itself, as well as whatever else its creators said it was supposed to mean.

An architect who had seen it take shape later said that four men designed Freedom Tower: Daniel Libeskind, David Childs, Guy Nordenson, and Matt Higgins—the genius, the bureaucrat, the engineer, and the operative. This was partly true. Daniel Libeskind had given Freedom Tower its patriotic cues, though without Nina no one would have known. David Childs could take credit for its final shape—all but that vestige on top—but he was putting into form the lease-blessed numbers of Larry Silverstein. Guy Nordenson had given the building a twist—like the high-wire walker Philippe Petit and so many other amateur designers who had first put that simple idea in the air. Matt Higgins, with Kevin Rampe and a host of other Pataki appointees, had left their mark by enforcing the clock, though they were acting for a higher power.

The efforts of many others will be recorded in the dimensions of the freighted building. The first skyscraper scheduled to go up at Ground Zero, the symbolic heart of the redevelopment, was shaped by a cascade of cause and effect rolling back through Andrew Cuomo's campaign trail gaffe and the formal free play in the Max Protetch Gallery to all those renderings of five-towered fuck-you fists that first equated architecture with defiance in the days after September 11. The diehards of Team Twin Towers should be recognized for sustaining the equation, and their spokesman, Jon Hakala, for putting it into words that never failed to entice the press. Freedom Tower was shaped by the biases of newspapers, the martyrdom of Beyer Blinder Belle, the inspiration of the countless amateurs, the families' devotion to the footprints, the Port Authority's passion for revenue, the public's acquiescence, George Pataki's ambition. Freedom Tower was also the embodiment of more distant political forces—the Republican convention, the war in Iraq—unleashed in Washington but blowing back to reveal themselves in the form of that monumental model lit up by flash-bulbs in a building five blocks from Ground Zero. Freedom Tower, New York City's first viable architectural response to September 11, was the perfect product of an imperfect process. It had a thousand authors and none at all.

Daniel Libeskind, in the end, left almost no mark; his political capital was spent. Freedom Tower had been taken away and in the following months he would also lose his "Wedge of Light," devastated by the Port Authority's plans for the train station, as well as the very foundations of "Memory Foundations"—the sunken pit, erased by a competition-winning design for the memorial. He still had that off-center spike on the tower, its height pointing to the Declaration of Independence, but its future was in doubt. After the model of the new Freedom Tower had been applauded and photographed, as images of it were racing around the world, workers preparing to remove it from Federal Hall snapped Libeskind's little stick right off—something the level-headed architects of SOM were itching to do.

From the moment he wowed the Winter Garden with his first

presentation, Daniel Libeskind lasted a year and a day in the process. Now it was time for him to say good-bye. "When the developers and politicians and architects are long gone to other projects," he told reporters after the event at Federal Hall, "I'll still be here making sure that ten years from now, or twelve or fifteen, that everything on this site is important, that this is not just business as usual."

12

SO MOVED

WHILE THE redevelopment process bumped along, the pace at the site never slowed. By early 2003, the physical work of preparing Ground Zero for its future was well advanced. At the bottom of the pit, construction on the temporary PATH commuter rail station moved ahead quickly through the year, meeting Governor Pataki's deadline in November, when the last train that got out on the morning of the attack rolled back in with a cargo of VIPs. To the north, on an adjacent block uncomplicated by the loss of life, rapid progress was being made on a building to replace the fallen 7 World Trade Center, a fifty-two-story prism designed for Larry Silverstein by David Childs. To the south, just across Liberty Street, work continued behind a black shroud to prepare the mortally wounded Deutsche Bank tower for its piece-by-piece dismantling. There was too much resurgent city life around it to allow a safe implosion, and anyway no one wanted to see another building blown up.

With the effort to pack onto the site everything that had been there before, plus the new features planned in response to the disaster—a memorial, a memorial museum—the Deutsche Bank land had become a coveted frontier. In April 2003, Governor Pataki called in former senator George Mitchell—the man who brokered the Good Friday Agreement peace accord in Northern Ireland—to negotiate an end to a simmering legal battle between Deutsche Bank and its insurers. Settling the dispute cleared the way for the

large block to be rolled into the master plan, where it was needed
for another of Larry Silverstein's office buildings (to decrease
crowding on the site itself), but also for a frangible open space,
soon called Liberty Park, under which incoming trucks could be
screened for bombs.

Next door to the crippled Deutsche Bank tower stood another
shrouded building, 90 West Street. Until it blew down in a gale, an
enormous advertising banner, ten stories tall, was installed on it—
an image of the Statue of Liberty and the reduced skyline of
Lower Manhattan fading into a giant flag-striped heart over the
motto "The human spirit is not measured by the size of the act
but by the size of the heart." The banner was a gift to the city
from the comedian Yakov Smirnoff; it was hung in front of scaf-
folding that had been in place on September 11, and that two years
later was still yielding body parts. As those discoveries were made,
more red dots were added to the map of Ground Zero, and the con-
tours of sanctity at the site became that much more convoluted.

Were it not for signage—the comedian's donated Hallmark
heart, some interpretive panels hung on the perimeter fence—364
days a year Ground Zero could have been mistaken for a large urban renewal site. On one day—the anniversaries of the attack—
the World Trade Center site was transformed into a giant stage for
civic memory: relatives of the victims stood on the bedrock floor
of the Pit and thousands of others gathered in respectful inaction
on the surrounding streets as a long recital of names echoed off
into the Financial District. But, in general, most otherwise-
engaged New Yorkers never came downtown to see the site, and in
a way there was nothing to see. Construction machines queued on
West Street, waiting for a turn on the long ramp into the pit; water trucks sprayed the bottom to keep down the dust. The best reminders that the place was special were the tourists—bused in,
approaching tentatively, looking for something to hang on to. With
the scene of the devastation at once so vast and so sterile, it was
not always clear where they should focus their sacraments. So they

scanned the commemorative hats and snow globes spread for sale on folding tables, photographed one another in front of the noth- ingness, and after it reopened in November 2003, pestered the res- idents of "Ten House," the little fire station on Liberty Street from which the first of September 11's first-responders had come. The firemen there eventually printed out a page of FAQs and taped it to the door, adding a reminder that even polite questions stirred memories of what had happened across the street.

A few steps away, around the base of the Deutsche Bank tower, there was a block-long plywood construction fence. Before being painted over in preparation for the formalities of the second an- niversary, it had collected thousands of handwritten notes. Many were god-fearing, some were bloodthirsty, but most were just shout-outs from some distant point: *We came from far away; this place is important; we will never forget.* At one end of the wall, a regu- lar at the site set up shop with his folk art—paper matchbooks pared down into the image of the old Lower Manhattan skyline, the two matches representing the Twins partly burned. On most days, too, on the far end of the wall, one could find Harry Roland, Ground Zero's unofficial greeter and guide, drawing crowds with his call, "This is history! Don't let it be a mystery!" He fielded questions from confused pilgrims: *Where were the towers? Which way did the planes come? What are they building here?* Another fixture at the site, an aged beatnik with a head of wild white hair, would play his flute for solace and spare change, stopping periodically to sell the visitors on his personal cosmology: on September 11, 2001, time itself had reset, and those sixteen acres behind the fence were now the navel of the universe. He cited as a portent the name of a pop- ular discount department store, Century 21, that was doing a booming business again right across from Ground Zero.

The tourists were not the first to confront the obstacles to sim- ple reverence at the site—the victims' families had beaten every- one to that experience—but in their plight they dramatized the quandaries to come. What sort of sanctity is possible at such a

place? How do you honor the dead even as their graves are under-
mined by the daily grind of the living? The process had ensured
that any future memorial would have trainloads of New Jersey
commuters rumbling through its cellar, an underground shopping
concourse abutting it, and, competing for attention on the
street—if all went well—a concentration of office buildings, cultural facilities, and big-name stores as crowded and vibrant as any
in the world. And somewhere in the mix, not far from the cash reg-
isters, the families would have their Tomb of the Unknowns, a
repository for twelve thousand remains awaiting advances in DNA
identification.

The greatest challenge of the redevelopment was to foster a
form of sanctity that could endure and transcend the banalities of
a reconstituted commercial center. At his debut, Daniel Libeskind
said he had "meditated many days on this seemingly impossible dichotomy," which he then tried to defuse with his slogan "Life victorious!" Other professional and amateur architects suggested
their own solutions for managing the sacred within the profane.
But in the end, the problem fell to the political guardians of the
site, the officials at the Lower Manhattan Development Corporation. They had to consider the intractable whole: the bodies, the
money, the leases, the land, everything. It was their task to invent
a new model for preserving memory at compromised hallowed
ground, and they went about it with full faith in the rituals of bureaucracy. Between the paradox of the site and the bland LMDC
offices across the street, the unsettled act of remembering September 11 was fearlessly normalized into meeting minutes, bullet-
pointed presentations, and the cold comforts of *Robert's Rules of
Order: All in favor? . . . Aye! . . . So moved.*

The meetings of the LMDC board were predictable events, as
regular and reliable as a Sunday Mass. One morning each month,
just after eight o'clock, the dozen or so directors convened at a
large *U*-shaped table that framed a stenographer; key staff lined
up behind them; reporters buttonholed sources and filed in to find

familiar seats; cameramen set up their tripods in the back of the
room, their number, varying from zero to more than twenty, reflecting the anticipated import of the day's agenda. During the
meetings, Kevin Rampe, the LMDC president, could often be seen
waiting nervously for John Whitehead, the aging, genteel, and
renegade chairman of the board, to stray from message discipline,
and Matt Higgins, managing the press, would be quick to squelch
the questioning if he did. Security would fluctuate. After a tenants' group had broken in to protest the distribution of residential
assistance grants, attendees at the next meeting were greeted by
cops and a cattle run of velvet ropes. On several occasions there
were silent demonstrations at the board meetings themselves,
which, though open to the public, were not, as John Whitehead
once said, "a speaking opportunity." But such diversions were
rare; most discussion was preordained, and nearly every motion
was passed with a unanimous chorus of "ayes."

That dependable rhythm was broken, briefly, on April 10,
2003—as Daniel Libeskind sold himself to New York City, as
Baghdad fell—by the first and only moment of public discord between board members. It took place as the directors were considering a particularly jarring piece of bureaucratic liturgy, a
resolution approving the mission statement and competition program that would steer the open search for a memorial design:
"WHEREAS, the LMDC is committed to the creation of a fitting memorial at the World Trade Center site; WHEREAS, the LMDC
Memorial Mission Statement states that the memorial shall 'Remember and honor the thousands of innocent men, women, and
children murdered by terrorists' . . . WHEREAS, the heroism of
those who risked and gave their lives to save others . . . provided
strength and inspiration to our city . . . WHEREAS, the international design competition shall seek a large number of creative design proposals . . . With all of those whereas's, NOW, THEREFORE BE
IT RESOLVED." The dispute that day centered on the meaning of a

word in the mission statement that would not have been in play at other construction sites or in doubt at other cemeteries: *sacred*.

Madelyn Wils, the tenacious, effective Community Board 1 chair and the only local resident on the LMDC board, had never given up her campaign to prevent the site from becoming frozen in mourning—"a graveyard," as her constituents usually put it. For this stand, and for her opposition to the placement of a temporary memorial in Tribeca's only park, she had early on been targeted by the Coalition of 9/11 Families, even receiving several death threats from relatives of the deceased clinging to the site. "They want it so badly they'll kill you for it," she said. With many of her neighbors in Tribeca and Battery Park City, Wils wanted Ground Zero to belong again to Manhattan—a place for work and shopping and sidewalk life, as well as for an appropriate yet modestly scaled commemoration. She understood that the scope of the site's sanctity would be determined by the shape of the memorial, and that the memorial would be born from piles of official paper.

At the LMDC board meeting, just before the vote was to be taken on the resolution authorizing the memorial competition, Madelyn Wils interrupted the proceedings. She wanted the record to reflect a specific, limited definition of the word *sacred*, one that would not mark the entire site as a place apart. The word had been used once in the memorial mission statement—"Respect this place made sacred through tragic loss"—a four-sentence eulogy that had been painfully debated for more than a year by the family members, residents, rescue workers, and survivors of the attack who made up several committees of the LMDC. Wils's opponent that day, lying in wait, was fellow board member Paul Crotty, a telecommunications executive and a former corporation counsel for the City of New York under Mayor Giuliani. Crotty had been tipped off about Wils's plan to restrain the meaning of the word. Why else would he have had his own dictionary on hand? As captured by the stenographer, the exchange went as follows:

DIRECTOR WILS: I just want to request that in the Memorial Mission Statement, it referred to the word "sacred." And I think that that's a very personal term for
many, many people and everyone should have the
right to translate that as they wish. But I would like it
to be on the record that the word "sacred" for our
purposes be clarified to and be acknowledged as a definition in the Webster's dictionary as "entitled to respect and reverence." And if that could be shown on
the record.

DIRECTOR CROTTY: Mister Chairman?

CHAIRMAN WHITEHEAD: Yes, Paul.

DIRECTOR CROTTY: I don't think that's a very good suggestion. This is a process that has been open to everybody . . . I think we ought to leave it to the memorial
[committee] and not put any gloss on the words they
chose. Sacred means a lot of things to different people. And I think that it should be infused with the
meaning that people want to give it. Literally, I think
almost 3,000 people were sacrificed on September
11th. The word "sacrifice," if you look at the etymol-
ogy of that word, means really to make sacred by the
loss of their lives, how they perished. So sacred is con-
centrated, it's holy, it's hallowed. And it has a number
of meanings. I think for us to impart—import a particular meaning to the word is inappropriate. And I
think the word "sacred" covers how people will react
to it in their own different and diverse ways which I
think is really at the heart of the Memorial Statement. It ought to be a broadly based, universal appeal
to mankind and let mankind respond to it as they
choose. But I don't think we ought to be limiting any
particular word by interpretations that seem to find
favor with one or another board member . . .

DIRECTOR WILS: Well, I guess this is just a, you know, a place of disagreement. But the purpose is just so that there is—the interpretation allows secular uses on the memorial site and that it just not be confused with the inability to have secular uses on the site or the interpretation of that . . .

DIRECTOR CROTTY: I don't know why we are so concerned about the religious interpretation of the word "sacred." And the word "sacred" is in the dictionary and it will be interpreted any way people want. I don't know why we insist on a secular—that it only be secular/sacred—

DIRECTOR WILS: I'm not saying it should only be secular.

DIRECTOR CROTTY: Well, that's what you said. So I think—

DIRECTOR WILS: Well, secular is up to different people with different interpretations.

DIRECTOR CROTTY: I think "sacred" is up to anybody who wants to approach the memorial in the spirit in which it is going to be created, they can bring their interpretation to the word "sacred." I don't think it's appropriate to limit.

CHAIRMAN WHITEHEAD: I would like to ask if there are other Board Members who have views on this. No other views? Well . . . regardless of the substance of the issue, the process has taken us through a long consultation with the various advisory committees, including the Residents and the Families, a representation of all people. And the word "sacred" was discussed by those people and they felt that the word should be used as is. So I think I would recommend to the Board that they pass the resolution as it is written, but let the record show, as it will, as it does, that you have spoken on this and suggested the alternative language, that for you it means entitled to reverence and respect, which is the definition in the dictionary—

DIRECTOR CROTTY: Only one.

CHAIRMAN WHITEHEAD: —that can be found.

DIRECTOR CROTTY: There are many definitions.

CHAIRMAN WHITEHEAD: Well, there are many definitions.

DIRECTOR WILS: Absolutely.

CHAIRMAN WHITEHEAD: But you [Wils] have effectively represented your view and represented with the first definition.

DIRECTOR CROTTY: No, it's not the first definition.

DIRECTOR WILS: No, no, no. Let me—the concern that I had, just to be clear about it, is that some of—one of the interpretations in the dictionary was that it could only be used for one holy purpose only, and that was where I thought that the dictionary meaning of entitlement to "respect and reverence" would better suggest the ongoing work that has to go on with the [memorial designer] and the interpretations of their work on the memorial site. And that was my purpose on this. I will vote for this resolution. It was not my intention not to. But I felt it was important to clarify that because of the difference in the interpretation in the dictionary.

CHAIRMAN WHITEHEAD: Very good. Well, I think we've done that.

DIRECTOR CROTTY: Mister Chairman, I just don't want to go away from this with any sense that the interpretation that Ms. Wils wants to put on the word "sacred" reflects the consensus of the Board. If that's her interpretation, I respect that interpretation. But I don't think we ought to channel the interpretation saying that's the Board's interpretation because when I look at the Webster's dictionary, what Ms. Wils suggests is the one, two, three, four, five, sixth interpretation of the word "sacred." So I'm content to have the dictionary define it and I'm content to have the men and women of the world who come and show reverence to this site, have them define the word "sacred" as they choose in their own particular fashion. And I hope that's what our [designers] do and I hope that's what the [competition] jury does. . . . That you have to go to the sixth definition for the word "sacred" to get something that's meaningful to one Member of the Board. . . .

CHAIRMAN WHITEHEAD: Well, seeing no further hands raised, I gather we are ready to vote on the resolution. It looks like we have—everyone who had an interpretation of what "sacred" means, it's been an interesting discussion and I guess it means something different to different people, and those who wanted to express their views on it have had a chance to put their views on the record. Now it's time to vote on the resolution. And I'll ask that all those in favor say "aye." . . .

With that unanimous vote, nineteen months after the attack, the process reached an important milestone; the long-awaited competition for a memorial design, deferred until the establishment of the site's commercial framework, was cleared to begin. But what exactly was the competition seeking? The ten members of the diverse LMDC committee that drafted the mission statement had arrived at their compact formula—"Respect this place made sacred through tragic loss"—but they offered no elaboration of it. "The memorial mission statement serves as a compass to guide not only the creation of the memorial, but also its evolution through the ages," the committee wrote in a preamble, "ensuring the symbolic representation never diverges from the mission."[1]

Those were confident words, but regarding the tenor of that symbolic representation, officialdom was punting; the solution to the
puzzle of death and life at Ground Zero had now fallen to some as-
yet unknown designer and to the jury charged with recognizing a
breakthrough.

Three weeks after that revealing April board meeting, the
marble-floored, palm-planted hangar of the World Financial Center Winter Garden found itself repurposed once again as a backdrop for a major media moment, the announcement of the
competition jury. A podium was set up between flags, and behind
it hung a poster with a first look at the new graphic identity the
LMDC had devised for the memorial competition: a soft field of
white-and-gray clouds in a light blue sky with the word "Remember" fading away in archaic script. This kinder, gentler LMDC introduced a thirteen-member jury rich in artists and academics and
light on politicians, including the sculptor Martin Puryear; the
Mexican architect Enrique Norten; Lowery Stokes Sims, director
of the Studio Museum in Harlem; and Maya Lin, the architect who
had revolutionized the idea of physical remembrance with her
competition-winning design for the Vietnam Veterans Memorial, a
black granite chevron cut into the Washington Mall.

The jurors who chose to speak confirmed the almost desperately vague quality of the coming search. Paula Grant Berry, who
lost her husband in the World Trade Center, was the sole victims'
family member seated on the panel. "We must never lose sight of
why we are doing this and who we are doing it for," she said. "Magnificent people died, and we must be magnificent in how we honor
them." James Young, a history professor who specialized in the
study of Holocaust memorials—and who had served on the jury
that selected Peter Eisenman's design for the Holocaust memorial
in Berlin—added some pointedly open-ended comments: "We
want architects and artists—anybody who submits—to feel they
can go where their imaginations, where their mourning needs to
take them in order to articulate some relationship to this terrible

loss." His revelation—that the rules, so painstakingly drafted, reviewed and approved, could be broken—was seconded in statements by Kevin Rampe and Maya Lin, and it framed all the press coverage of the announcement. The memorial competition, already open to anyone anywhere over eighteen years old, would now officially welcome any proposal, whether or not it fit neatly into the 4.7-acre socket Daniel Libeskind had prepared for it at the center of his "Memory Foundations" master plan.

To illustrate his point, James Young went on to say that Daniel Libeskind had "had to break all kinds of rules" to come up with the plan that had prevailed in the Innovative Design Study. But the rule Libeskind had most clearly broken was the study's prohibition against designing the memorial itself. In theory, he had just created a setting for it; his seventy-foot-, then thirty-foot-deep pit encompassed the tower footprints but did not specify a treatment of them; his plan showcased the exposed concrete retaining walls but did not go so far as to inscribe them with the names of the dead. Still, it was very clear from Libeskind's design that he was having trouble keeping his hands off the memorial. His proposed museum forced its prow sharply into the memorial zone, and two long "cultural" wings spreading out from the building would span the entire north footprint and hang over a corner of the other. The south footprint was also shown flanked on one side by a towering, two-hundred-foot-wide water wall—a mostly overlooked extravagance that one reporter eventually noted would be higher than Niagara Falls. To reach the bottom of the pit, Libeskind had proposed a bank of escalators and several long, narrow ramps, all intruding at his signature awkward angles. And along the one edge of the memorial site, after the floor of the pit had been raised to accommodate the trains below, he had added a deep slot to reclaim some physical access to the bedrock that the families, with so little else to hold on to, considered sacred ground.

All of these elements were carefully drawn in the plans that were sent out to the memorial competitors—and just as carefully labeled as fixed givens in the design: out of bounds. The LMDC's competition guidelines were thus asking entrants to wrestle with an erratic, many-sided site hemmed in by Daniel Libeskind's idiosyncrasies in full flower; the rules condemned the designers to attempt a memorial-within-a-memorial, and it was those rules the jurors now wisely invited them to break. Putting a finer point on it, Maya Lin was soon telling friends that she intended to use the power of the jury to roll back Libeskind's influence on the memorial.

John Whitehead had delayed the announcement of the jury until it was clear that George Pataki would not interfere with it; the memory of the governor's hand in the selection of the master plan was still raw. And though Pataki did have one agent on the panel—Michael McKeon, his former communications director—the competition was laid out according to accepted norms of fair play: the designs would be judged blind and known only by a six-digit code; all entrants would have to limit their graphic output to a single thirty-by-forty-inch presentation board; the deadline was eight weeks hence; the jury, though not sequestered, would meet in an undisclosed location (a vacant office in a building near Ground Zero owned by Larry Silverstein), and they would deliberate under a gag order barring contact with the press. Most important, though an earlier announcement had set the revelation of a chosen design for September 11, 2003, all parties now stressed that the jury alone would decide when to pick a winner, regardless of the symbolic or political calendars. Among the redevelopment's usually and justifiably skeptical reporters, a surprising consensus emerged: the jury was clean enough, the rules appropriately flexible, the commitment to decency impressive; this time the LMDC was doing it right.

Of course, the LMDC was freer here to be fair than at any other stage of the process. There was no real resistance to building a memorial (only a few of the most militant reconstruction activists

ever spoke out against it), there was no knotted skein of jurisdic-
tions (the Port Authority seemed happy to leave this hot potato to
its sister bureaucracy), and there was no money riding on the outcome; the memorial, eventually priced at $350 million to con-
struct, was the only element of the master plan not conceived in
the service of profit, and ample funds to build it were expected to
come in from private sources. Still, because of the way the site's
different uses overlapped and interlocked, the memorial was subject to the same accelerated timeframe as the rest of the redevelopment; nothing could go forward beneath or around it until a
design had been selected and refined. As a result, the LMDC was
forced to conduct the memorial competition in haste, before attitudes toward September 11 had matured, before the emotional
challenges of the site had been considered in any great depth, and
with the images of the day itself so relentlessly fresh, long before
the preservation of memory had become a necessity.

One of the final questions asked of the forty-five hundred people who participated in the second "Listening to the City" meeting had concerned the memorial's timing: should the various
authorities wait to finalize the site plan as ideas about the memorial ripened, or should they just designate a spot for it and move
on? Most, almost 80 percent, said wait. That was in July 2002, ten
months after the attack, but feelings about the event had not
evolved much by the following summer, when the memorial competition was under way. As Madelyn Wils and Paul Crotty had
shown in their boardroom dialectic, the particular nature of sanctity at Ground Zero was still far from understood. And without
honestly facing the predicament—that there was no simple sacred
ground at Ground Zero—any memorial design risked a descent
into falseness, and perhaps, depending on the manner of its vain
search for unhampered holiness, even kitsch. To resolve that sacred "means something different to different people," as John
Whitehead had while tabling his colleagues' debate, was to resolve

nothing at all for the people who would try to communicate that idea through a physical object suspended at the center of one of the most valuable urban properties in the world.

In the absence of reflection, the memorial was doomed to fall victim to the same kinds of day-before assumptions and day-after tropes that had so curtailed any critical exploration of planning options for Ground Zero. There, items on old wish lists had carried the day, fating the site to be a record of the path of least resistance between conventional civic wisdom and the needs of commerce. In the premature search for a commemorative form, ideas that the process itself had generated—particularly the crutch of the sacred footprints—condemned the memorial to superficiality. The unspoken hope for the competition was that it would discover genius—a surpassing feat of imagination that could act as a solvent on the entrenched presumptions. Such an idea might have realigned the crude forces acting on the site into something new, fitting, magnificent. But, as with the earlier search for architectural genius, there were no messiahs coming. The preceding years were so light, the state of the art so meager; an appropriate depth would have to be relearned. Barring the passage of time, the memorial could be only a hollow form decorated with the pieties of the process itself, a memorial to solipsism. The LMDC was mostly "doing it right" in the mechanics of the competition, but it was doing it way too soon.

In the eight weeks between the announcement and the deadline for submitting proposals, more than thirteen thousand people registered and received the competition brief—a thirty-three-page booklet detailing the now partially suspended rules. To handle the expected deluge, the LMDC contracted with a warehouse on a dowdy, garage-lined block of West Thirty-sixth Street in the workaday wasteland between the Javits Convention Center and the mouth of the Lincoln Tunnel. The day of the deadline, June 30, 2003, ideas came in by the truckload, in tubes and brown paper–wrapped packages, totaling 5,201, a record for an architec-

tural competition. Trying to impose order, the LMDC had specified that no personal deliveries would be accepted, but designers
always work until the last minute on their presentations, and hundreds came rushing over, solutions in hand. The team of LMDC
staff on duty had to turn them away (some rules are rules), but
then contrived an ingenious and, in the tortured logic of government, gracious compromise. On the fly, the staffers hired a local
messenger service, Quick Trak, which parked its red van about
fifty yards away. Entrants who had missed the fine print about submission protocol were sent up the block to the prepaid messen-
gers, who returned the entries in batches to the warehouse. Your
tax dollars at work.

The harried to-and-fro only added to the carnival atmosphere
that seemed to descend on every site the process touched. After
handing over their babies, many of the competitors stuck around,
sharing war stories and watching anxiously as the submissions arrived and the piles grew, up to the five o'clock deadline and even
sixty-six generous, rule-bending minutes beyond, until the last
dreamer came down the street to file her dream with the bureaucracy. Fred Schwartz, the Think team architect defeated by
George Pataki and the Libeskinds, had parted from his presentation board and planted himself with a beer on a stoop across the
street. Taking the jury at its word, he had broken the rules; his
proposed memorial to the World Trade Center dead took the form
of a giant concrete bowl set into the site, carefully obliterating all
signs of the plan that had beaten his the winter before.

After the doors closed at the warehouse, the competition went
underground. As they assessed their haul, using a system of colored stickers to signal their approval, jury members were in all but
complete lockdown. The only news that leaked out hinted at the
difficulty of their job. By mid-August, they had reviewed just five
hundred boards, and some jurors were grumbling about the quality of what they had seen.

The second anniversary rolled around with no word on the

competition. But everyone was talking about the memorial. On September 10, members of the Coalition of 9/11 Families staged their largest demonstration yet at Ground Zero to repeat their claim that the tower footprints were sacred "from bedrock to infinity." Kevin Rampe responded within hours. "I want to make this very, very clear," he said at a hastily arranged press conference at the LMDC. "From bedrock to infinity, we will never, ever build commercial or retail space where those towers once stood." It was a kind gesture by the LMDC, but the issue had been decided long before, when the governor blessed those two hotspots in similar words, freeing the rest of the site for the dollar; what the families were asking for, uncomplicated sanctity, was not the LMDC's to give.

The next day, under a perfectly hideous cloudless blue sky, the mourners descended to the bedrock for what many feared could be the last anniversary visit. They stood around an impromptu memorial—two small square enclosures: the footprints in effigy—as children of the victims read for hours through the list of names. The floor of the pit was a lot smaller than it had been the year before. The Port Authority's temporary train station was nearly complete, occupying about a third of the width of the bathtub. Plans for the permanent station already showed its platforms and tracks covering almost all of the south footprint and clipping a corner off the north. So much for sacred ground at Ground Zero.

Unlike the ceremonies on the first anniversary, there was no presidential visit in 2003. Vice President Cheney had been scheduled to come, but the security needed to protect him in wartime was seen as too great an imposition on the event. The Secret Service had insisted that if Cheney attended, family members would have to pass through metal detectors on their way down into the Pit, and the mayor's office rejected that mood-breaking hint of terror. So instead, the night before, there was a small dinner at the White House for the leaders of the family groups, attended by George Bush, George Pataki, National Security Adviser Condoleezza Rice, and Secretary of Defense Donald Rumsfeld. One fearless firefighter's widow found herself at a table with Rumsfeld, then very busy trying to get control of the nation he had conquered the spring before. He asked her what she thought of the war in Iraq. "You don't want to know what I think of it," she answered, and when Rumsfeld said he did, she told him: "I resent that you are exploiting the death of my husband." The secretary of defense stormed off, leaving his wife behind to patch things up.

With its promise of defiance, Freedom Tower had become the lightning rod for the politicization of the redevelopment at the national level, leaving room to hope that the memorial could move forward free of rhetorical abuse. The site itself was still a political chit—when Bush spoke at the United Nations later that September he referred to Ground Zero as "a battlefield and a graveyard and the symbol of an unfinished war"—but the process of choosing a memorial would only be manipulated locally.[2]

By the end of September, the jury had made its decisions, and it sent nine finalists' boards down to the LMDC. Six weeks later, after one of the designers had been disqualified for submitting two entries under different names (and his attempt at an injunction to prevent the release of the other plans had been thrown out of court), eight memorial designs were unveiled at the Winter Garden. The exhibition set up for the occasion included the original boards submitted by the chosen solo practitioners and small teams—all youngish professional architects, though a huge number of amateurs had entered the competition—but there were also elaborate new models, renderings, and digital fly-throughs to enrapture the public. During those six weeks out of sight after their selection, the finalists' designs had been punched up with a budget of about $130,000 each.

After the failure of the staid Beyer Blinder Belle presentation and the success of the glossy Innovative Design Study images, the LMDC had learned well the value of seduction. But you can't put big money into the representation of a design without changing it, developing it, matching the resolution of the idea to the resolution of the new media. And there were significant changes. All of the designs now appeared with press-friendly titles to suggest the various and predictably callow mechanisms with which the proposals tried to imbue the site with sanctity. Several of the names—"Passages of Light," "Garden of Lights," "Inversion of Light"—seemed intended to conjure a connection to the beloved "Tribute in Light," which had been rekindled for one night at the recent anniversary. Others were in the more ponderous spirit of Daniel Libeskind's "Memory Foundations": "Reflecting Absence," "Dual Memory," "Votives in Suspension." Alarmingly, as they were getting their new names and new glam, some ideas found on the original boards had been edited out. In the submission for the plan now called "Suspending Memory," two New York architects had devoted about half their space to illustrating a lucid concept: a network of kiosks throughout the city that would frame views of the empty sky where the Twin Towers once stood. When the design was unveiled, that idea was nowhere to be found, leaving only the architects' considerably less affecting proposal to flood the pit and turn the footprints into two forested islands studded with glass totem poles, one for each victim.

Who had overseen this off-the-radar phase of the competition? Who had directed the redesign of the finalists' plans? When those questions were posed to Matt Higgins—interrupted in the Winter Garden as he and Kevin Rampe were escorting New York City's fire commissioner through the show—he didn't answer right away. Was it the jury? No. Was it the LMDC planning department? That got a laugh. Then who? "LMDC staff," Higgins said, smiling. As with Freedom Tower, it seemed, the memorial would have its share of unlikely authors.

The plan that was altered the most by the LMDC's intervention was the one that would eventually be selected as the winner: "Reflecting Absence," designed by Michael Arad, thirty-four, an architect with the New York City Housing Authority and the son of a former Israeli ambassador to the United States. His plan, as originally submitted, seemed to channel the desires of the jury to free the site from Daniel Libeskind's grip. It showed two square, cascade-lined pools set deep into the footprints below a purposefully barren street-level plaza. Four ramps led down to concrete-walled galleries around the sunken pools—termed "voids"—where visitors could look out into the emptiness through veils of falling water to contemplate what Arad called "the enormity of the destruction."[3] All of Libeskind's encroachments—the museum, the cultural wings, the access ramps, even the foundation walls that had given his scheme its name—were preemptively razed. "With respect to the master plan in the competition brief, this scheme suggests an alternative view of how the site can be integrated into the fabric of the city," Arad wrote in the statement accompanying his competition entry.

> It suggests continuity by remaining at street level, with a large open square that will become defined as buildings rise around it. This large open field should be punctuated only by the footprints of the two memorial pools, while other buildings that are associated with commemorating the events of September 11, such as a museum or visitor center, can be placed across the street from the open square in one of the adjacent blocks. This will allow the site to function both as a sacred memorial ground for those who descend to the memorial pools, and as a large urban plaza that will benefit the residents of the city in their everyday lives as they cross the site on their way to work or play.

That was Arad's vision—his straightforward attempt to balance the sacred and the secular—and that's what the jury had wanted us to see. But as it came out of the LMDC's closed-door design charette, the site was no longer a pure, open plane. The plaza had been dotted with wiry Dr. Seuss trees, and flanking its entire edge against West Street was a long building designated for the museum. There's an old architecture school adage that anything you can snap off of a model shouldn't be there in the first place, and this was clearly such a case. As mocked up for the finalists' show, the interloping museum was so unconvincing that several published accounts mistook it for a monumental sculpture. Arad had broken the rules, the jury had rewarded him for it, and the LMDC, as it had to, was trying to piece the master plan back together to make it work. There was no room on Larry Silverstein's oversubscribed acreage for a museum "across the street," and there was no way to get rid of the museum building: another competition was already under way to find an institution to fill it.

"Reflecting Absence" was further revised in the weeks before a final version was unveiled at Federal Hall—a period of contentious haggling that was a miniature version of the war over Freedom Tower. Daniel Libeskind fought a last-ditch battle to preserve the memorial area, the core of his master plan, but all he could salvage was a rump of the museum building. It was brought back to the northeast corner of the site but in a new form: a leaning iceberg, broken by a crevasse through which pedestrians could reach the memorial area from the "Wedge of Light" (soon to be lost itself when the Port Authority revealed its design for the permanent PATH station). Adding insult to injury, not only did the new memorial fill in Libeskind's "Pit," but also, to accommodate the slight slope of the site, the plaza had been raised above some of the surrounding streets.

Other changes to the design were made to bring it into compliance with long-standing process assumptions. During the last stage of the memorial selection, the jury had considered "Reflecting Absence" against two of the other finalists. "Garden of Lights," by a team of architects from New York, California, and France, took a shotgun approach to finding appropriate forms for the memorial; its many devices included an apple orchard, a wall of repurposed

World Trade Center steel, a channel filled with floating rose petals, and individual altars to the victims set within a dark crypt. "Passages of Light," the other runner-up, featured a below-street-level promenade with a spotlight in the walkway for each victim beaming up into a bridge made from ten thousand glass cylinders. Michael Arad's plan certainly had simplicity on its side—it was the closest thing to the model everyone had in the back of their minds: Maya Lin's Vietnam Veterans Memorial—and it led in all of the newspaper polls. The jury, which had been unimpressed by the sparse addition of trees the plan had gotten in its first makeover, had urged Arad to team up with an experienced landscape architect. From a list the jury provided, Arad chose Peter Walker, a veteran who had worked with many of the profession's stars. He filled Arad's plaza with trees in a random pattern, destroying the integrity of the original vision, but realizing the popular notion—dating back to the week of the attack—that Ground Zero should be a soothing green oasis in the city. One juror, James Young, had proposed that very thing earlier in an essay.[4]

Another venerable idea for the memorial, to incorporate the wreckage from the towers, was also accommodated. During the cleanup of the site, the Port Authority had deputized a local architect to scan outgoing trucks for exceptional pieces of the debris, and it had also collected an assortment of destroyed vehicles and large sections of the Twin Towers' facades, labeled for reassembly. The existence of those relics made their use inevitable, and back they came, into an instant "Memorial Center" that was added under the southwest corner of Michael Arad's now comfortably shaded plaza. In another change, intended to satisfy the families' increasingly disruptive calls for access, a private cavern containing a sarcophagus for the unidentified remains was drawn in at bedrock beneath the reflecting pool in the north footprint. No one was certain if it would be possible to isolate that space from the rumble of the trains passing just on the other side of its concrete walls, or just what that diversion would add to the experience.

After it emerged from this buffeting, Michael Arad's severe memorial had become a multifarious affair, its many elements tuned to the needs and tastes of the various process constituencies; like Freedom Tower, it was a thoroughbred camel. But "Reflecting Absence" remained at its core what it had been from the beginning: a big plaza with two big holes in it, a commemoration of the empty footprints. Though its ability to communicate would be assisted by the literalism of the wreckage and by the displays in the future museum, though its claims on sanctity would perhaps be ballasted by the presence of the bedrock shrine, the memorial's two thirty-foot-deep, two-hundred-foot-square "absences" would be asked to do the heavy emotional lifting.

With historical perspective still so many years away, maybe the best the process could do was to provide those two empty vessels and wait for them to fill up with meaning. But what filled the voids at their debut were the residues of the process itself. Michael Arad had given back to the process that which it had already made. The list of names, the healing waters, the sanctity of the footprints, the faith in architectural salvation—these things were well established before Arad arrived, and even in the form he had first proposed it his memorial did not advance the conversation. It wasn't a critical work, leaning toward some future understanding; it was a summary of what was known. And two years after the attack, what was known about what a memorial to September 11 should be could have filled a space much smaller than the two gaping acres his memorial set aside. The process had stopped short of investigating the limits, and perhaps even discovering the opportunities, of the site's peculiarly compromised sanctity—and with its retreat to the footprints, so too did "Reflecting Absence."

When the competition jury met for its final long day of judging, Maya Lin arrived with a letter to her colleagues. Over the preceding days, "Reflecting Absence" had been losing the jury's support, but she had come to realize how powerful it could be.

That power, she wrote, resided in the the footprints: "This design works because it has the strength to let the footprints be the memorial—not to try to upstage such a real and historic place with extra aesthetic form added to the site for arbitrary and additional meaning." No one was surprised when it was revealed that Lin had pushed for the plan in this way. She had sketched some memorial ideas for Herbert Muschamp's "Masters' Plan," one of which showed a park with twin reflecting pools in the footprints.

The reverence of the footprints was perhaps the least questioned of all the conventional wisdoms the process generated. They were certainly historic, as Maya Lin had written, but not quite as "real" as she and everyone else seemed to believe. There was nothing inevitable about regarding those two offset squares as sacred. The families' justification was that concentrations of remains had been found there, but there were other areas of similar density, and if a sacrosanct zone were to be delimited by the places where people came to rest, it would have to extend many blocks beyond the spots where the towers had stood. That was the logic behind the early calls for holding the entire site as sacred, and indeed the families had come to focus on the footprints only after having been denied everything else. What had been born from emotional necessity was then codified by political necessity. George Pataki had seen what catering to the families had done for Rudy Giuliani's reputation, and when the governor decreed the sanctity of the footprints during his 2002 reelection campaign, he was attempting to get a little bit of that for himself.

Architects had also been instrumental in the process of exalting the footprints. Some of the first plans to center on them were shown among the other fantasies at the Max Protetch Gallery four months after the attack, something that should have been a red flag. The footprints were just the sort of trace on a site that architects find irresistible—a preexisting formal cue that spares them the terror of a blank slate, with its infinity of options, no course clear, and all possible. The footprints were a crutch, and clinging to them was a concession that architecture had reached the limits of what it could say. There was no architectural language on hand that could convey even simple ideas in a comprehensible way, let alone the difficult things that had to be said in a memorial to September 11.

Maya Lin helped to sway the jury in favor of Michael Arad's plan by extolling its trust in the footprints and its refusal to force "arbitrary and additional meaning" on the site. But what did the footprints mean? If a memorial were to let that meaning shine through, what would it be memorializing? In "Reflecting Absence," the names of the dead were to be inscribed on a low wall in the viewing galleries wrapping each footprint, hard against the sheets of falling water that Lin wrote reminded her of tears. The order of the names was itself the subject of a fierce and unresolved debate; Arad had initially proposed a random listing, to evoke the randomness of death that day. Many of the other finalists' designs had done much more to render the human victims as unique, proposing life histories etched in glass, various architectural objects devoted to each, or even poster-size transparencies of every face in an installation that looked like a trade show. Michael Arad was probably wise to eschew those extremes, but his minimal, almost recessive treatment of the names left open the possibility that his voids, so lovingly recording the towers' outlines, would be interpreted first as a memorial to the buildings themselves.

Consider a group approaching the memorial some year after the redevelopment of the site is complete—in 2012 or 2020 or whenever the last lot is filled and the process, having done its work, goes away. The visitors will step off their tour bus or come up from the subway into a corner of Manhattan like any other. They will be surrounded by skyscrapers, newer than their neighbors but otherwise indistinguishable; in the end, one office building looks pretty much like the next. They may lift their eyes and see Freedom Tower, and if they know its name and how it came about, they may know that they are supposed to feel proud. Maybe they'll find a sign explaining its height, and if not they might move on toward the souvenir stands. In all likelihood, the site will still attract its share of entrepreneurs and sidewalk philosophers, working the five million visitors the memorial is expected to draw each year. It will be hard to enforce good taste; the city is incorrigible. All around, New Yorkers long inured to the ghosts of the place will be carrying on, moving in and out of the bright lobbies, shopping along the lines of bright stores. Our visitors will be standing on the site itself, but without a guide, they won't know it, and that fact alone will serve to tame the scale of the catastrophe. *Where did September 11 happen? In that park across the street?* They'll move toward the memorial—perhaps they'll hear the crashing fountains, perhaps they'll have to ask where it is—and when they work their way through the trees they'll find the footprints.

Because they were so plain, it was hard to gauge the size of the Twin Towers. But they were as big in life as they have become in death. The memorial that borrows their dimensions will be overwhelming. The name given to it will be mercifully forgotten, but the absences will still be there, exactly as big as the buildings, and to a visitor confronting the memorial, so much bigger at that moment than the memory of those who died all around. How will the dead compete with all this reverence for lost construction? Even if it communicates nothing else, the design will immortalize the measure of the Twin Towers and the fact that they did once really stand. Architecture remembering architecture—that is beyond question something this memorial can do. Whether it will also distinguish between the site of the attack and its victims, whether it will "respect this place made sacred through tragic loss," whether it will redeem Ground Zero, only time will tell.

EPILOGUE

Emotions will run high. We will not agree. But in the end, there is no right way to remember. It is only right that we do remember.

—GOVERNOR GEORGE PATAKI

THE LAST major piece of the site plan fell into place on January 22, 2004, when the Port Authority took over the Winter Garden to reveal its design for the long-heralded Downtown Grand Central Terminal. The Port had made an end run around the usual uproars by tapping Santiago Calatrava, the world's undisputed champion of transportation architecture. He responded with a light, bony pavilion in glass and white-painted steel that he compared to a dove released from the hands of a child—not only because, like many of his buildings, it had wings, but because it was at Ground Zero. When he had proposed similar structures over the years in his native Spain, he said they were inspired by a charging bull.

Calatrava only designs symmetrical buildings, and to find room for symmetry in Libeskind's plan he had had to destroy it. The station was centered on one long side of the triangular "Wedge of Light," but it bulged into the space in a broad sweep, putting an end to any question of how and when the plaza would trap the sun. When they first learned of the design, Daniel and Nina Libeskind tried to dig in, but they were too tied up with the fight over Free-dom Tower to open up a second front. So Calatrava's station—the closest thing to Rudy Giuliani's "soaring, beautiful memorial" that the site was likely to see—slid by without a fuss.

In any case, by then the process was palpably winding down. The big, easy question had been answered—How would the site be used?—and the difficult one—How would it remain sacred?—had been fudged with help from Michael Arad's memorial. Quietly, SOM was rushing to ready Freedom Tower for its strategic ground-breaking, which would take place the following Fourth of July. Planners at the Port and the LMDC were working to adapt the memorial design to the realities of subsurface train lines and truck ramps. Larry Silverstein's insurance lawsuit was ambling to-ward a losing verdict. Matt Higgins left the LMDC, moving on to another Manhattan land-use battle that shared all the elements of the process except for those that had made its search for symbols imperative. There were a few more blowups—like Libeskind be-fore him, Arad fought for full control of the project—but for longer stretches than in any of the years before, there was no news. All but a few of the beat reporters got pulled away to cover other stories—the presidential election or the Martha Stewart trial. There was only one thing to report at Ground Zero: the pro-cess had done its necessary work, not neatly, not purely, not with-out selfishness or rancor or vice, but in a manner that was recognizable as essentially New York—fast, vital, vain, and not too hung up on the past.

A plan was in place, but for a while it wasn't represented any-where. The final version of Freedom Tower had been unveiled with Libeskind's museum and "Pit" and "Wedge" still intact. Images of the memorial included the right tower but the wrong train station. And the Port Authority presented Calatrava's dove as if it had alit on "Memory Foundations" fully realized. The plan was finally fixed in one state, yet, fittingly, it didn't even exist on paper. SOM hadn't seen a unified drawing. The LMDC didn't have one. And no one knew what the Port might have tucked away. All the other parties were waiting for that irredeemable bureaucracy to take a survey of the site that would allow precise, dimensioned drawings. Two and a half years after the attack, Ground Zero had not yet been mapped.

But there was one place in town where the site's future could be seen: at the Winter Garden. The LMDC had mounted yet another display, this one retrospective, a time line of the process smoothing all the burrs. "The remembering continues," one panel read. At the end of the long line of glass cases, hidden by a video screen, was a single very tentative model, about the size of a card table, that showed Freedom Tower twisting, the memorial waters flowing, and the train station soaring, the whole composition clumsily rendered in plastic and cardboard, but each revelation in its place.

Think of all that had gone into that little model, with its random shapes distilled from so many specific human moments. It would have looked different if architects had not been called on to perform miracles, or if they had. It would have looked different if an election had swung another way, or if someone, anyone, had challenged the terms of Larry Silverstein's lease. Nice as the popular idea might be, architecture is never simply frozen music. As the attempt to bring meaningful forms to Ground Zero made clear, in the harsh, telling light of caricature, architecture is frozen conflict. Architects can try to apply meanings to their buildings up front, off the shelf. But when the captions fall off, when the stories are forgotten, the constructions that remain have other things to say. Action, antagonism, and compromise shape them; buildings are given meaning by the process of their birth.

If there was any doubt that an end—not the end—had arrived, it was put to rest at the public hearings that took place on February 18 at Pace University, downtown. The LMDC had called two sessions that day to hear comments on the fast-tracked environmental impact review—a federally mandated study that greenlighted the redevelopment—but, not surprisingly, what remained of the riled public used this last chance at an open mike to make other points. Dr. Robert Jarvik, the inventor of the artificial heart, was there. He had submitted an idea to the memorial competition (a map of the world, a pentagonal slab, three thousand sculptures of swimmers) and he now wished to open up a broad attack on the legitimacy of the LMDC, echoing some early statements by the Port Authority that the agency lacked jurisdiction over Ground Zero. A woman from Brooklyn rose to call Freedom Tower an erection ("Yeah, that's the kind I mean"). There was even some brave soul, a new face, trying to drum up concern about plate glass, flyways, and "avian mortality." Even so, it was a calm and tired room. The big fights had been fought and, for this crowd, mostly lost.

The crusaders of Team Twin Towers were well represented at that ebb-tide meeting. And as always their simple call for reconstruction would get the biggest applause, though here, with so many empty seats, it was no more than a smattering. Jon Hakala testified in his dual capacity as Team Twin Towers spokesman and concerned former World Trade Center tenant, but the energy that had in the past brought this very room to its feet, and the hope that rabble-rousing would make a difference, was gone. Earlier that day he had presided at the press-deprived unveiling of the only design proposal his organization chose to endorse. Previously, Team Twin Towers had tried to communicate its beliefs through a barrage of papers and the stirring cadences of Hakala's speeches. Now, as everyone else headed to the locker room, Team Twin Towers was getting into the architecture game. An architect who had worked on the design of the World Trade Center drew up the plan for them: two 112-story towers, both square, both with closely spaced steel-grille facades, both rising sheer from the ground, the tower to the north topped by a single TV transmitter. They called it "The Plan of the People," and still it probably was.

As the hearing rolled on, Jon Hakala exited to the lobby, got himself together, and prepared to walk out into the cold. "I think they've heard enough from me," he said to explain why he was leaving. As he stood in the doorway, his eye caught a poster that some LMDC advance man had brought in for decoration: a money shot of Freedom Tower at dusk. A few months earlier, just after the final design was revealed, the *New York Post* had published a letter from Hakala: "The latest version of the so-called 'Freedom Tower' is a monstrous abomination—a FrankenTower. I leased space on the 77th floor of One World Trade Center, and will take the terrorism risk of returning, but only to towers truly worthy of that risk." Now he looked at the image of the building for a silent moment with what might even have been resignation. "The defiance argument is overrated," Hakala said, gesturing at the poster, but also taking in the whole sad scene in the lobby: the bitter-enders from various groups conspiring in small klatches, a few bored guards, the long table of LMDC press handlers setting out their catered sandwiches, a lonely camera crew documenting all this victorious life as Act One of the process faded slowly into gray. "The terrorists who did this, in case nobody has noticed, are dead," he continued. "They're dead. This is for us. This is about healing."

NOTES

PROLOGUE

1. Dan Levy, "Twin Towers Were Architectural Icons: Skyline Won't Be the Same," *San Francisco Chronicle*, September 12, 2001, p. B6.
2. Alexis Chiu, "Fire Crews Battle Fatigue, Despair with Comrades Missing, Rescuers Brave 'Living Hell,'" *San Jose Mercury News*, September 13, 2001, p. 4A.
3. Minoru Yamasaki, *A Life in Architecture*, New York: Weatherhill, 1979, p. 112.

1: FIRST RESPONDERS

1. Steve Cuozzo, "Back to Downtown," *New York Post*, May 2, 2002, p. 41.
2. Arthur Lubow, "Rem Koolhaas Builds," *New York Times Magazine*, July 9, 2000, p. 30.
3. Giorgio Baraville, *Newyorkseptembereleventhtwothousandone*, New York: de.Mo, 2001, unpaginated.
4. William Heyen, ed., *September 11, 2001: American Writers Respond*, Silver Spring, Md.: Etruscan Press, 2002, p. 346.
5. Ralph Appelbaum, cited in Richard Meier, "To Rebuild or Not: Architects Respond," *New York Times Magazine*, September 23, 2001, p. 81.
6. Liz Diller and Ric Scofidio, cited in Meier, "To Rebuild or Not."
7. "Rebuilding New York and the Pentagon," *Talk of the Nation*, NPR News Special, September 27, 2001.
8. Ed Koch, week of Sept. 11, on TV, http://slate.msn.com/id/115641.
9. Eric Glanz and James Lipton, "The Height of Ambition," *New York Times Magazine*, September 8, 2002, p. 36.
10. *Hardball with Chris Matthews*, MSNBC, September 17, 2001.

11. E-mail to author, September 13, 2001.

12. Interview with author, March 25, 2003.

13. Herbert Muschamp, "The Commemorative Beauty of Tragic Wreckage," *New York Times*, November 11, 2001, p. II37.

14. Jean Baudrillard, *The Spirit of Terrorism: And Requiem for the Twin Towers*, New York: Verso, 2002, p. 7.

15. Wim Cuyvers, "Behind the Iconostasis," *Archis 6* (December 2001): 58.

16. Stephane Fitch, "Elegy for a Landmark," *Grid Breaks*, September 17, 2001.

17. Lecture for Friends of the Upper East Side Historic Districts, New York School of Interior Design, September 19, 2001. Transcript provided by the architect.

18. Juliet McIntyre, *21 Days at Ground Zero*, New York: Bell Harbor Press, 2002, p. 105.

19. http://www.cafeshops.com/newwtc;
http://www.cafeshops.com/rebuildworld.

20. Adam Nagourney, "In New York, Bush Visits Sites Evocative of His Philosophy," *New York Times*, July 11, 2001, p. A1.

21. Interview with Daniel Libeskind, August 6, 2003.

2: OUR BUILDINGS, OURSELVES

1. Minoru Yamasaki, *A Life in Architecture*, New York: Weatherhill, 1979, p. 15.

2. Ibid., p. 17.

3. Paul Heyer, ed., *Architects on Architecture: New Directions in America*, New York: Walker, 1966, p. 19.

4. Thomas Meehan, "The World Trade Center: Does Mega-architecture Work?" *Horizon* 18, no. 4 (autumn 1976): 11.

5. Letter from George Haskell to Peter Blake, April 2, 1962.

6. Yamasaki, *A Life in Architecture*, p. 114.

7. Ibid., p. 112.

8. Meehan, "The World Trade Center," p. 11.

9. Ibid.

10. Ibid.

11. William Heyen, ed., *September 11, 2001: American Writers Respond*, Silver Spring, Md.: Etruscan Press, 2002, p. 13.

12. Interview with Jaquelin Robertson, March 11, 2003.

13. http://www.nytimes.com/pages/national/portraits/.

14. Edward Wyatt, "At Hearing: A Resolve to Rebuild Twin Towers," *New York Times*, May 26, 2002, p. 33.

15. "Half of New York Wants the Twin Towers Rebuilt," *New York Post*, July 14, 2002, p. 1.

16. Richard Meier, "Filling the Void, to Rebuild or Not: Architects Respond," *New York Times Magazine*, September 23, 2001, p. 81.

17. Alexander Butzinger, statement, July 26, 2003.

18. J. L. Sert, F. Léger, and Siegfried Giedion, "Nine Points on Monumentality" (1943), in Siegfried Giedion, *Architecture You and Me*, Cambridge: Harvard University Press, 1958, p. 48.

19. Ibid., p. 50.

20. Siegfried Giedion, "In Search of a New Monumentality," *Architectural Review* (September 1948): 117.

21. Philip Johnson, "Where Are We At?" *Architectural Review* (September 1960): 175.

22. Thomas H. Creighton, "The Sixties: A P/A Symposium on the State of Architecture: Part II," *Progressive Architecture* 42, no. 4 (April 1961): 32.

23. Minoru Yamasaki, "Minoru Yamasaki," *Art in America* 50, no. 4 (winter 1962): 50.

24. Meehan, "World Trade Center," p. 11.

25. Yamasaki, "Minoru Yamasaki," p. 50.

26. Yamasaki, *A Life in Architecture*, p. 113.

27. Ibid., p. 12.

28. Laurie Kerr, "The Mosque to Commerce," *Slate*, December 28, 2001, http://slate.msn.com/id/2060207/.

29. Editorial, "What Should Rise from the Ashes?" *City Journal* (autumn 2001), http://www.city-journal.org/html/11-4-whatshouldrise.html.

30. Ibid.

31. Philippe de Montebello, "The Iconic Power of an Artifact," *New York Times*, September 25, 2001, p. A29.

32. Herbert Muschamp, "The Commemorative Beauty of Tragic Wreckage," *New York Times*, November 11, 2001, p. 37.

33. Vincent Scully, *Modern Architecture: The Architecture of Democracy*, New York: G. Braziller, 1961, p. 44.

34. Alec Appelbaum, "Q and A with Vincent Scully," *Metropolis* (December 2001): 102.

35. Heyer, *Architects on Architecture*, p. 195.

3: THE COOPERATION OF MEN

1. James Glanz, "From Torn Steel, Cold Data of Salvage," *New York Times*, October 9, 2001, p. B13.
2. Richard T. Pienciak, "Anguished Search for Traces of the Missing," *New York Daily News*, January 6, 2002, p. 8.
3. Susan Edelman, "9/11 Kin Rip 'Heartless' Bloomberg," *New York Post*, June 22, 2003, p. 4.
4. Ada Louise Huxtable, "The New York Process: Don't Expect Anything Uplifting from the Pols and Realtors Now Pondering the WTC Site," *Wall Street Journal*, September 17, 2001, p. A20.
5. Gary Taushire, letter to the editor, *New York Post*, October 27, 2003, p. 28.
6. *America Rebuilds: A Year at Ground Zero*, PBS, September 10, 2002.
7. Robin Finn, "Undaunted and Planning the Next Great Skyline," *New York Times*, February 15, 2002, p. B2.
8. Huxtable, "The New York Process," p. 4.
9. Andrew Rice and Tom McGeveran, "Who's at Center of Ground Zero? Permanent Elite," *New York Observer*, April 1, 2002, p. 1.
10. Discovery Times, *Engineering the Future WTC: Rebuilding Ground Zero*, 2002.
11. Frank J. Prial, "Governors Dedicate Trade Center Here; World Role is Cited," *New York Times*, April 15, 1973, p. A1.
12. Gael Greene, "The Most Spectacular Restaurant in the World," *New York*, May 31, 1976, p. 53.
13. Letter from Theodore Kheel to Paul Goldberger, undated.
14. Karrie Jacobs, "Strange Bedfellows," *Metropolis* (June, 2003):116.

4: AMATEUR HOUR

1. http://www.cnn.com/SPECIALS/2002/wtc.ideas/.
2. Letter to author, October 6, 2003.
3. http://home.iae.nl/users/lightnet/world/blackmagic2.htm.
4. Discovery Times, *Engineering the Future WTC: Rebuilding Ground Zero*, 2002.
5. Howard McDonald to Michael Bloomberg, December 18, 2002.
6. Tom McGeveran, "At Tower Site Vast Top Seen as Memorial," *New York Observer*, June 17, 2002, p. 1.

5: CIRCUS MAXIMUS

1. *11 O'clock News*, WCBS, January 17, 2002.
2. David Seifman and Todd Venezia, "Downtowners Worried Sick," *New York Post*, January 12, 2002.
3. "Job Loss from September 11 to Impact for Years," *Newsday*, January 11, 2002.
4. Charlie LeDuff, "Still Digging for Lost Sons After a Million Tons of Pain," *New York Times*, January 8, 2002, p. A1.
5. Max Protetch, *A New World Trade Center: Design Proposals from Leading Architects Worldwide*, New York: Regan Books, 2002, p. 5.
6. Ibid., p. 37.
7. http://www.maxprotetch.com/SITE/PREVIOUS/ANEWWTC/ FORM/index.html.
8. Edward Wyatt, "Blueprint for Ground Zero Begins to Take Shape," *New York Times*, May 4, 2002, p. A1.
9. http://www.maxprotetch.com/SITE/PREVIOUS/ANEWWTC/ KOVAC/index.html.
10. Michael Graves in Max Protetch, *A New World Trade Center*, p. 53.
11. Michael Benedikt, *For an Architecture of Reality*, New York: Limen Books, 1981, p. 4.
12. "Gallery Shows WTC Design Proposals," *Associated Press*, January 18, 2002.

6: LISTENING MODE

1. John Whitehead, remarks, Crain's breakfast forum, March 26, 2002.
2. Roger Ebert, "Make It Green," *Chicago Sun-Times*, September 14, 2001.
3. Herbert Muschamp, "One Vision: A Hill of Green at Ground Zero," *New York Times*, September 11, 2003, p. E1.
4. Ebert, "Make It Green."
5. *America Rebuilds: A Year at Ground Zero*, PBS, September 10, 2002.
6. Leonard Post, "Community Has Its Say on World Trade Site's Future," *Tribeca Tribune*, February 2002, p. 2.
7. Mike Wallace, *A New Deal for New York*, New York: Bell & Weiland/Gotham Center Books, 2002, p. 93.
8. Louis Epstein, "Anatomy of a Disgrace," pamphlet.
9. Agreement of Lease, July 16, 2001, p. 172.

10. http://www.americaspeaks.org/welcome.html.
11. http://www.americaspeaks.org.
12. Michael Sorkin, *Starting from Zero: Reconstructing Downtown New York*, New York: Routledge, 2003, p. 58.
13. Adam Nagourney, "Cuomo's Criticism of Pataki's Role After 9/11 Sets Off Furor," *New York Times*, April 17, 2002, p. B1.
14. Lower Manhattan Development Corporation, "Principles and Preliminary Blueprint for the Future of Lower Manhattan," p. 1.
15. Ibid., p. 9.
16. Alexander Garvin, *The American City: What Works, What Doesn't*, New York: McGraw-Hill Professional, 1995.
17. Interview with author, July 16, 2003.
18. Herbert Muschamp, "Marginal Role for Architecture at Ground Zero," *New York Times*, May 23, 2002, p. B1.
19. David Dunlap, "Limiting Possibilities Downtown," *New York Times*, July 18, 2002, p. B1.
20. Interview with author, July 16, 2003.
21. Edward Wyatt, "Six Plans for Ground Zero, All Seen as a Starting Point," *New York Times*, July 17, 2002, p. A1.
22. Ada Louise Huxtable, "Another World Trade Center Horror," *Wall Street Journal*, July 25, 2002, p. B13.
23. Tom McGeveran, "At Tower Site Vast Top Seen as Memorial," *New York Observer*, June 17, 2002, p. 1.
24. George Pataki, speech, February 2, 2002.
25. Edward Wyatt, "Pataki's Surprising Limit on Ground Zero Design," *New York Times*, July 2, 2002, p. B1.

7: STAR LIGHT, STAR BRIGHT

1. Henry-Russell Hitchcock, "The Architecture of Bureaucracy and the Architecture of Genius," *Architectural Review* 101 (January 1947): 3–6.
2. Ibid., p. 5.
3. Ibid.
4. Steve Cuozzo, "The Wrong Stuff: Keep World's Architects Away from Ground Zero," *New York Post*, May 28, 2002, p. 27.
5. Herbert Muschamp, "Filling the Void: A Chance to Soar," *New York Times*, September 30, 2001, p. B1.
6. Herbert Muschamp, "An Agency's Ideology Is Unsuited to Its Task," *New York Times*, July 16, 2002, p. 6.

7. Lower Manhattan Development Corporation, "Request for Qualifications: Innovative Designs for the World Trade Center Site," p. 3.

8. Ibid., p. 4.

9. Interview with author, May 8, 2003.

10. Herbert Muschamp, "Don't Rebuild, Reimagine," *New York Times Magazine*, September 8, 2002, p. 46.

11. *Charlie Rose Show*, PBS, September 13, 2002.

12. http://ndm.si.edu/NDA/WINNERS/2003/ARCHITECTURE/SCHWARTZ/1.shtml.

13. Alastair Gordon, "Frederic Schwartz: The Man Who Dared the City to Think Again," *New York Times*, September 19, 2002, p. F1.

14. Philippe Petit, *To Reach the Clouds: My High-Wire Walk Between the Twin Towers*, New York: North Point Press, 2002, p. 241.

15. Muschamp, "Don't Rebuild, Reimagine," p. 58.

9: WHEN ARCHITECTS ATTACK

1. http://www.archinect.com/discuss_cgi/groups/0965.html.

2. Interview with author, October 10, 1998.

3. Julie Iovine, "Turning a Competition into a Public Campaign: Finalists for Ground Zero Design Pull Out the Stops," *New York Times*, February 26, 2003, p. B9.

4. Deborah Solomon, "The Way We Live Now: Questions for Frank Gehry, Towering Vision," *New York Times Magazine*, January 5, 2003, p. 11.

5. *NewsNight with Aaron Brown*, January 9, 2003.

6. Julie Iovine, "Appraisals of Ground Zero Designs," *New York Times*, January 9, 2003, p. E3.

7. Herbert Muschamp, "Visions for Ground Zero: An Appraisal; the Latest Rounds of Designs Rediscover and Celebrate the Vertical Life," *New York Times*, December 19, 2002, p. B10.

8. Herbert Muschamp, "Balancing Reason and Emotion in Twin Towers Void," *New York Times*, February 6, 2003, p. E1.

9. Herbert Muschamp, "Don't Rebuild, Reimagine," *New York Times Magazine*, September 8, 2002, p. 46.

10. William Neuman, "Libeskind Pushed Ground Smear-O," *New York Post*, December 9, 2003, p. 4.

11. Steven Malanga, "Disneyland of Death," *New York Post*, October 31, 2002, p. 33.

12. http://www.gothamgazette.com/rebuilding_nyc/chat/libeskind-transcript.shtml.

13. Marvin Trachtenberg, "A New Vision for Ground Zero Beyond Mainstream Modernism," *New York Times*, February 23, 2003, p. B54.

14. Paul Lieberman, "Building Resolve," *Los Angeles Times*, February 23, 2003, p. E43.

15. JCRC Update, Jewish Community Relations Council, March 6, 2003.

16. Robin Finn, "A Visionary of the Skyline, with Three Pairs of Glasses," *New York Times*, January 22, 2003, p. B2.

17. Jess Bravin, "Ground Zero Finalist's Past Draws Questions," *Wall Street Journal*, February 26, 2003, p. B8.

18. William Neuman, "Sham Plan for New WTC: Bigs Look Certain to Cut Heart Out of Tower Design," *New York Post*, February 21, 2003, p. 6.

19. Edward Wyatt, "Practical Issues for Ground Zero," *New York Times*, February 28, 2003, p. A1.

20. Edward Wyatt, "Panel Supports Two Tall Towers at Disaster Site," *New York Times*, February 26, 2003, p. B1.

21. Charles Bagli, "Agencies Jockey to Control Future of Any Design for Ground Zero," *New York Times*, February 7, 2003, p. B1.

22. Elisabeth Bumiller, "President, No Matter Where, Keeps Battlefield Close," *New York Times*, March 30, 2003, p. B1.

23. http://www.webforums.com/forums/f-read/Next154.69.75.html.

10: SHOW AND TELL

1. Daniel Libeskind, "Conflict Resolution," *New Statesman*, June 24, 2002, p. 36.

2. Kurt Forster, *Daniel Libeskind: Radix-Matrix*, New York: Prestel, 1997, p. 10.

3. Philip Nobel, "The Mystic of Lindenstrasse," *Metropolis* (January 1999): 83.

4. Edward Wyatt, "Shadows to Fall, Literally, Over 9/11 'Wedge of Light,'" *New York Times*, May 1, 2003, p. B1.

5. Daniel Libeskind, *Fishing from the Pavement*, Rotterdam: NAI Publishers, 1997.

6. "Ground Zero 'Poet' Exposed," *New York Post*, June 4, 2003, p. 10.

7. Deroy Murdock, "The Nutty Architect," *New York Post*, June 28, 2003, p. 19.

11: THE ART OF THE POSSIBLE

1. Maggie Haberman and Greg Gittrich, "Gov's WTC Plan for GOP Parley," *Daily News*, May 2, 2003, p. 10.

2. Maggie Haberman, "Dems Rip GOP '04 Convention Plans," *Daily News*, May 4, 2003, p. 53.

3. "NY Rallies at Ground Zero for Troops," CNN.com., April 11, 2003.

4. Nathaniel Owings, *The Spaces in Between: An Architect's Journey*, New York: Houghton Mifflin, 1973, p. 99.

5. Ibid., p. viii.

6. Ibid., p. 113.

7. Andy Geller, "Corporate Allure Blocks Childs-Like Vision," *New York Post*, July 17, 2003, p. 4.

8. William Neuman, "Libeskind Power Play—Demands Control of Tower, Rail Hub," *New York Post*, June 17, 2003, p. 5.

9. "Control Freak," *New York Post*, June 17, 2003, p. 30.

10. William Neuman, "Libeskind Pushed Ground Smear-O," *New York Post*, December 9, 2003, p. 4.

12: SO MOVED

1. http://www.renewnyc.com/Memorial/memmission.shtml.htm.

2. "In Bush's Words: Advance of Democratic Institutions in Iraq Is Setting an Example," *New York Times*, September 24, 2003, p. A12.

3. Eva Hagberg, "Reflecting Absence Unveiled," *The Architect's Newspaper*, February 3, 2004, p. 1.

4. James E. Young, "Remember Life with Life: The New World Trade Center as Living Memorial," in *Properties*, February 2002, p. 332.

ACKNOWLEDGMENTS

All writers owe a debt to their editors but mine is deeper than most. Riva Hocherman has been devoted to this book and has improved it immeasurably. She conceived the idea for the book at a time when my mind was on other things, and then Sara Bershtel more or less dared me to write it. Without the promise of their intelligence to lean on going forward, I would never have considered saying yes; without the inspired industry of my agent Bill Clegg, I would never have been in a position to. Having taken on the project, I was very fortunate to draft Eva Hagberg to work on it with me. An original thinker and a ferocious writer, her contributions make a mockery of the term "research assistant."

Many of the ideas here first took shape in articles I wrote for a variety of periodicals, before and after September 11. Martin Pedersen, my editor at *Metropolis*, has been a source of unblindered perspective on the redevelopment since the earliest days. He edited several columns and essays that have been put to new use in chapter 5. Noel Millea, equally at home with words and buildings, edited a *Metropolis* profile of Daniel Libeskind that underpins parts of chapters 8 and 10. In the fall of 2001, Jack Bankowsky and Jennifer Liese gave me space in *Artforum* to consider the role of architects at Ground Zero; echoes of that piece can be found in chapters 1 and 7. At the suggestion of Ariel Kaminer, the sharpest knife in the drawer, I wrote a story for the *New York Times* that helped me dig much deeper into the world of the LMDC. The earliest glimmers of the scope of the book appeared in two articles I wrote for *The Nation*, bits of which are repurposed in chapters 6 and 8. Those stories were expertly edited by Art Winslow and generously proposed by Elizabeth Pochoda. Betsy also gave me critical and encouraging notes on the first half of the manuscript at a time when I very much needed both.

The job of making sense of the redevelopment was made easier—and much more enjoyable—by the collegiality of the exceptional critics and reporters who assembled to cover it, including Andrea Bernstein, David Dunlap, Alex Frangos, Paul Goldberger, Julie Iovine, Karrie Jacobs, David Levitt, Julia Levy, Cathleen McGuigan, and Suzanne Stephens. I was particularly fortunate to make the acquaintance of Maggie Haberman and Willie Neuman, two formidable journalists who gave me what amounted to a running master class in how to think like a reporter.

Tom Kuntz and Stephanie Schwam of New York Times Television opened many doors for me—including the gates to Ground Zero itself. John Schiumo, who hides a killer reporter's instinct behind his anchorman demeanor, invited me to be a member of his "Architecture Round Table" on the local all-news channel, NY1. On and off the air, the discussions with John and my fellow panelists—Joseph Giovannini, Tony Vidler, and Alex Washburn—were tremendously important in helping me think things through. Like everyone who writes about architecture, I am deeply indebted to Kristen Richards and her daily digests of international design news posted at ArchNewsNow.com.

Jessica Scaperotti put a friendly face on the LMDC and was an invaluable guide there. Elsewhere, many others made themselves available for my sometimes hasty queries. At various critical moments I got essential insights and aid from Kurt Andersen, Michael Bierut, Ray Gastil, Rosalie Genevro, Alex Gorlin, John Keenen, Stuart Klawans, Joshua Micah Marshall, Jacob Tilove, and Claudia Wagner. Many more assisted me whom I cannot mention by name: thank you.

A handful of professors have had a disproportionate effect on my understanding of architecture. Narciso Menocal at the University of Wisconsin–Madison taught skepticism under the guise of lectures on Frank Lloyd Wright. Had I not had the good luck and great pleasure to work with Joan Ockman, director of the Buell Center for the Study of American Architecture at Columbia University, whole chapters of this book would look very different. She introduced me to Henry-Russell Hitchcock's essay, "The Architecture of Bureaucracy and the Architecture of Genius," as well as to so many other ideas that have since merged with my own. In the design studio, Anne Perl de Pal and Peter Testa showed me what architecture is and what it should never try to be.

Surviving as a freelance writer for many years, I have been fortunate to have two patrons who have given my life a semblance of stability. Horace Havemeyer, publisher of *Metropolis*, has always supported me as I took risks in the pages of his magazine; Paige Rense, editor in chief of *Architectural Digest*, has very graciously given me a second home in hers.

As this project consumed me, several of my friends revealed new depths of patience and generosity. Mayer Rus, whose unrivaled wit has always been an inspiration, appeared out of nowhere to offer me the perfect place to hide and write. Jody Rosen's step into high-five-digit word counts gave me the courage to attempt it myself, and his well-timed interventions helped me keep the words coming. Ari Kelman saw that I could write this book long before I did; through his example he showed me that I could finish it. Mark Lamster—editor, writer, and Catskills humorist—helped me figure out the mechanics of getting this done while staying (mostly) sane. Andrea Schwan was always there to remind me that, away from Ground Zero, architectural folly continued apace. Chris Strom gave me timely advice on several chapters and, with his experience in the field, kept me focused on what was new and what was not new in this one corner of New York real estate.

It is safe to say that no one is more relieved than my family to see this chapter closed. My parents, Ken and Phyllis Nobel, outdid themselves in running interference with their grandchildren, giving me time and space to immerse myself in this difficult story. They were joined by my sister, Julie Nobel, and by Mark Fraser, Stephanie Fraser, and Howard Fraser, my father-in-law, who loves New York City more thoroughly and knowledgeably than anyone I know.

No dedication or end-of-book niceties can do justice to the contributions of my wife, Caroline, who somehow managed to remain my essential creative collaborator even as I neglected our family to follow the news and then disappeared for weeks on end to write. I will never be able to repay her for her heroism in raising our two sons: Oscar, born with the book, and Alexander, three, who when asked what it's about always answers correctly: "A construction site."

INDEX

ABOUT THE AUTHOR

PHILIP NOBEL writes about architecture for *The New York Times* and *Architectural Digest*. He also contributes a monthly column, "Far Corner," to *Metropolis* magazine. Trained as an architect, he lives in Brooklyn, New York.